The Scott Family

OF

DIPPLE PARISH, MORAY, SCOTLAND

AND

"DIPPLE," STAFFORD COUNTY, VIRGINIA

Originally published as a portion of *Virginia Genealogies: A Genealogy of the Glassell Family of Scotland and Virginia; Also of the Families of Ball, Brown, Bryan, Conway, Daniel, Ewell, Holladay, Lewis, Littlepage, Moncure, Peyton, Robinson, Scott, Taylor, Wallace, and Others, of Virginia and Maryland*

BY

Rev. Horace Edwin Hayden

HERITAGE BOOKS
2013

HERITAGE BOOKS

AN IMPRINT OF HERITAGE BOOKS, INC.

Books, CDs, and more—Worldwide

For our listing of thousands of titles see our website
at
www.HeritageBooks.com

A Facsimile Reprint
Published 2013 by
HERITAGE BOOKS, INC.
Publishing Division
100 Railroad Ave. #104
Westminster, Maryland 21157

Originally published in the late 1800s

— Publisher's Notice —

This volume was originally published as a portion of *Virginia Genealogies: A Genealogy of the Glassell Family of Scotland and Virginia; Also of the Families of Ball, Brown, Bryan, Conway, Daniel, Ewell, Holladay, Lewis, Littlepage, Moncure, Peyton, Robinson, Scott, Taylor, Wallace, and Others, of Virginia and Maryland*

International Standard Book Numbers
Paperbound: 978-0-7884-5457-8
Clothbound: 978-0-7884-6975-6

SCOTT,

OF DIPPLE PARISH, MORAY, SCOTLAND,

AND " DIPPLE," STAFFORD COUNTY, VIRGINIA.

ARMS, from tomb of Rev. Alexander Scott, M. A. *"On a bend a star between two crescents, in a bordure eight stars."*

CREST. *"A dove."*

MOTTO. *"Gaudia Nuncio Magna."*

ARMS, from book plate of Hon. Gustavus Scott *"Or, on a bend azure, a bezant between two crescents of the field, in a bordure argent eight bezants."*

CREST. *"A dove ppr. holding in its beak an olive branch:"*

MOTTO. *"Gaudia Magna Nuncio."*

98. Martin Pickett Scott, M. D., C. S. A., p. 646, was educated University Virginia 1840–41; graduated M. D. University of Pennsylvania, 1846, thesis "Dysentery;" studied medicine also in Paris, France; was Professor of Chemistry, Medical College of Virginia, Richmond, 1854–1861; appointed surgeon Confederate States Army, with rank of Major, May, 1861, serving until the war ended. After the war he was Professor Medical Department, Washington University, Baltimore, Maryland, and later elected to the chair of Agriculture and Biology, Virginia Agricultural and Mechanical College, Blacksburg. Is a member American Medical Association, Maryland Academy Science, and American Association for Advancement of Science. He married, October, 1854, Caroline Pocahontas, daughter of John H. Bernard, Gaymont, Caroline county, Virginia. Had i. Gay Bernard; ii. Elizabeth Blackwell; iii. Lelia Bolling; iv. John Bernard; v. Caroline Louise.

93. Arthur Alexander Morson (page 653), was born Stafford county, Virginia, 1801; died Richmond, Virginia, January 13, 1864. He graduated A. B. Yale College, 1822. Studied law at Litchfield, Connecticut; began to practice at Fredericksburg, Virginia, 1823, and took at once a high rank in his profession. In 1844 he located at Richmond where he practiced until his death. The Virginia Law Reports, 1845–1863, show the extent and variety of his attainments. He was associated at the Richmond bar with such men as Patton, Stanard, Moncure, Green, Robinson, and Robert E. Scott. To have held his own against such antagonists required the highest degree of learning and forensic skill and ability. Yet it was in such associations that Mr. Morson attained his distinguished reputation. There was an unyielding courage and an unbending integrity about him, combined with a charity that never closed its hand in the presence of want, and these hardy virtues were softened and refined by the utmost gentleness and grace of manner. Judge Barton of Fredericksburg who knew Mr. Morson well, said of him: "Were you to draw a character and give to it the virtues which we ascribe to the ideal gentleman, you would find upon your canvas a portrait of Mr. Morson."

ERRATA.

P. 655, No. 97, "Caskey" should be "Caskie," also on page 657, Nos. 167 and 169.

P. 655, line 8 from bottom read "This was one of the volunteer companies which Governor Wise," &c.

P. 657, No. 167, read "Col. George V. Scott."

P. 658, No. 181, children, read "i. Marian; ii. Charles Love, &c., died August, 1869."
    Also Foulke note, line 6 read "Thornburg" for "Themburg."

SCOTT.

This Virginia family traces its descent from Rev. John Scott, M. A., of Dipple, Morayshire, Scotland, cir. 1650. Every effort to learn his birth place or family connexion has failed. Armed with a *carte blanche* from the late Hon. William L. Scott, of Erie, Pa., to prosecute the search regardless of expense, I applied to the Lyon Herald, College of Arms, Edinburgh, and to my valued correspondent, Mr. J. O. Mitchell, of Glasgow. These parties were unable to add anything to the data I had already secured, but they returned the following reply, in substance, viz:

"It would be throwing away money for your American friends to pursue their researches for the ancestry of Rev. John Scott. It is absolutely impossible to have a middle class family *unconnected with land* earlier than the 17th century, when almost all Scotch parish registers begin. In the cases of Burgesses of an important town, say Aberdeen, one *might* get a little further back, but even this is very problematical. As to the Scott arms, the bend with the mullet, or star, between two crescents appears in the shields of Buccleugh, and Lord Napier, a Scott of Thirlstane, but the border of mullets or bezants on the American shield looks as if the Rev. Alexander or Gustavus Scott had obtained a grant *with a difference*. These arms are not in the Lyon College Register. They may be in the College of Arms, London. There is no use in pursuing the genealogical search unless the birth place of Rev. John Scott of Dipple was known."

This decision was made to apply also to the Scotch families of Glassell, Gordon and Moncure, given in these pages. The history of the Peyton family shows the great difficulty of tracing American families in Great Britain in the absence of landed estate. The Wallace pedigree, it will be noticed, was not completed through the parish registers of Scotland; but through family letters of the 18th century, and the indenture of the first American settler of the line. The use of "Arms" by Rev. James Scott and his son Gustavus in colonial times, under a Royal supremacy, on tombstones and on official papers, justifies crediting to them the right to bear arms. The late Dr. Burnett, the Lyon Herald, also wrote me thus:

"I have done all that was possible in the way of making and directing such searches as the case required. I wish I could say with complete success. The main lines of the families of Scott and Gordon are well known. The difficulty has been to trace your friends back to any known branch of either, and I have been unable except hypothetically to do so though my searches have been very extensive in public and local records including those of the Universities and the different classes of records of Aberdeen, also in private charters, charts, etc. Of the Scotts you have already most of the matter I could have furnished you with. I am unable to go beyond the minister of Dipple, John Scott, whose wife, Helen Grant, survived him, though much of my searching has been directed towards discovering his paternity. Neither the arms on the bookplate nor those on the tombstone are recorded here. The latter would suggest a descent from the Scotts of Scotstarvet."

I am especially indebted to my valued friend, Miss A. L. Peyton (PEYTON, p. 540), Dr. G. S. Franklin (SCOTT 180), and Hon. Wm. L. Scott, 123 (who bore the expense of the search in Scotland), in the preparation of this family history. Personally and by proxy the records of the various counties in which the Virginia members lived have been carefully examined.

Rev. Mr. Gordon writes me that the only representatives of this family now alive (1887) are Mrs. Gull or Gall and her family, and her sister, Mrs. Kennedy.

On five monumental tablets on the wall of the Church of Spynie are the following epitaphs of this interesting family:

1. *Rev. Mr. Robert Paterson*, 22 years minister of Spynie, d. July 31, 1790, æ 56. "He was eminent for the faithful discharge of his pastoral office, and as a husband and father he was nearly as perfect as human nature will admit." Also *Alexander Paterson*, his 3d son, who survived his father 9 months, having d. April 13, 1791, æ 17, "after having finished his academical studies." Also *Margaret Collie*, spouse of Mr. Robert Paterson, minister of New Spynie, and only child of Mr. William Collie, late minister of Drainie, and Margaret Mackenzie, his spouse. * * * She d. July 23, 1782, æ 34.

3. "Consecrated by the Rev. James Paterson, Min. of Birnie, to the memory of his brothers, *Mr. William Paterson*, who d. Apr. 5, 1829, æ 59, and *Dr. Robert Paterson*, H. E. I. C. S., who after 20 years service in India d. Calcutta Dec., 1829, æ 48. Also sacred to the memory of *Rev. James Paterson*, Minister of Birnie, whose benevolent life adorned the doctrines which he taught. B. Apr. 13, 1778; d. Feb. 23, 1840."

4. *Rev. John Paterson*, Minister of the Gospel at Auldearn, 1794–1813, when he d., æ 41. "An accomplished scholar and an eloquent preacher. His character was adorned by integrity, candour and benevolence, still more than by those attainments." Here also lies "his sister Helen, spouse of Rev. Thos. Macfarlane of Edinskillie," who d. Apr. 7, 1810, æ 34. The other stone, the 5th, was placed by Mrs. Robert Paterson to "Mr. Hugh Anderson, and Margaret Munro, his spouse, also Mr. William Collie, his successor, and 27 years Minister, and Margaret Mackensie, his spouse." Wm. Collie d. Apr. 29, 1768, æ 73, and his wf. Apr. 27, 1773. (Shaw's Moray, II. 143-4.)

Rev. James P. was ord. Asst. Min. Birnie, Jan. 26, 1808; Minister, Dec. 19, 1816; demitted Oct. 26, 1832.

The following letter from Rev. Robert Paterson is full of interest:

January, 1784.

My Dear Sir: I had occasion to write you once and again of late. My last letter was sent by a young man, Mr. Brander, nephew to your old Tutor, Mr. John Brander. The young man went to take possession of his Uncle's Estate & Property. I refer to that letter, which I hope was carefully delivered. In it I informed you of the state of my family, & of my sad loss by the death of my Dear wife, July 28th, 1782, who left me with seven young children. Five of which are sons, & Two Daughters. We all much lament the Death of your Father. Tho' his family & Friends are great losers by that event,—I hope he has gone to a better place than this world could afford. We also much regret the last accounts of your Mother's dangerous illness [which] we had from Prof. Gordon, who is very kind in communicat[ing] every information about our Friends which he receives [from] you.

My family is in the same state as when I wrote you last. Your Aunts stay with me, Grissel is my house-keeper, & Isabel is in the family. My children, thank God are in good health at present, and promise well.

Mrs. Gordon of Comrie is still in life but an old woman & feels the bodily infirmities of old age. Her sister, Mrs. Innes, is much stouter, but somewhat ailing now & then.

I presume you remember Dr. James Hay when he was Minister of Dyce near Ab'dn. He was removed to Elgin between 4 & 5 years ago [July 8, 1779]. He died of a short illness on the 22d inst. much regretted [Jan. 22, 1784, æ 48]. He married a second time, & has now left behind him by his first wife six children. His second wife, whom he has now left a widow, had no children to him.

This country has been in great distress almost for three years by Dearth. The last year was peculiarly distressing to the Poor, & this year appears not to be favorable. The Parliament last year appointed £10,000 sterling to be laid out in providing meal for the North of Scotland, more especially for the Highlands where they had scarcely any crops at all,—and many private gentlemen were highly liberal to their Tenants, otherwise many must have inevitably perished. I hope you will soon be in Britain, & that we shall ere long have the pleasure of seeing you in this house,—on which account I make my letter short. I most sincerely wish you, Mrs. Scott & family, an agreeable Voyage & all happiness. Your Aunts join with me in good wishes & compliments to you all. This is intended to go by one of two gentlemen who are called to be teachers of an academy meant to be established at Dumfries. If any accident should detain you longer in Virginia than you intended, I hope you will do me the pleasure to write me. Please remember us affectionately to all our Relatives & connections on the other side of the Atlantic, & believe me to be with true regard, My Dear Sir,

Your affectionate Kinsman & most obedient servant, ROBERT PATERSON.

New Spynie, January 28th, 1784. | The Rev'd Mr. John Scott, Dumfries, Virginia.

SCOTT FAMILY.

1a.   REV. ALEXANDER[2] SCOTT, M. A. (*John*[1]), of Overwharton parish, Stafford county, Va., b. Dipple parish, Elgin, now Moray, Scotland, July 20, 1686; d. "Dipple," Stafford county, Virginia, April 1, 1738; will dat. Jan. 19, 1737. He m. Va., May 20, 1717, SARAH (GIBBONS) BRENT, b. England, 1692; d. "Dipple," Va., Oct. 29, 1733; daughter of William Gibbons, Wiltshire, Eng., Gent., widow of William Brent, Richlands, Stafford county, Va., and sister of Sir John Gibbons, member of Parliament for Middlesex.

Rev. Alexander Scott received his Master's degree in Great Britain, and was pro. ordained and licensed for Virginia by the Lord Bishop of London about 1710. He first appeared in Virginia as Rector of Overwharton parish, Stafford Co., 1711, to which parish, as his tombstone states, he ministered "near 28 years." He came to Virginia doubtless to escape the political troubles in Scotland. The records of the Brent family, in possession of the late John Carroll Brent, of Washington, D. C., contain the statement that Mr. Scott came to America with the Rev. David Stuart of K. G. Co., Va., 1717. That this date is an error appears from Mr. Scott's report to the Bp. of London. Meade says that David Stuart was in K. G. Co. many years before 1722. He also states, in speaking of Mr. Scott's parish, that "in 1724 there were within its limits 650 families, 80 to 100 communicants, one church, and several chapels, as full as they could hold." Mr. Scott was possessed of a large estate in Virginia. He rented the parish glebe, and built a house for himself on his own land in Staff'd and called it "Dipple," from the Scotch parish of that name, where he was born. He was present at a convention of the Va. clergy held at W. & M. Coll., April —.

Meade states that Mr. Scott never married. This is an error. Among the Brent papers it is recorded that

"William Brent, 2d son of Giles Brent, heir entail to the estates in Virginia, and next after his brother Giles heir to the estates of Cosington in England, went there in 1708, and was m. in London on the 12th May, 1709, to Sarah Gibbons of Box Parish, dau. of William Gibbons of Wiltshire, Gent. He d. Nov. 26, following. His son William, b. Mar 6, 1710, was heir entail to the estates in Eng. and Va. His mother brought him to Va. Jan., 1717, and on the 20th May, 1717, was herself m. to Rev. Alexander Scott, Rector of Overwharton Par., and d. Oct. 3, 1733. This family of Brents, descended from Giles, are called the Richland Brents.") *v.* Hen., V. 292; also DeBow's Review, XXVI. 489.)*

Mr. Scott and his wife lie buried in "Dipple" grave yard, an enclosure located on the property of Mr. Scott, two miles from Richland Station, Staff'd Co. The tomb of Mr. S. was at one time a raised marble slab supported by four or six pillars, and about two feet high. It now lies flat on the ground, but the slab is in a good state of preservation. At the top of the slab appears, in relief, an hour-glass, beneath which is a skull and cross bones, and under that an angel, head and shoulders, winged. Then follows this inscription :

" Here lyes the body of the Rev'd Alex. Scott, A. M., & Presbyter of the Church of England; who lived near twenty eight years minister of Overwharton Parish, and died in the fifty third year of his age. He being born the twentieth of July, 1686, and departed this life the first day of April, 1738."

---

* Mrs. Scott had by her 1st mar.—i. William Brent of Richland, b. Mar. 6, 1710, who d. Staff'd Co. 1742, leaving William of R., m. Eleanor, daughter of Dan'l Carroll, Rock Spring, Md.; was justice, burgess, mem. Conv. 1776, delegate, &c. Had Anna, m. Daniel Carroll ; Richard, U. S. Senator 1809 ; Col. Dan'l rroll ; Eleanor, m. Clement Hill ; William, Col. in Cont. Line. (Critic, II. 27.)

Beneath this inscription is the "coat of arms" of Mr. Scott, surrounded by the motto, "*Gaudia Nuncio Magna ;*" i. e., Arms, "*on a bend a star between two crescents, in a bordure eight stars.*" Crest, "*a dove ;*" beneath the crest an Esquire's helmet with visor closed. The dove has no olive branch in its beak, as appears in the book plate of Gustavus Scott.

On the right side of Mr. Scott's tomb there is a second tomb, raised on pillars about two feet from the ground. The top slab of gray stone is unbroken, and the effigies are complete, but the inscription is nearly illegible. Above the inscription there are, in relief, two winged angels, each holding a globe in the one hand, and a palm branch in the other. Under these are the words, "*memento mori,*" with the usual skull and cross bones. Then follows this inscription in sunken letters:

"Here lyeth the Body of Sarah, the Wife of the Rev'd Alex'r Scott, A. M., Minister of Overwharton Parish, & Formerly Wife & Widow of Wm. Brent of Richmond, Gent. She exchanged this Life for a Better About the 41st year of her Age on Monday at one o'clock of Oct'r 29th, 1733. * * *Proh, Moritur* * * *tegitur mea Sara Sepulta labe* * * * *"

This inscription was copied from the tomb some years ago by Rev. John Moncure (MONCURE 121, p. 457), who says that reference was also made on the tomb to Mrs. Scott's children, by her first husband. I visited Dipple grave yard on one of the hottest days of June, 1887, and deciphered enough of the nearly extinct inscription to assure me of the correctness of the first half, as recorded above. It is not known that Mr. Scott had any children.

Bishop Meade says: Mr. Scott, some years before his death, invited his younger brother, Rev. James Scott, to remove to Va. and inherit his estate.

Mr. Scott's official report of his church work, made to the Ld. Bishop of London, who had direct supervision of the Church in America, sometime in 1724, gives an interesting account of his charge, and is reprinted here from Perry's Va. Church Papers, p. 311–313.

"Overwharton Parish, 1724. I went from England in the year 1710 in the latter end thereof and arrived here in 1711. I have had no other Church or Parish but this. I was Licensed by the Rt. Rev. Henry, Lord Bishop of London, to officiate in this Colony of Virginia. I was sent to this Parish with a Letter from the Governor and another from the Commissary to the Vestry who received me without induction, that being not common. I do ordinarily reside in the parish wherein I do now exercise my function. The bounds of my Parish is not known it being a frontier parish but is inhabited near 80 miles in length and in some places near 3 miles, in others near 20 miles in breadth and about 650 families. There are no Indians nor other Infidels among us but Negro Slaves the Children of whom and those of them who can speak and understand the English Language we instruct and baptise if permitted by their Masters. Divine Service is performed but once every Sunday either in Church or Chappels by reason of the Great distance the inhabitants have to Church'or Chapel, Some living about 15 miles distant from either & the plantations being but thin seated. Notwithstanding I have then generally as full a congregation as either Church or Chappels can contain and can well be expected in such a thin seated place. I administer the Sacrament of the Lord's Supper 6 times a year, and generally have betwixt 80 & 100 Communicants each time. I catechise the youth of my parish in Lent and a great part of the Summer.

Our Church is tolerably well provided our two Chappels want a pulpit Cloth, reading Desk Cloth, Communion table cloth, and vessels for the Communion. The value of my living is very uncertain being paid in Tobacco the quantity 16,000 lb Tobacco yearly & being in a frontier place may be worth *communibus annis* 5 shillings for each hundred pounds and very often not so much worth. The glebe lies so inconvenient at the lower end of the parish that I was obliged to lease it out and purchase a convenient plantation near the middle of the parish for myself. There is no house upon it for its being so inconvenient that it must be leased out it did not seem needful to build one. I preached at the Church and one of the Chappels near to which the inhabitants are thickest seated every Sunday by turns and at the other Chappel 6 times a year. There is no public school for the instruction of youth, and there is no Parochial Library.   ALEXANDER SCOTT."

2. REV. JAMES[2] SCOTT, M. A. (*John*[1]), of "Dipple" and "Westwood," Virginia, b. Dipple parish, Elgin, Scotland, —; d. Virginia, —, 1782; will dat. Aug. 22, 1782.* He m. "Rich Hill," Charles county, Maryland, cir. 1738, SARAH BROWN, b. Aug. 29, 1715; d. —, 1784; daughter of Dr. Gustavus and Frances (Fowke) Brown. (BROWN 8, p. 154.)

Rev. James Scott came to Virginia before 1739. Bishop Meade says that his brother Alexander invited him to come to Va. and inherit his estate. There is no evidence that he was ever Assistant to his brother. Rev. John Moncure (MON-CURE 1, p. 424) became the Assistant in Overwharton Par. before 1738, and succeeded Rev. Alexander Scott as Rector in 1738. Rev. James Scott, however, inherited his brother's estate and lived at "Dipple," Va., until he went to Pr. Wm. Co. His five eldest children were born at "Dipple," and their births are recorded in Overwharton Par. register 1739-1745, and were baptized by him. In 1745 he became Rector of Dettingen Parish, Pr. Wm. Co., Va., continuing in charge until his death, a period of 37 years.

His connexion with this parish was effected doubtless by the following letters to the vestry by Gov. Wm. Gooch of Va. and Commissary Dawson of Va. (Meade, II. 208):

"WILLIAMSBURG, April 26, 1745.

"*Gentlemen:* As your parish is at present unfurnished with a minister, I recommend to your approbation and choice the Rev. Mr. Scott, who, in my opinion, is a man of discretion,

---

* In the name of God Amen I *James Scott* of the County of Prince William and Commonwealth of Virginia being in good health do make this my last will and testament & revoke all other wills before this date.

Impris I give my immortal soul to Almighty God and humbly hope for pardon of all my sins by the merits & mediation of Jesus Christ my savior and redeemer, my body I desire may be buried in a decent manner without pomp or parade and what estate God hath given me I leave as follows: I give and confirm to my son *John Scott*, clerk, the lands in Fauquier and Fairfax Countyes already given by deeds. Item I give to my son *Gustavus Scott* all the lands in Stafford and Fairfax given him and confirm by this will the deeds made to him. Item I give to my son *William Scott* the lands in Fairfax given him and hereby confirm the deeds made him. Item I also confirm the deeds of the lands made to my Grandson *Alex. Scott* son of *Robert* dec'd after the death of his Grandmother. Item I confirm the half of a tract of land given to *Dr. Brown* & my daughter *Catherine* by a deed. Item I give to my beloved wife Sarah Scott the dwelling house where I live called Westwood with five hundred acres of land adjoining & the use and occupation of all my personal estate except as hereafter excepted, also the rents of all my lands now rented or may be rented at my death. Item I give to my son the following slaves, Josh, Ben, Jane, Nell & Joe & after his mother's death, Elgin, George, Suck, Milley, Sarah & their increas to him and his heirs forever. Item I give to my grandson *Alexander Scott*, before named after the death of his Grandmother these slaves, Ceasar, Manuel, Stephen, Charlotte, Simon, Daniel & Bett with her two daughters Daphne & Nance, but if he should die before he is in possession of them or without lawful issue his lands go according to the deeds & his slaves to be equally divided among all my children. Item Whereas I some years ago made a purchase of slaves belonging to *Col. Thos. Blackburn* which slaves were under Execution for debts due from the said *Blackburn* & for which I made myself liable by Bond, now my will and desire is and I hereby declare that those slaves shall be only considered as under a mortgage for the payment of my engagements & that they shall still as they have done hitherto remain in the possession of the said *Blackburn* liable only to a discharge of those debts contracted for him & shall after such discharge revert to the full & entire possession & be the legal right of the said *Blackburn* his Ex'rs and Adm'rs as fully as I had never made such purchase, I hereby forbid and annull any claim which my heirs or any of them may set up to the said slaves or anything else in consequence of my purchase under these executions further than the balance of such part of my engagements as still remain due. Item I give to my grandaughter *Sarah Scott* a bond for a 100£ due from her father's estate, to her & her heirs forever. Item I will and desire that my esteemed friend *Thomas Mc-Kie* be supported and kept during his natural, with good bed and board at the expence of my estate and that my wife keep him but if they should not agree I give him four thousand lbs. of Tobo. yearly out of my estate. Item I give and bequeath to my above named wife *Sarah* the use of all my slaves not devised the stocks of Horses and all kinds, also the utensils of my quarter and home house and all my personal estate during her widowhood. I also give her during that term the use of the land left to my Grandson *Alexander* and at the old Court house in joint tenancy between Mr. & Mrs. Daniel & and after death or marriage my will is that my estate in her possession not given (except a girl named Merinda and the silver plate which I leave at her disposal and everything made with her own hands) be sold and equally divided between my three daughters *Helen Christian* and *Catherine*. Item I give to my son William a set of Chinz curtains made by his mother with a pair of sheets, Blankets, Bedstead in the Parlour a Quilt. Item I give to *Catherine* the wife of *Dr. William Brown* a set of dark coloured curtains with Bedstead, bed sheets, blanket and quilt or counterpain. Item I give to my grandson *Alexander* a set of Striped curtains, Bedstead, bed, Blankets, Sheets & quilt. Item I leave my friend *Colo. George Mason* my agent to manage my shares of the Ohio Company and to pay the money of my part to be added to my personal estate Item Whereas I have an

understanding and integrity, and in every way qualified to discharge the sacred office to your satisfaction. I am your affectionate friend and humble servant. WILLIAM GOOCH."

[From the Commissary.]

" *Gentlemen :* I hope and believe that your parish will be worthily supplied by the Rev. Mr. James Scott. His merits having been long known to you, I need not dwell upon it. That you may be greatly benefitted by his good life and doctrine, and mutually happy with each other, and all the souls committed to his charge may be saved, is the daily prayer of,
"Gentlemen, your most affectionate humble servant,
" William and Mary College, April 26, 1745. WILLIAM DAWSON."

Bishop M. also states that Mr. Scott lived the most of his time that he held the charge of Dettingen Par. "at his own estate of 'Westwood,' the gift, it is believed, of his brother." However, the parish purchased for him a glebe of 400 a. on Quantico Creek, paying Thomas Harrison £135 str. for it. The vestry also passed the following resolutions at the time of his call to the charge of the Church : "Ordered that the Rev. James Scott be received into this parish on condition of his removing into it as soon as a glebe and house is prepared."

In Hening (VII. 630) is recorded "An Act to confirm and establish an agreement made between James Scott the elder, Clerk, and James Scott the younger, his son," which shows that Rev. Alexander Scott left by will to his "dear and loving brother James Scott," in fee taile, eight tracts of land, *i. e.*, 800 acres, Stafford Co., 2,823 acres on Carter's Run, Fauq'r Co., 2,050 acres same county, 1,000 Fairfax Co., 2,000 elsewhere same county, total 8,673 acres, with 30 slaves. In order to make proper provision for his younger children, being *seven in number* [Alexander was then dead], Rev. James Scott and his eldest son, and heir, James Scott, applied for right to dock the entail of 3 of the above 8 tracts of land, "in order to raise a provision for his said younger children ; by means of which his

---

Act of Assembly for 2950 acres of land in Kentucky for our importation of fifty-nine Servants [?] my will is that if my son *Gusty* pays the expence of the whole he shall have half of it, and the other half shall be divided between *William* the son of *Dr. William Brown* and *James* the son of *James* but if *Gusty* declines the terms that the whole shall then be divided equally between *James Scott* son of *James* and said *William Brown.* Finally I appoint my beloved wife *Sarah* Executrix. and my sons *John and Gustavus* Exrs of this my last will and testament. IN WITNESS WHEREOF I have hereunto set my hand and seal this 2d day of August in the year of our Lord 1782 written with my own hand.

JAMES SCOTT [Seal]

Signed, sealed, acknowledged and declared to be my last will and testament in presence of John
his
Macmillian Geo Graham Robert R Young David Crowley.
mark

IN ORDER to explain any doubts which may arise upon my will bearing date the second day of August in the year of our Lord One thousand seven hundred and Eighty-two wholly written with my own hand except the figures 1782 I do annex this codicil to my said will declareing my meaning and intention to be that my dwelling house of Westwood with the five hundred acres of land adjoining left to my wife during her widowhood should after her death or marriage descend to my Grandson *Alexander Scott* the son of my late son *James Scott* deceased and to his heirs forever. Item I do declare it to be my meaning and intention that the residue of my tract of land adjoining to my house of Westwood descend to my said Grandson *Alexander* son of *James* and his heirs forever. Item I do declare it to be my meaning and intention that should my Grandson *Alexander Scott* the son of my late son *Robert Scott* deceased die without issue before he attains the age of twenty one years that the negroes bequeathed him by my said will shall be equally divided amongst all my children. Item I do declare it to be my meaning and intention that the money goods and debts only of my share in the Ohio Company are to be considered as personal estate, included in the bequest to my wife and daughters, but that my share of the lands as a member of that Company shall be equally divided share and share alike to take as tenants in common and not as jointenants between my said Grandson *Alexander Scott* son of *James* my three sons *John Gustavus and William* and my Grandson *Alexander Scott* son of my late son *Robert Scott* deceased and their heirs forever, but if my Grandson *Alexander* the son of *Robert Scott* should die without issue before he arrives at the age of twenty one years then his share of my lands in the Ohio Company is to be equally divided between my Grandson *Alexander* the son of *James Scott* and my said sons *John, Gustavus and William* and their heirs forever as tenants in common. Item I declare it to be my meaning and intention that my lands at Prince William Old Court house my share of the money goods or debts in the Ohio Company, all the negroes and personal estate left by said will to my wife during her widowhood [except the slave Meranda the plate and the annual rents and profits left at her disposal and the negroes particularly bequeathed after death to my son *William* and my Grandson *Alexander* son of *Robt*] be sold after the death or marriage of my said wife, by my surviving Executors or Executor and the money arising therefrom be divided into three equal parts, the one third of which I give to the separate use of my daughter *Helen Bullet* during her natural life without the interposition of her husband *Cuthbert Bullet Esq* and without the interposition of any future husband that My said daughter may hereafter marry and I give to my said daughter full power by her last will and testament whether she be married or single to

SCOTT FAMILY.

said eldest son, who is *now married*, would have no provision for or be able to maintain his wife and family during his said father's life," unless the Assembly should empower him to make the following arrangement: Rev. James Scott being seized of 2,000 a. in P. W. Co. which he had bought of Sam. Jackson, Abraham Farrow, and Wm. Ashmore, which improved was as valuable as all the other lands of which he was seized in taille under the will of said brother Alexander, agrees by this Act to put his said son James into immediate possession of the 2,823 a. on Carter's Run, Fauq'r Co., and also the said lands in P. W. Co. which he had bought of Jackson et al., with 17 slaves from Alexander Scott's estate, and 16 slaves from James' estate, all in fee taille, he the elder James to stand seized in fee simple of all the rest of the estate of Alexander Scott, dec'd. This Act passed the Assembly November, 1762.

Rev. James Scott was pro. educated at Aberdeen Univ.; but, as in the case of Rev. Alexander Scott, I have applied in vain to learn from Aberdeen or Edinburgh Universities whether he studied at either place. He was also pro. ordained and licensed for Virginia by the Lord Bishop of London cir. 1735. He was one of the Justices of P. W. Co. 1769–70, and pro. later. (C. P., I. 261.) It is believed that he and his wife were buried in "Dipple" grave yard, as here lie the remains of his wife's mother, Frances (Fowke) Brown, Christian (Brown) Graham, Rich'd M. Scott, &c., but no stone exists to show his grave or that of his wife. The late Mrs. W. E. Moncure of "Somerset," adjoining "Dipple," who knew more about the grave yard than probably any one living, stated in 1883 that "A very aged lady, then over 80, whose home adjoined old Dipple estate, told me that her old black nurse was present at Rev. James Scott's funeral and saw him buried in the Dipple grave yard. She says also that there was a lady in the Scott family who was so

dispose of the same in any manner she shall think proper to any child or children that she now hath or hereafter may have by the said *Cuthbert Bullet Esq.* and in case my said daughter shall make no such disposition then I direct the same after her death to be equally divided between all the children of the said *Cuthbert* and *Helen Bullet* which shall be then living and the children of such as shall be dead the children of those that are dead taking such part as their deceased parent would have taken if living. Item I give one other third of the money arising from such sales to the separate use of my daughter *Christian Blackburn* during her natural life without the interposition of her husband *Thomas Blackburn Esq* and without the interposition of any future husband that my said daughter may marry hereafter and I give to my said daughter full power by her last will and testament whether she be married or single to dispose of the same in any manner she may think proper to any child or children that she now hath or hereafter may have by the said *Thomas Blackburn* Esq. and in case my said daughter shall make no such disposition then I direct the same after her death to be equally divided between all the children of the said *Thomas* and *Christian Blackburn* which shall be then living and the children of such as are dead, the children of those that shall be dead taking such part as their deceased parent would have taken if living. Item I give the remaining third of the money arising from such sales to the separate use of my daughter *Catherine Brown* during her natural life without the interposition of her husband *Doctor William Brown* and without the interposition of any future husband that my said daughter may marry hereafter and I give to my said daughter full power by her last will and testament whether she be married or single to dispose of the same in any manner she may think proper to any child or children that she now hath or hereafter may have by the said Doctor *William Brown* and in case my said daughter shall make no such disposition then I direct the same after her death to be equally divided amongst all the children of the said Doctor *William Brown* and his said wife which shall be then living and the children of those who shall be dead, the children of those who shall be dead taking such part as their deceased parent would have taken if living. Lastly I do by this my codicile confirm my said will and do annex this codicile thereto and desire it may be considered as a part thereof.

IN WITNESS WHEREOF I have hereunto set my hand and affixed my seal this twenty second day of August in the year of our Lord one thousand seven hundred and eighty two.

his
JAMES S. SCOTT [Seal.]
mark

Signed, sealed, published and declared by the Testator before use to be his last will and testament who witnessed the same in the Testators presence and in the presence of each other.

his   his
Thomas Mason, David D. Jaminesson, Robert R. Young.
mark   mark

Sarah Scott's will dat. Jan. 10, 1783; pro. June 8, 1783; directs her burial beside her husband at Dipple, and tombstones erected over the two graves; names Sarah and Eleanor Brown, daus. of Dr. Wm. B.; gives gold watch and best diamond ring to son William S., other diamond ring to Alex. S., son of Robert, also a sett of breast buckles for knee breeches to same; divided much handsome silver between the two last named; son Wm. S. sole exc'r.

9

devoted to his memory that she desired to be buried at the gate of the grave yard that no one might reach his grave without passing over hers." The will of his son William (q. v.) also indicates that Rev. James and Sarah Scott were buried at "Dipple."

Children—the first five b. Overwharton Parish, Staff'd Co. :

+ 3.   i.   HELEN,[3] b. June 7, 1737 (O. R.); d. —; m. —, Hon. Cuthbert Bullitt.

  4.   ii.   ALEXANDER, b. July 10, 1740; B. July 15, 1740 (O. R.); d. before 1762, and not named in father's will. It is said that he was drowned at sea on his return from the University at Aberdeen, where he was educated. In 1762 James was called the eldest son.

  5.   iii.   CATHERINE, b. Jan. 22, 1741 (O. R.); d. —; m. —, William Brown, M. D. (BROWN 36, p. 177.)

+ 6.   iv.   JAMES, b. Jan. 8, 1742 (O. R.); d. —, 1779; m. before 1762, Elizabeth Harrison.

+ 7.   v.   CHRISTIAN, b. Mar. 4, 1745 (O. R.); d. —; m. —, Col. Thomas Blackburn.

+ 8.   vi.   JOHN, b. cir. 1747; d. Apr. —, 1785; m. June 10, 1768, Elizabeth Gordon.

  9.   vii.   ROBERT, b. cir. 1749, b. before 1782, lost at sea; will dat. Dec. 17, 1770; pro. June 2, 1783; m. —, Catherine Stone, Charles Co., Md. (BROWN 19, p. 175, n.)

        Robert Scott, in his will, sworn to June 2, 1783, by John and Wm. Scott and C. Bullitt as in his own handwriting, leaves his wife Catherine S. and his son Alex'r S. to the tender care of his parents, Rev. J. S. and Sarah S.; directs his son be sent at 16 to Aberdeen (unless W. and M. Coll. sh'd be under better regulation), to remain until he take his A. M., studies Divinity and takes Orders; leaves no estate, but appoints Gustavus S. guardian to his son.

        Children :

        i. Alexander of Georgetown, D. C., b. —, d. —; minor in 1782, as per will of Jas. Scott, Sr.; m. —, Elizabeth Blackwell, dau. of Capt. Wm. Blackwell. (CONWAY, p. 268, No. 44.) Had—i. Elizabeth. ii. Ann. iii. Frances. iv. Sarah. v. Juliet. vi. Mrs. Brown of N. C., who had Kate, m. Col. John S. Popham, Culp'r Co., Va. vii. and viii. unknown.

 10.   viii.   WILLIAM, b. cir. 1751; d. s. Dec., 1787; buried "Dipple;" will dat. July 4, 1785; pro. Fairfax Co., Dec. 17, 1787.†

+11-12.   ix.   GUSTAVUS, b. cir. 1753; m. Feb. 16, 1777, Margaret Hall Caile.

---

† In the name of God, amen, I, William Scott of the County of Fairfax and Commonwealth of Virginia, of perfect strength of mind and memory do make and ordain this my Last will & Testament in manner following; Imprimis, I commit my Soul to God in humble confidence of his mercy, through our Lord Jesus Christ at whose awful tribunal I fully expect to appear at the great day when the secrets of all hearts shall be disclosed.

Item, it is my will and desire that my body may be decently interred in the family burying ground at Dipple where there may be a tomb errected over my Grave with a proper inscription on it, and if it should so happen that the grave yard should not be enclosed at my death, I desire it may be decently paled or walled in at the expence of my estate.

Item, I desire that a tomb may be erected over the grave of my dear and honored father and mother, properly inscribed, [if I should not have it done in my life time agreeable to my mother's request], at the expence of my estate. Item, I bequeath all the real and personal estates I die possessed of or may have a right to after the payments of my just debts, inclosing the grave yard, and erecting the above mentioned Tombs to my dear brother *Gustavus Scott* of Dorchester County, Maryland, and his heirs forever, incumbered with the legacys after written which I desire may be paid in four years after my demise by him my said brother *Gustavus Scott*, one hundred pounds current money Virginia to my sister *Hellen Bullett*, £100 like money to my sister *Christian Blackburn* and twenty pounds like money per annum to my sister *Catherine Brown* during her natural life. It is my intention that the above legacies to my sisters above mentioned should be absolutely at their own disposal & not subject the debts or controul of their husbands.

Item, I bequeath the following legacies also to be paid by my brother *Gustavus Scott* out of my estate in five years after my death, one hundred pounds current money of Virginia to my nephew *John Scott* son of late brother the rev'd *John Scott* deceased & £100 apiece to each of his daughters namely *Elizabeth Scott* & *Margaret Scott* in like manner and to be paid in like manner, also £100 Current Money of Virginia to my nephew *Thomas Blackburn* Son of Colo Thomas and Christian Blackburn to be paid in like manner by my said brother *Gustavus Scott* out of my estate.

Item, I request that an elegant ring with a lock of my hair under the stone of it, be presented to miss *Ann Martin* Daughter of *Thomas Bryan Martin* Esq, as a pledge of my friendship for her.

Lastly I appoint my much esteemed friends, *Gustavus Scott, Thomas Blackburn & Cuthbert Bullett* Esqrs Executors of this my Last will and Testament written with my own hand. I hereby revoke all wills preceeding this date.

Witness my hand and Seal this fourth day of July one thousand seven hundred and eighty five.
Strawberry vale July 4th 1785.

                          [Signed] WM. SCOTT. [L. S.]
    A Copy.   Teste P. WAGENER, C.

3. HELEN[3] SCOTT (*James,[2] John[1]*), b. Overwharton parish, Stafford county, Va., June 7, 1739; B. by Rev. James Scott, June 8, 1739 (O. R.); d. Va., Sep. 15–16, 1795 ; will dat. July 26, 1795 ; pro. Prince William county, July 3, 1797 ;* m. cir. 1760, HON. CUTHBERT BULLITT, b. —, 1740; d. Prince William county, Va., Aug. 27, 1791 ; will dat. May 16, 1791 ; pro. Oct. 3, 1791 ;† son of Benjamin and Elizabeth (Harrison) Bullitt, Fauquier county, Va.

Hon. Cuthbert Bullitt studied law and practiced in P. W. Co., Va. He was a delegate to the Va. Assembly, 1777 and 1787, and at one time Speaker of the House. He was also a mem. of the Va. Conventions of 1775, 1776 and 1788, and of the P. W. Committee of Safety. In 1777 the Va. Assembly appointed him, with six others, on a commission to ascertain the losses sustained at the hands of the British by the people of Norfolk in the burning of that town, Jan., 1776. (Hen., IX. 328.) He was a legatee of his brother Col. Thomas Bullitt, as Mar. 29, 1784, Cuthbert B. and Ellen, his wife, of P. W. Co., and Alexander S. B., their son, deeded land devised to Cuthbert by the will of his brother Thomas. In a letter to Gov. Henry, written from "View Mount," P. W. Co., Dec. 30, 1784, he complains that he is

"Condemned for bread to drudge on in the practice of the Law, and applies to be appointed Attorney for the Commonwealth in one or more of the Districts on the Circuit where he lived ; Hopes the application may not be improper ; he is at present Attorney for the Commonwealth in two of the Counties comprising the District, and resides a few miles from where the Circuit Court is to be held." (Cal. Pap., III. 639.)

He was elected Dec. 27, 1788, by joint ballot of the Senate and House of Del., Additional Judge of the General Court of Va. (*id.,* IV., 537.) Two other letters to the Gov. relative to his app't by the Ass'y to receive rents from the Bristoe lands, P. W. Co., are in Cal. Pap., V. 272, 283. Judge B.'s connexion with the Scott-Baylis affair will be noticed under Rev John Scott. In 1787 the Ass'y incorporated the town of Newport, for which 30 acres were appropriated from the lands of Cuthbert Bullitt in P. W. Co. Here, in 1788, Mr. B. erected a tobacco warehouse, which was in 1792, and later, an authorized point for the inspection of tobacco. In 1788 he was appointed Trustee for the town of Carrborough, P. W. Co. (Hen., XII., 684, 695; XIII., 480.) Many of these early Va. towns have disappeared. Cuthbert Bullitt entered 8,000 a. land on N. fork Licking Creek, Ky., May 16, 1788. (Ky. Rep.)

Children (BULLITT):

13.   i. COLONEL ALEXANDER SCOTT,[4] b. P. W. Co., —, 1761 ; d. Jeff. Co., Ky., Apr. 13, 1816 ; m. Oct. —, 1785, Priscilla Christian, dau. of Col. Wm. Christian, who em. to Ky., 1783–4, and his wife Anne, sister of Patrick Henry. (For Christian *v.* Life and Times of Judge Caleb Wallace of Ky., 66–80, and Peyton's Augusta Co., Va.) Col. B. was a delegate from P. W. Co., Va., 1783. In 1784 he located near Bullskin Stream, Shelby Co.,

---

* Helen Bullitt's will names children Sarah Barnes, Helen Grant Huie, Sophia Bullitt, Alexander Scott Bullitt, and Thomas James Bullitt, whom she made ex'r. In his acc't, Sep. 17, 1795, is an item of £8.3.4 for funeral expenses.

† Hon. Cuthbert Bullitt's will gives grandson Cuthbert B. 750 a. land in Ky.; his own son Thomas B. land in Quantico and 800 a. in Fauq'r, 600 a. bought of the wid. of Rev. Jno. Scott, 200 a. bought of John Waller, 1500 a. on the waters of Pleasant Run and Beechfork, Ky.; names daus. Frances, Sarah, Helen and Sophia; sons Alexander and Thomas; son-in-law Wm. Garrard; and friends Thomas Blackburn, Alexander Henderson and George Graham, ex'rs; Rev. Thomas Harrison and Mr. John Pope, guardians of his children. Wit., Thomas Harrison, Jr., Thomas Ball, Cuthbert Harrison, Thomas Harrison, son of Thomas. (PEYTON, p. 512.)

Ky., but was forced by Indian raids to seek a safer place. He then entered and settled on a tract of land near Sturgus' Station, Jeff. Co., Ky., where he spent the rest of his life. He took a very active part in the affairs of his State. In 1786 his name appears on a petition from Jeff. Co. to the settlers in adjoining counties for aid against the Indians who had, just before, slain Col. Wm. Christian. (C. P., IV., 161.) He was appt'd County Lieut. for Jeff. Co., 1787. He was Pres. of the Court Martial which, Mar. 21, 1787, tried and convicted Col. Hugh McGary* of Mercer Co., Ky., for the murder of Malunthy, a Shawnee chief who had surrendered as Prisoner of War (IV., 258) to Gen'l Clarke, and other misdemeanors. He was also mem. Ky. Conv., 1788, and of the Const. Conv., 1792, also the Conv., 1799 of which he was President; mem. Ky. Senate, 1792, and Speaker of the same, 1792–1804. In 1800 he was elected Lieut. Gov. of Ky., the first to hold the office. He continued to represent this Co. in Leg. until 1808 when he retired from public life. In 1789 the Va. Ass'y appt'd him a Trustee of the town of Louisville, Ky. (Hen., XIII., 91.) Bullitt Co., Ky. was named in his honor. (Collins' Ky.)

Children:

i. Cuthbert, b. —; d. —; m. —. Had—i. Henry Massie, M. D., d. Ky., Feb., 1880, an eminent physician of whom I can learn nothing more. ii. Priscilla Christian, b. —; d. July 3, 1872; m. —, Archibald Alexander Gordon. (CONWAY 53, p. 251.)

ii. William Christian, b. —; d. —; m. —, Mildred Ann Fry, dau. of Joshua and Peachy (Walker) Fry of Ky. Had—1. Joshua Fry, b. —; m. Elizabeth R. Smith. He was a lawyer; Mem. Ky. Leg. from Louisville 1851–3; elected Judge Ky. Ct. of Appeals Mar. 20, 1861, holding the office until June, 1865, the last year as Chief Justice; arrested by Gov. Bramlette Nov. 22, 1864, charged with belonging to the "Sons of Liberty," and nominally sent into the Southern Confederacy, but really placed in prison in Louisville; exchanged Jan. 4, 1865, and resumed his seat. Mar. 1 he was summoned for trial before the Legislature; removed from office June 3, 1865. In the Legislature of Ky., Mar. 2, 1868, and Mar. 16, 1869, resolutions were offered stamping this action of the Legislature of 1865 "as a flagrant outrage upon constitutional right, and an insult to the honor and dignity of Ky." They were adopted Mar. 16, 1869, by a vote of 64 to 17 in both houses. In 1871 Judge B.'s political disfranchisement was removed. (For full accounts of this political crime v. Collins' Ky., I. 148, 151, 157, 160, 188, 196, 213 (II. 310); had Joshua, John C., James Bell. 2. Alexander Scott, d. 1840; grad. A. B., Univ. Pa., 1813; A. M. 1817. 3. John C., b. Feb. 10, 1824; m. Theresa Langhorne. He is in the foremost rank at the Philadelphia, (Pa.) bar, and the leader in commercial law. Is principal mem. of the legal firm of Bullitt and Fairthorn. Full sketches of Mr. B. will be found in Biog. Cyc. of Pa., &c., &c. He had Theresa, m. Dr. Jno. W. Coles, Asst. Surg. U. S. N., May 6, 1863; Pass'd Asst. Jan. 14, 1867; Surg. Oct. 6, 1873; Wm. Christian, grad. A.B., Univ. Pa., 1876; Julia; Logan McKnight; James; Helen Key; John C. 4. Martha Bell. 5. Susan Peachey, m. Hon. Archibald Dixon, b. Caswell Co., N. C., Apr. 2, 1802; moved to Henderson Co., Ky., 1805, with his father; studied law; Mem. Ky. Leg. 1830 and 1841; Senate 1836 and 1840; Lt. Gov. of Ky. 1844–1848; Mem. Constit'n Conv. 1849; U. S. Senate, succeeding Henry Clay, 1852–1855; author of the famous Kansas-Nebraska bill, which was accepted by Judge Douglas, repealing the Mo. Compromise act of 1821; elected 1862 to the Border State Conv., Louisville, where he failed to influence that body to conciliatory measures to avert war (Collins); had Kate, m. David Burbank;

---

* Col. McGary was one of the 1st Justices of Ky., 1781; Maj. July 1781, 1st Ky. Mil., having removed to Ky., 1777. (Collins Ky.)

William B.; Thomas B.   6. Sarah Bell, d. inf.   7. Helen Martin, m. Dr. Henry Chenowith ; had Martha Ann, m. John Stiles ; Fanny Bell ; Susan B.; Henry; James.   8. Capt. Thomas Walker, C. S. A., b. May 17, 1838 ; m. his cos. Annie Priscilla, dau. of Capt. W. Logan, b. Apr. 26, 1847 (Marshall Fam., 278); grad. Centre Coll., Ky.; lawyer; private C. S. A. 1861; rose to a captaincy (*v.* Bivouac, 1886, Vol. I., 51, 116) ; had William Marshall, b. Mar. 3, 1873 ; James Bell, b. June 18, 1874 ; Agatha Marshall, b. Nov. 24, 1875 ; Alexander Scott, b. Jan. 23, 1877 ; Mildred Ann, b. Oct. 12, 1879 ; Keith, b. Feb. 18, 1881 ; Mira L., b. July 12, 1885.   9. James Bell, C. S. A., killed by U. S. troops while carrying a flag of truce.   10. Henry Massie, C. S. A.; m. Mary L. Frederick.

  iii. Annie, b. —; m. —— Howard.
  iv. Helen Martin, m. (I.) Gen. Henry Massie, for many years of Chillicothe, O.; (II.) John L. Martin ; (III.) Col. Marshall Key, father of Judge Thomas M. Key of Cin., O., and Mrs. Hon. Thomas H. Nelson of Ind.

14. ii. THOMAS JAMES of Easton, Md., b. —; d. Dec., 1840 ; will dat. Nov. 16, 1837 ; pro. P. W. Co., Va., Jan. 2, 1841 (O. 470) ; m. —, Mrs. —— (Caile) Harrison, Balto., Md., sister of Mrs. Gustavus Scott, and dau. of —— Caile. (SCOTT, No. 11, Ex. Caile.)   She was the mother of William and Hall Harrison of Balto., Md.   Judge Scott studied law with his bro.-in-law, Hon. Gustavus Scott, and was one of the Judges of his county.   "He was one of the most elegant grandees of his day, he always appearing in top boots with knee buckles."   His will gives son Alex. C. lands in P. W. and Fauq'r Co., Va., and dau. Elizabeth Haskins Hayward lands in Talbot Co., Md., and makes her ex'x.
    Children :
   i. Thomas, d. s. p. —; m. in Balto., Md.
   ii. Alexander C.   iii. Elizabeth Haskins, m. Hayward.

15. iii. FRANCES, b. —; d. —; m. —, Capt. William Garrard of Staff'd Co., Va., and Bourbon Co., Ky.
    Children :
   i. Sophia Bullitt, named in will of 19.

16. iv. SARAH, b. —; d. —; m. —, William Barnes, Justice, P. W. Co., Va., 1793. His est. audited, P. W. Co., Feb. 3, 1825.   (O. 30.)
    Children :
   i. Mary, will of 19.   ii. Richard, d. s.
   iii. Helen M.   iv. Thomas B.
   v. Catherine A., m. Wileman Thomas.
   vi. Eliza L., m. —— Addison.   vii. Thomas.
   viii. Alexander B.   ix. William C.

17. v. HELEN ELEANOR GRANT, b. —; d. Sep. —, 1815 ; will dat. July 20, 1815 ; pro. P. W. Oct. 2, 1815 (K. 456) ; m. —, James Huie of Dumfries ; dead 1815, when she called herself "widow."   In deed Sep. 5, 1807, from Jas. Huie to Dr. Geo. Graham he refers to deed of Sep. 8, 1798 as "made before his marriage with Helen Eleanor Grant Bullitt."
    Children, from will :
   i. Helen Scott, m. John King.   ii Ann Foster.
   iii. Thomas J.   iv. James Blackburn.
   v. George William.

18-20. vi. SOPHIA C. M., b. —; d. s. Dec., 1803 ; will dat. May 27, 1803 ; pro. P. W. Jan. 2, 1804 (L., 14) ; names sisters Frances Garrard, Sarah Barnes, Helen Huie ; nieces Sophia Bullitt Garrard, Helen Scott, Ann Foster Huie and Mary Barnes ; nephew Thomas Barnes, and bro. Thos. J. Bullitt.

EXCURSES—BULLITT.

BENJAMIN BULLITT, gent., was Justice P. W. Co., Va., 1743 ; d. P. W. Co. 1757. Thomas and Cuthbert Bullitt were on the bond of his ex'rs. Benjamin Bullitt, son of Joseph Bullitt of Maryland, d. Hamilton Par., Fauq'r Co., Va., Jan. 9, 1766 ; will dat. May 3, 1766 ; pro. Fauq'r Co. Oct. 27, 1766. It is said that he m. (I.) 1727, Elizabeth Harrison of the Chappawamsie family (PEYTON, p. 512), and by her had Joseph, Thomas, Cuthbert, Elizabeth and Benjamin. His will names wife Sarah and the following children: i. Joseph, to whom he gives "all he now has." ii. Thomas, to whom two tracts of land in Maryland, one in the forks of Mattroman Creek, owned by my father Joseph, who is buried on Daniel's Branch on the same land. iii. Seth, wife of John Combs, to whom "all she now has." iv. Cuthbert, ditto. v. Elizabeth. vi. William Burditt, alias Bullitt. vii. John. viii. George. ix. Benoni. x. Parmenas. xi. Burwell, alive, P. W. Co., Oct., 1789 (Land Causes, A 2); names wife Sarah and sons Thomas and Cuthbert ex'rs. Green, in his "Historic Families of Ky.," p. 150, gives an account of this family, which is incomplete and partly incorrect, as probably the above pedigree is, because, as in this case, the family silently declined to give any information. For Col. Thomas Bullitt, prominent in the Revolution, see Olden Times, I. 180; Penn'a Arch., III. 370; Force's Arch., S. 4, Vol. V. and VI., S. 5, Vol. I, &c. Colonel Thomas Bullitt was entitled to about 6,000 a. land for Revolutionary services, which land appears to have been distributed among the descendants of his brother Cuthbert, as 555 a. were issued to Ellen Earnest; 555½ to Sophia Gwathmey; 1,481½ to Ann Huie, and Helen J., Ann E., Luby F., R. W. and W. King; 740¾ to James B. Huie; 370½ to William C. Raines; 370¾ each to Helen M., Thomas B. and Alexander B. Barnes, Catherine A. and Elizabeth L. Thomas.

Of Hon. William Christian Bullitt, son of 13, Colonel Alexander Scott Bullitt, the Louisville papers stated, that, " Mr. Bullitt was in public life but once, when elected a member of the Constitutional Convention of Kentucky, 1849-50. When the War between the States began he took sides with the South. He believed in secession as an abstract right, and the only remedy for the condition of things which had been caused by the Republican party. He did not defend slavery as a necessary evil, but as an absolute good, elevating the character, tone and bearing of the superior race and placing the negro in a better condition than he could attain in a state of freedom. He desired no office, and held his views from no desire to advance himself. He was a type of the most extreme of Southern enthusiasts. In integrity which was never suspected, a love of truth that was never questioned, and a self-respect that preferred death to dishonour, he was the model of the very highest type of the gentleman wherever he may be found." (For Fry *v.* Slaughter's Mem. of Col. Joshua Fry, Green's His. Fam. of Ky., Collins' Ky.)

6. CAPTAIN JAMES[3] SCOTT (*James,[2] John[1]*), of "Clermont," Fauquier county, Va., b. Jan. 8, 1742; B. Jan. 10, 1742. (O. R.); d. —, 1779; m. cir. 1760, ELIZABETH HARRISON, b. Feb., 1740; d. "Sunday, 8 o'clock P. M., Nov. 9, 1823, aged 83 years and 9 mo.;" daughter of Cuthbert and Frances Harrison. (PEYTON, p. 513, No. 11.)

There is an accepted tradition in the family that the eldest son of Rev. James Scott was drowned at sea while on his way from Scotland, after receiving his education there. "The second son, James, being wild and difficult to manage, had caused his father considerable expense in paying his debts, and had spent his share of his father's estate. He was apprenticed to a carpenter, but on hearing of his eldest brother's death he threw down the tool he was using exclaiming, "Farewell jackplane." Mrs. Allen of Strasburg, Va., says that the table on which he was working is in her possession. He knew he would inherit the eldest son's portion of his father's estate."

The est. of Rev. Alexander Scott was entailed by his will on the eldest son of his brother James. This entailed estate came to Capt. James by the death of his bro. Alexander. It will be seen under Rev. James S., No. 2, that the Va. Ass'y, in 1762, empowered him and his son Capt. James to break the entail, the latter receiving in lieu of his right 2,283 a. improved land in Fauq'r Co. His will devised all his estate to his wife and children, making no provisions for his debts. The Ass'y of 1786 therefore empowered his Exec'rs to sell so much of his landed estate as would pay his debts. (Hen. XII., 382.) Capt. S. was a mem. of the Va.

Ho. of Burgesses, and Va. Conv., 1775-6. "He was Captain of a Fauq'r Co. in the Revolutionary War, located at Long Bridge, Norfolk. He was ordered to Penna. with his Co., then incorporated in a Va. Reg. He d. during this war from hardships incurred in the field. His memory was long cherished by his surviving comrades." I do not find his name in any list of Va. officers.

Capt. Scott's will, pro. Fauq'r Co., Nov. 22, 1779; names wife Elizabeth, to whom he gives life interest in his est.; daus. Sarah, Frances, Elizabeth, Nancy, and sons Alexander, James, Cuthbert and Thomas; these 8 to share alike in his est. after wife's death or marriage, except his Ohio lands which he gives to his four sons; names wife, son Cuthbert, and Cuthbert Harrison, Exec'rs, who were "to have my sons well educated out of the profits of my estate, and that they shall be got into such business as they shall think will best suit their genius;" His father to have son James, if desired.

Miss E. Whiting writes of Mrs. Scott, that,

"She always superintended her farm herself, in person and on horseback, until a few years before her death, when by a fall she dislocated her hip. After that she never walked, but was wheeled about the ground in an arm chair. I have no recollection of her before this, but as I was much at the 'Grove' from childhood, I retain a vivid memory of her. She was a fine, amiable and very affectionate lady, had beautiful black eyes, soft and kind in expression, and with very winning manners."

Mrs. Scott is buried at "Clermont." A portrait of her is owned by her descendant, Mrs. Elizabeth (Hollis) Hupp, Strasburg, Va. (BROWN 86, p. 161.)

Children :

+ 21.   i.   ALEXANDER[4], b. 1762 (?); d. June 29, 1819; m. (I.) —, 1786, Frances Whiting. (II.) July 13, 1813, Sarah Butler (Henry) Campbell.
22.   ii.   FRANCES HARRISON, b. 1764-5; d. —, Nov. 27, 1837; m. Apr. 14, 1786, Gustavus Brown Horner, M. D. (BROWN 62, p. 186.)
23.   iii.   SARAH, b. —, d. s.; named in Rev. Jno. Scott's will.
24.   iv.   ANN, b. —; d. —; m. 1800, William Brown. (BROWN 86, p. 161.)
+ 25.   v.   ELIZABETH, b. July 17, 1771; d. May 16, 1858; m. April 15, 1788, Major Lawrence Ashton.
26.   vi.   CUTHBERT HARRISON, b. —; d. —, æ 90; m. —— Waugh, who is buried at "Meadow Grove."

Children :

    i. Betsy, m. Joshua Bishop.
    ii. Jane, m. Beverley Martin.
    iii. Ann, m. —— Howe.
    iv. Mary, m. (I) —— Denning, had 1 son.- (II) —— Stevens, had Lizzie, d. yng., and Whitfield, C. S. A., d. 1862.
    v. Thomas Waugh.   vi. James.   vii. Frances.

27. vii.   JAMES, b. —; d. s.—;   28. viii.   THOMAS, b. —; d. s. —.

7. CHRISTIAN[3] SCOTT (*James,*[2] *John*[1]), b. Mar. 4, 1745 (O. R.); d. 18—; m. —, COLONEL THOMAS BLACKBURN, b. cir. 1740; d. "Ripon Lodge," Va., Oct. 27, 1807; will dat. June 15, 1807; pro. P. W., Jan. 4, 1808. (I., 369); son of Richard Blackburn* of Ripon, Yorkshire, Eng., and his wife Mary Watts, of the same family as Dr. Watts the Hymnologist.

---

* *Edward Blackburn* of Bermudas, Jan. 9, 1734, gave power of atty. to "my brother Richard Blackburn of the Parish of Hambledon." (P. W. Co., Deed Bk., B., 427.) This Richard was a carpenter in 1733, and made a great many leases and contracts. There is a tradition that Col. Thos. B. had 3 sons and 1 dau., and that he built Mt. Vernon for Lawrence Washington by contract, 1743. Lieut. Christopher Blackburn served in the Cont. Line from Va. as Adjutant during the Revolutionary War and rec'd therefore 2,666⅔ a. land. (Rec. Sec. Tr., 1834.) His heirs lived in Caroline Co. One of the same name was Cornet Capt. Hill's Co., 45th Va. Reg., Staff'd, 1813-14, and one was Adjt. Gen., 1814.

Richard and Mary (Watts) Blackburn had also—1. Cary, d. yng. 2. Alice, m. Col. Thos. Elzey. Gen. Samuel B. of Bath, Va., was also of this family. Edward B. was Justice, P. W. Co., 1775. (C. P. I., 267-8.)

Col. Thos. Blackburn lived at "Ripon Lodge," near Dumfries and 12 m. from Mt. Vernon. He was a Justice P. W. Co., Va., 1769. (C. P., I., 261) Charles Brockden Brown, in his notice of the death of Col. B., says:

"He was one of those firm and unshaken partiots who fought and bled for that Independence which we now enjoy. At an early period of the Revolution he took a decided part in favour of the rights and liberties of his country, and at the battle of Germantown received a severe and dangerous wound. Distinguished for his generosity, his bravery and nice sense of honour, he was no less eminent for his hospitality, benevolence, and charity. For those domestic virtues which adorn and dignify the human character he was equally conspicuous; an affectionate husband, an indulgent parent, and a humane master. He has finished a well spent life; he has left an unsullied reputation, and is removed from a world of trouble to the mansions of infinite and eternal bliss." (Am. Reg. I., 1807.)

Col. B. was a man of large estate. During the Revolution he quartered a Regiment of Continental troops on his place a whole winter, clothed and fed them and in the spring sent them back to the army free of expense. In 1771-2 he was appt'd by the Assembly one of the Commissioners for disposing of tobacco damaged in public warehouses, and giving relief to the sufferers whose tobacco was hurt or damaged by water. (Hen. VIII., 494, 627.) In 1774 (Dec. 9) he was elected one of the Committee of Safety for Pr. William Co., in pursuance of the 11th Resolution of the Continental Congress. This Com. met on the 21st of the same month, and among other things "Resolved, as the opinion of this Com., that no person or persons whatever in this country ought to make use of East India Tea, until American grievances are redressed, and that all Public Balls and Entertainments be discountenanced in this County from this time as contrary to the sentiments of the Continental Congress." (Force's Arch., I., 1034.) He was a mem. of the Special Committee for the same county, held May 22, 1775, which unanimously thanked Capt. Patrick Henry for extorting £330 from the Receiver General for the powder Lord Dunmore removed from Williamsburg. (*id*. II., 667.) He was elected a member of the Virginia Convention of 1775 from P. W. Co., and was appointed by the Conv., with Rich'd and Henry Lee, Francis Peyton and Josiah Clapham, one of a Commission to examine, state, and settle the accounts of pay, provisions, arms, etc., furnished the Militia of certain counties in Va. (III., 423.) In 1775 the Ass'y of Va. appt'd him, with others, to settle the accounts of Militia lately employed against the Indians, and to provide for raising forces to be used in defense of the Colony of Va. (IX., 62.) In 1776 the Ass'y appt'd him a Trustee of the town of Dumfries, and in 1787 of the town of Newport (XII., 372, 603), and in 1792 of the town of Centreville, Va. (XIII., 580.)

Col. B.'s family were staunch adherents of the Prot. Epis. Ch. in Va. Bp. Meade says:

"The family of Ripon Lodge had long been the main support of the Church at Dumfries and Centreville, and their house the resort of the Clergy. On a paper dated 1812, for the support of the Rev. C. O'Neill the clergyman of the parish, Col. B. subscribed $50 the highest amount given. Old Mrs. Blackburn with her four granddaughters, Jane, Polly, Christian, and Judith Blackburn, daus. of Mr. Richard B., were much at Mt. Vernon. I became acquainted with them during the years 1812 and 1813, while I was ministering in Alexandria. They were the first fruits of my ministry in that place and very dear to me. Two of them, Jane and Polly, m. nephews of Judge Washington, and settled in Jefferson. One of them, Judy, m. Gustavus Alexander of K. G., and Christian, d. unm. By my intimacy with these four most estimable ladies, and with Mrs. Blackburn and her sister, Mrs. Taylor, I have from time to time become acquainted with the state of things at Ripon Lodge and Mt. Vernon as to the Clergy." (II., 236.) Of Mrs. B., Mrs. Alexander writes, "a lady of elegant manners and great mind, of wonderful information and Christian grace, she died in full faith and full of peace and hope." Bp. M. says: "She was long known, loved, and revered as one of the most exemplary members of our Church in the parish of Wickliff in old Frederick Co. From my first entrance on my ministry her house was my frequent resort. I have never known a family of children and servants more faithfully regulated by Christian principles than was hers, and by herself, for she was a widow at an early age. She left three children, who are members of the Episcopal Church, and who seek to follow her example in the regulation of their households." (II., 208.)

The will of Col. B. gives Ripon Lodge to the children of his deceased son Richard, and as his wife and daughters are provided for, the rest of his estate is given to his son Thomas; names wife, son-in-law Judge Washington, Mr. Crawford, Mr. Turner, his son Thomas B., and Matt. Harrison, Exec'rs.

Children (BLACKBURN):

+ 30. i. RICHARD SCOTT,⁴ b. —; d. —, 1804-5; m. (I.) —, Judith Ball. (II.) —, Ann Blause.

+ 31. ii. THOMAS, b. —; d. —; m. —, Elizabeth Sinclair.

+ 32. iii. JULIA ANN, b. —; d. s. p., Nov. 9, 1829; m. —, 1785, Hon. Bushrod Washington.

+ 33. iv. CATHERINE, b. —; d. —; m. —, 1796, Henry Smith Turner.

34. v. SARAH, b. —; d. —; m. —, Thomas Crawford of Pr. Geo. Co., Md.
Children:
i. Thomas. ii. Nathaniel.
iii. David. iv. Bushrod.

35. vi. MARY ELIZABETH, b. —; d. æ 15 of Consumption, in the Bermuda Isles.

8. REV. JOHN³ SCOTT, M. A. (*James,² John¹*), of Dettingen parish, Prince William county, Va., b. "Westwood," P.W. Co., —, 1747; d. at residence of Gov. James Wood of Va., Frederick county, Va., April —, 1785; will dat. Apr. 29, 1784; pro. Apr. 27, 1785;* m. Aberdeen, Scotland, June 10, 1768, ELIZABETH GORDON, b. —; d. —; daughter of Thomas Gordon, M. A., Provost, and Professor of Philosophy, King's College, Aberdeen, and his wife, Miss Forbes. (Excursus, Gordon 15.)

* In the name of God Amen, I *John Scott* of the Parish of Dettingen and County of Prince William Clerk, being in good health of body and sound and disposing mind and memory praised be God for the same and being desirous to settle my worldly affairs while I have strength and capacity so to do Do make and publish this my last will and testament hereby revoking and making void all former [wills] by me at any time heretofore made, And first and principally I commit my soul unto the hands of my Creator who gave it hoping in the merits & mediation of our Lord Jesus Christ and my body to the Earth to be interred at the discretion of my executrix hereafter named and as to such worldly estate, wherewith it has pleased God to intrust me I dispose of the same as followeth, Imprimis I will order and direct that all my just debts together with my Funeral expenses be justly and fully paid and satisfied, Item, I devise give and bequeath unto my dear children all my estate real and personal that I have in possession or reversion in America or Great Britain equally to be divided between them share and share alike subject however to the legacies Conditions Provisions and exceptions hereafter to be recited. Item I give and bequeath to my dear and loved wife *Elizabeth* during her widowhood one half of all my estate above mentioned on condition she accept the same in lieu of all marriage settlements and dower but if (contrary to my present hopes and oppinion of her respect to my memory and tenderness for the welfare and happiness of her infant children) she should marry then it is my will that this bequest be wholly void and that she have only such part of my estate as the law will give her. Item, it is my will and desire that the share of each of my children in one half of my whole estate at his or her age of twenty-one years or in case of daughters at marriage if made with consent of their Guardian and if it should happen that my wife marry again in that event it is will and desire that the share of each of my children in my whole estate be paid at his or her age of twenty one years or in case of daughters at marriage if made with consent of their Guardian. And if any of my sons shall be of the age of twenty one years or any of my daughters of the age of twenty one years or married with the consent of their guardian at the time my wife married again in that case it is my will and desire that the share of such of my children in my whole Estate shall be paid to them immediately, Item, I do will and desire that if my aunt *Elizabeth Innis* of the Kingdom of Great Britain shall have entailed or shall hereafter entail any Estate on me or any of my children which he shall have or inherit the devisee or legacy hereby given to such child shall be void to all intents and purposes as if there had been no such child and if paid either in part or in full shall be repaid to my Executrix or my Executors to the use of this my will, And I do further direct if any of my children should *dye* unmarried before the age of twenty one that that the share or shares of such my Children shall be equally devided among the surviving children & paid at his or her age of twenty one or in case of Daughters at marriage with the consent of their Guardian. Item, I do will order & appoint that all my estate reall and personall be

Mr. Scott's birth and death are not recorded in the Overwharton Par. Reg. The P. W. Co. records show that John Scott, son of Rev. James Scott, aged about 15 years, made deposition before Henry Lee, J. P., Sep. 13, 1762. (Deed Bk. P., 251.) Lieut. William B. Wallace (WALLACE 34) wrote his brother, Dr. James W., from Fredericksburg, Va., Oct. 23, 1785:

"The rev'd Mr. John Scott died since I wrote you last and Old Mrs. Scott his mother. This has been a remarkably sickly season throughout this State almost."

Mr. Scott grad. M. A., King's Coll., Aberdeen, Scotland, 1768.

"In 1768 on the 29th March the degree of A. M. was conferred on 'Joannes Scot, filius Magri Jacobi Scot de Westwood in provincia Virginiae,' the promoter being Mr. Thomas Gordon, Professor of Philosophy." (King's Coll. Rec.)

Tradition says that Mr. Scott's marriage was without the immediate knowledge of Prof. Gordon. If so, it did not long disturb the pleasant relations between the Gordons and himself, as his correspondence shows.

Mr. Scott's early life was marked by an event that doubtless shaped very materially his subsequent career. Bp. Meade says, that

"He was very probably set apart for the ministry in his early youth, but at the age of 18 years, having conceived that his father and himself had been insulted and injured by the misrepresentations of one who, according to report, was a most unworthy and dangerous man, deemed it his duty to seek reparation by a resort to arms. He determined to challenge, and applied to Mr. Bullitt, his brother-in-law, to be with him in the contest. Mr. Bullitt dissuaded him from the challenge in a letter which contained some of the many unanswerable

---

sold by my Executrix or Executors hereafter named, (as the case shall require at such time when my eldest son *Robert* shall attain his full age of twenty one years or if he dies before his full age at such time when he would have attained his full age of twenty-one years if he had lived so long.) Item, I give and bequeath to my dear wife *Elisabeth* a mulatto woman slave named Aminta ernestly requesting in consideration of the true and faithful services that she has received from the said slave that she may never sell or hire her out during her life time and that if the said slave should survive her she may be left free and moreover that such of her children as she shall have at the time of her freedom not above four years old shall be free also and I will and direct that five pounds sterling be paid out of my estate to the said mulatto woman slave Aminta if she survives her mistress hoping it be imployed in taking care of herself and children when she is left at her own disposeal. Item in consideration of the entire confidence reposed in my ever dear and effectionate wife I do will and appoint that she shall have the sole guardianship and tuition of all my children so long as she continues single and in case of her death or marriage during the minority of any of my children then I will and appoint that my much esteemed and sincere friends *Thomas Blackburn* and *William Alexander* Esqrs shall have the guardianship and tuition of them during their minority : and I do entreat that the utmost care may be taken of their educations and morrals, I do will and constitute my dear wife sole Executrix so long as she shall continue unmarried of this my last will and testament and do direct that no security shall be required from her for the due performance and execution thereof, and in case of her death or marriage I do appoint my son *Robert* and my above mentioned friends *Thomas Blackburn* and *William Alexander* joint Executors of what shall then remain to be executed of this my last will and testament. Witness my hand this ninth day of February in the year of our Lord one thousand seven hundred and eighty three.

JOHN SCOTT, Clerk.

Republished this 29th of April one thousand seven hundred and eighty four in presence of *Cuthbert Bullitt Alexander Scott Thomas Fitzhugh.*

I *John Scott* Clark do make & annex the following codicill to this my last will and testament, whereas I have since the making the same which is all wrote with my own hand sold my negroes & purchased several tracts of land from *Alexander Scott Bullitt* Esqr it is my will and intention & I do desire the same to be regulated pass & go in the same manner and be sold by my Executrix or Executors at the same time that my other lands are to be sold and the money arising from such sale to be equally divided among all my children and their Heirs or such of them that arrive to the age of twenty one years or marry subject to like provisions for my wife as is mentioned in my said will and further it is my will and intention that in case of a Provision made for either of my children by my Aunt *Elisabeth Innis* and it should not be aequall to what my other children will enjoy and have under my said will and codicill that in that case the child or children so provided for shall have such provision made equal to their other brothers and sisters out of my estate it is also my intention that in case of my wife's marriage she shall have one third of the profits of my real estate after my debts paid until the same be sold and after one third of the money arising from the sale to be put out on interest on proper security and the interest paid her during her life and I direct and desire that my children with all convenient speed be carried to and educated in Scotland untill they arrive to the age of twenty one years and empower my Executrix or Executors after selling my other Estate for the purpose to sell as much of my reall estate immediately as will pay all my just debts and to rent out the remainder and residue untill my youngest son *John* arrives to the age of twenty one years at which period and not before the said residue is to be sold and the money disposed of as directed by my will and this codicill and in case of my wife's marriage I add to my other Executors my friend *William Fitzhugh* Esqr of Fauquier and my kinsman the Rev'd Mr. *Robert Patterson* of Scotland, the latter only to be considered as Executor within the Kingdom of Great Britain. In testimony whereof I have hereunto set my hand this 29th day of Aprill 1784.

JOHN SCOTT, Clerk.

Signed published and delivered and in presence of *Cuthbert Bullitt Alexander Scott Thomas Fitzhugh.* A copy. Teste R. H. DOWNMAN, C. C.

SCOTT FAMILY.

arguments against duelling. Failing in his efforts, he attended him to the place of combat, the end of Old Quantico Chnrch, where the father of young Scott had so often read the words of Jehovah from Mount Sinai, 'Thou shall do no murder.' The result was that the second, who had warned against the act, and who, it was supposed, had gone in the hope of preventing the contest, was so treated by the challenged man on the ground, as to engage in a contest with him, in which the other was slain. He was tried and unanimously acquitted by the court upon the ground of self-defence. Mr. Scott was obliged to flee the country, and with his younger brother Gustavus went to Scotland." (Meade, II., 211.)

The following papers, prepared for him by Hon. Robert T. Scott, 143, formed the basis of Bishop M.'s account of this unfortunate event. They are given here because they effectually dispose of all other accounts of the affair, especially a very incorrect one preserved in the MSS. of Rev. Ethan Allan.

Memoranda concerning John Scott's duel with Baylis.

[John Scott's letter to Cuthbert Bullitt containing his challenge to Baylis.]

"*Dear Sir:* Enclosed I have sent you my letter to Baylis, which I have not sealed. If you have any material objection to it you must come up with my Father to-night and between us we will write another. But I would not have it postponed any farther if it is possible to avoid it, because as I am resolved to fight, nothing shall hinder me. I think we can't come together too soon, therefore you must not let a trifling objection prevent your giving him the enclosed. Pray don't talk to me any more about prudence, forbearance, and the consequences of what I have undertaken, for I am resolved to be deaf to all you can say. And if you are so unkind as to refuse to attend me, rather than submit to such insults as Baylis has offered me, I will engage him in private and run the risk of his taking advantage of his strength.
"Your ever affectionate brother,   "JOHN SCOTT."

[The challenge enclosed in the above.]

"WESTWOOD, Monday, September 2d, 1765.

"*Sir:* Your scurrility to me the other day, when you so manfully drew your sword upon a naked man, I should have passed by as unworthy of my resentment, nor should I have paid more regard to so palpable a falsehood as was contained in the advertisement you first set up at Tyler's, because I regard it as below the resentment of any gentleman. But as soon as I heard that you had dared to cast aspersions on the character of my Father (whose sacred function would have protected him from any but a wretch dead to every sentiment of virtue and honor), I no longer hesitate to call you to that account which your repeated insults to the best of men so loudly called for. I shall therefore expect you next Wednesday morning at the back part of Quantico church, armed with pistols and attended by some gentleman, furnished with a pair of the same instruments. I think it necessary that we should each come accompanied by some gentleman in whose honor we can confide, not only as it may be serviceable to the survivor to produce proof that he killed his antagonist in an honorable way, but because the great disparity in our strength might lay me open to advantages which I have too much reason to think you would very readily make use of. I therefore insist upon seconds, and I would have them to be of reputation. You are at liberty to choose whom you please for your attendant, and I shall endeavour to get one to attend me to whom you can have no exception.   "Your humble servant,   "JOHN SCOTT."

[Cuthbert Bullitt's reply to John Scott.]

"*Dear Sir:* I received yours. You request me not to dissuade you from your intentions. Did I not, from cool reflection, think they were better left alone, I would not. The danger I shall say nothing of, 'tho' much might be urged upon that head. Do you get anything by putting it in his power to take your life? Has he not an equal chance to prove fortunate? If so, the only thing you can gain is loss of life. If you kill him what great advantage do you get? You deprive a fellow creature of his life; you render his wife miserable; you ruin his innocent babes who have never injured you. Think! Oh think how heavy it will be on your conscience to have the curses of the widow and the orphan attending you to your grave. Sure to any man who is a Christian it will be a dreadful thought to take away the life of another deliberately and in cold blood. And what do you get by the victory? Nothing, believe me, dear Johnny. No man will think the better of you. If you kill Baylis, you must fly your country, give up your promising fortunes, and become an exile in a foreign land far from your friends and relations. What must I say to your father? What can I answer to your mother when, in the utmost distraction, she reproaches me with your death and asks her son at my hands. Dear Johnny, let me advise, let me entreat you to give over this rash enterprise. What you have yet done is unknown to every one but myself. No one will accuse you of want of courage, but all will of rashness. This one step will ever put it out of your power to pursue the vocation you are intended for. Let me know to-morrow what you intend. I shall not deliver yours until I receive an answer to this. If nothing can divert your purpose you must bring powder and bullets for the pistols you have with you. I shall only add that the consequences of the duel, that is Baylis' or your death, will be as fatal to me as to you. We shall both by the law forfeit our lives; this I do not mention by way of excuse. If you fight, by all that is holy I will go with you, nor shall anything hinder me. I shall wait your answer to-morrow impatiently. I am, dear Johnny, your attached "C. BULLITT."

[An extract from a newspaper of the day.)

"MR. GREEN: As it appeared at the Examining Court from the original letters and the deposition of the witnesses who saw it, that the following is the true and exact account of the late unhappy difference which arose on the 4th of September last past at the town of Dumfries between two gentlemen, I doubt not but your inserting it in your paper will not only be satisfactory to many of your readers, but serve to warn others from the like rashness and the gratifying their resentment at the expense of everything that is dear to them. A short time before the accident happened, John Scott, a young gentleman of good family, having had a difference with Col. John Baylis, a man of superior strength, Col. Baylis the next day set the following advertisement in the town of Dumfries:

" This is to give notice that Thomas Blackburn and John Scott are arrant cowards.
" JOHN BAYLIS."

At the bottom of this Col. Blackburn and Mr. Scott added these words:

" The author of this is a —— liar, which the subscribers are at any time ready to prove.
" THOMAS BLACKBURN,"
" JOHN SCOTT."

"I also add, he is a bully and dares not engage a gentleman on equal terms.
" JOHN SCOTT."

In answer to which Baylis set up a second advertisement, as follows:

"The best proof of Blackburn's and Scott's assertion would be to present to Baylis a pair of pistols in private, and if he refuse them, then their veracity for the future would not be suspected. But such a proposition will never be made, for as Blackburn and the son [obliterated in the MS.] they dislike the smell of gunpowder. "JOHN BAYLIS."

"In consequence of these advertisements Mr. Scott conceived himself obliged to call Baylis to account, in a way the world falsely calls honorable, and sent him a challenge. This challenge was conveyed to him by the hands of Mr. Cuthbert Bullett, a gentleman of good character and peaceable temper, who, having intermarried with a sister of Mr. Scott, was the rather to be depended upon. The challenge was left open for Mr. Bullett's perusal, and accompanied by a letter from Mr. Scott to Mr. Bullett, by which letter it appears that Mr. Scott had intimated to Mr. Bullett his intention of fighting Baylis before the letter was wrote, and that Mr. Bullett used every argument in his power to divert Mr. Scott from his purpose as appears from a letter sent to Scott by him the Monday night after he received Scott's letter. To this letter Mr. Scott returned for answer, that the injuries he had received were of such a nature that he could not overlook them unless Col. Baylis would acknowledge his being in the wrong, particularly in respect to his unprovoked reflection on the character of the Rev'd. James Scott, so that Bullett finding it utterly out of his power to change Scott's resolution at length yielded to his importunity and on Tuesday evening delivered Scott's challenge to Baylis and in about a quarter of an hour received the following answer:"

"To Mr. John Scott, Dumfries, Sept. 3d, 1765.
"Sir: I received yours this day by the hands of Mr. Bullett. I shall forbear to use that low, base scurrility that you do, but tell you at once I shall meet you according to your desire armed with a pair of pistols and a small sword to give that satisfaction you have demanded.
"JOHN BAYLIS."

"It also appeared from the course of evidence that Bullett did not enter into this affair without reluctancy, but he had great expectation of compromising it at the place appointed for this dreadful business. On Tuesday evening, after dark, Mr. Scott came out of the country to Mr. Bullett's lodging in town, and Wednesday, before sunrise, they repaired to the place appointed armed with a case of pistols each. In a short time Baylis, accompanied by one

Nathan Skipwith White, as his second, came on the field armed with pistols and a small sword. Baylis and Scott directly threw off their coats. Baylis cocked one of his pistols, presented it at Scott and bade him measure his distance. Scott instantly cocked and presented his pistol, calling to Baylis to put off his sword, and here probably the quarrel would have ended had not Bullett, agreeably to the plan he had preconcerted to bring about a reconciliation, rushed between them and entered into an expostulation with Baylis as well with regard to his second who was a man of no worth or reputation. This behavior of Bullett, however, had not the desired effect, for Baylis, resenting his interposition, proceeded to give him abusive language, asking him if he would take it upon himself, adding he would fight him anyway. Bullett, irritated at this treatment, too hastily accepted the proposal. Baylis threw off his sword and bade him follow. Bullett, recollecting that Scott's pistols were not only a better pair but much surer fire, exchanged with him and followed Baylis. Baylis, at about thirteen yards distance, stopped, asked Bullett if they were far enough, rested his pistol on his left arm, took aim and *snapt*. He then called to Bullett, whose pistol was cocked, not to take advantage of him. Bullett replied he would not, and dropped the muzzle of his pistol. Baylis again rectified his pistol, presented it at Bullett, fired, but missed. Bullett immediately returned the fire and wounded Baylis in the thigh groin. Baylis fell, calling to Bullett that he had broken his thigh. Bullett replied he was sorry for it and advanced some steps to his assistance, but observing Baylis to be getting up with his second pistol in his hand, stopt. Baylis, as soon as he was on his feet, again fired at Bullett, drew a third pistol which was concealed under his jacket, discharged it and then threw it at Bullett, who, with a loaded pistol in his hand, generously refused to take the life of a man who had already received a wound of which, in about five hours, he expired. Upon this testimony the Examining Court, which consisted of seven gentlemen of character who sat upon the trial of Mr. Bullett, was unanimously of the opinion that he killed Mr. Baylis in his own defense, and dismissed him from any farther prosecution. Poor Baylis has left a wife and children to lament his illtimed courage, and Mr. Bullett has a wife and three small children who share with him this great calamity. The pistols Mr. Bullett fought with were about eight inches by the barrel, and the report of his having threatened Baylis, preceding the duel, was altogether groundless."

[A Copy of John Scott's letter to C. Bullitt after the duel, and before he left the country.]

"Mr. Douglas,' Thursday Night.

"*My Dear Sir :* The gentlemen all advised me to provide for my safety immediately— and there is a writ out against me—three or four scoundrels are resolved to plague me. I have been prevailed with to go down to Mrs. Moncure's, but am resolved to go no further 'till I hear from you. For Heaven's sake ! My dear sir, if you think my remaining here can be of the least service to you, let me hear by Mr. Graham and I will immediately go up to Westwood. I gave my deposition without endeavouring to soften matters in the least, as you may see, and swore to Messrs. Douglass and Carr. Let me hear from you as soon as possible, and pray consult your own safety more than mine, for by Heaven it is dearest to your ever affectionate "JOHN SCOTT."

"There is a fact disclosed by the evidence, given in Court and omitted in the foregoing newspaper, which explains why the new and sudden quarrell with Bullett was made to take priority over that which had brought the parties to the field. Before repairing to the place of rendezvous, Baylis had declared his intention to fix a quarrel upon Bullett, whom he said he disliked more than his youthful antagonist. Baylis accomplished his purpose. The settlement of his difficulty with Mr. Scott was, thus for a time, postponed, and the death of Baylis postponed it forever. Amen."*

The following account of Mr. Scott's subsequent history, from a letter written by one of his granddaughters, Mrs. Margaret G. Lee, will also be found in Bp. Meade, II., 212:

"Immediately after the trial and acquittal of Mr. Bullitt my grandfather and his younger brother, Gustavus, left the country for Scotland. Soon after their arrival in Scotland they entered King's College, old Aberdeen, where they finished their education. My grandfather, who seems to have taken life by storm, married, while a student at King's College, Elizabeth, daughter of Thomas Gordon, one of its professors. He was afterwards ordained by the Bishop

* Col. John Baylis was Burgess from P. W. Co., 1761; elected May 11, 1761, over Col. Henry Lee (Deed Bk., P., 60); Justice Sep. 8, 1756—1762, with Rev. James Scott and others. His will dat. Oct. 22, 1764; pro. Oct. 9, 1765 (R., 119.) Jane B. his wife, Henry Lee and John Payne, Exec'rs; Oct. 9, 1765, Jane Baxter and Thomas Blackburn were bondsmen; Oct. 2, 1769, the Exec'rs sold Rev. James Scott 150 a. adjoining the glebe lands of Dettingen Par., and Nov., 1769, Jane Baylis sold him a number of slaves.

of London. It was during his residence in Scotland that my grandfather formed an acquaintance, which ripened into friendship, with Sir Robert Eden, an English or Scotch Baronet. When Sir Robert was appointed Governor of Maryland,* he invited my grandfather to Annapolis, promising to appoint him chaplain, and to use his influence to obtain for him the rich parish of Eversham. My grandfather readily accepted so advantageous an offer, and soon after sailed for America, leaving his infant son, Robert Eden Scott (who, it was feared, could not bear a three months voyage) with his maternal relatives. Upon his return to America he proceeded to Annapolis, was appointed chaplain to the Governor and pastor of the parish of Eversham. He resided in Maryland until the war between the mother country and the colonies broke out. An Englishman in principle, he adhered to the Royal cause, and, taking too active a part in politics, he became obnoxious to the Revolutionary party, into whose hands the government had passed, and was banished one hundred miles from tide water. Compelled to leave Md., he sold his property there for Continental money, and returned to Virginia, intending to return to Scotland as soon as he could make the necessary arrangements. While making these arrangements he resided on his plantation, which he called Gordonsdale, after the name of his wife. His health soon after failing, he was advised to try the waters of Bath in Berkeley Co., Va. On his return from Bath he stopped at the residence of General Wood, who had married his cousin, Miss Moncure, died there, and was buried under the pulpit of the old Episcopal Church in Winchester. My grandfather was a man of fine talents and remarkable eloquence, as well as the handsomest man of his day. His gayety and wit caused his society to be much sought after, and, from all that I have heard, rather unfitted him for his sacred profession. After his death my grandmother, who had been summoned to Winchester to receive his expiring adieu, returned to Gordonsdale. The distracted condition of the country (the Revolutionary war was then at its height) compelled her to relinquish all hope of a return to her native country. She continued to reside at Gordonsdale, devoting herself to the education of her children, a task for which she was eminently fitted, since she had received a college education. She lived to see her children grown and settled in life, and died lamented. Several years before her death she had the pleasure of welcoming to Virginia her eldest son, Robert Eden Scott, and although 21 years had passed since she had left him an infant in Scotland, she recognized him immediately. During his visit to Va. he received the office of professorship in King's College, Old Aberdeen, where he had received his education, and his maternal ancestors had held professorships for 300 years. He returned to Scotland, was made professor of mathematics, married a daughter of Sir Wm. Forbes, and d. yng. and childless."

Mr. Scott was ordained Deacon Mar. 5, 1769, by the Ld. Bishop of Norwich; licensed the same day to minister in the Province of Md. by the Ld. Bishop of London. He was ordained Priest in the Church of England in H. M. Chapel at White Hall, April 2, 1769, by the Ld. Bishop of Chester.† As Mrs. Lee has said (*sup*.),

* Robert Eden was appointed Governor of Md. 1769, succeeding Gov. Sharpe. He governed the Province until asked to resign by the Provisional Gov't of Maryland, May, 1776, and was sent home in June, 1776. He was a gentleman "easy of access, courteous to all, and fascinating by his accomplishments." His property was confiscated. But he returned in 1784 to reclaim it, died soon after and was buried near Annapolis. (v. Biog. Sketch, McMahon's Md., I., 435.)

† [Ordination of John Scott as Deacon.]

By the Tenor of these Presents, We by Divine Permission, Bishops of Norwich, do make it known unto all Men that on Saturday the Twenty-fifth Day of March in the year of Our Lord One Thousand seven hundred and Sixty Nine, We the Bishop before mentioned Solemnly Administering Holy Orders under the Protection of the Almighty, in Park Street Chapel near Grosvenor Square, Westminister did (at the request of Our Reverend Brother Richard Lord Bishop of London) admit our beloved in Christ John Scott M. A. of King's College, Aberdeen Scotland (concerning whose morals, Learning, Age, and Title the said Lord Bishop was well satisfied) into the Holy Order of Deacons, according to the manner & form prescribed and used by the Church of England, and him the said John Scott did then and there rightly & canonically Ordain Deacon he having first in our presence freely and Voluntarily subscribed to the thirty nine Articles of Religion and to the three Articles contained in the thirty sixth Canon, and he likewise having taken the Oaths appointed by Law to be taken for and instead of the Oath of Supremacy.

In Testimony whereof We have caused Our Episcopal Seal to be hereunto affixed, the Day and Year above mentioned and in the Eighth year of our Translation. PHILIP [Seal] Norwich.

[Rev. John Scott's License to preach.]

Richard, by Divine Permission Bishop of London, To our beloved in Christ John Scott Clerk, A. M. Greeting We by these presents Give and Grant to you, in whose Fidelity, Morals, Learning, sound Doctrine & Diligence. We do fully confide our License & Authority (to continue only during our pleasure) to perform the Ministerial Office of C. in the Province of Maryland in North America in Reading the Common Prayers and Performing other Ecclesiastical Duties, belonging to the said Office according to the Form prescribed in the Book of Common Prayer, made and published by Authority of Parliment & the Canons & Constitutions in behalf, lawfully established & promulgated and not otherwise, or in any Other manner (You having first

he came to Md. as the private chaplain of his Excellency, Gov. Eden. This relation to the Gov. did for a time stand in the way of his giving immediate support to the cause of the colonies during the Revolutionary war. There can be little doubt at this day that his position was much misunderstood by the Maryland authorities, and the means they used against him were unwise. Mr. S. was doubtless equally injudicious in his speech, but his letters unvaryingly asseverate his loyalty to the cause of American freedom. It appears from the *Maryland Journal*, 1775, that he signed the "Association Friendly to American Freedom" in Md. that year. During 1775 much disorder existed in Somerset and Worcester Cos., Md., between those who favoured the Crown and those who supported the Colonies. Many arrests were made, and the Co. Committees were busy trying cases. It was rumored that Mr. Scott was among the disloyal ones. He wrote to the Council of Safety the following dignified and manly defence:

"SOMERSET COUNTY, Md., Nov. 27, 1775.

"*Sir:* I have had the mortification to hear, more than once, within a few weeks past, that I am represented to the publick as an enemy to American liberty, and the chief promoter of those unhappy political dissensions which lately prevailed in this and Worcester County, but have not been able to discover where these reports, false and malicious as they are, originated. I am, therefore, reduced to this method of calling upon my accusers, whoever they are, to stand forth, or to lodge an information against me with the Provisional Convention, or Committee of Safety, where they shall always find me ready, upon the shortest notice, to attend them. Meantime, as I have the greatest reason to believe that no such publick accusation will ever be exhibited, and that I shall not be indulged with so favourable an opportunity of vindicating my conduct to my countrymen, with whom I profess entirely to coincide in my political creed, I hope the honest indignation I feel at being most insidiously attacked by private enemies, as well as my ardent desire to retrieve the good opinion of the publick, will excuse my inserting the following depositions.   "JOHN SCOTT."

Then follow six affidavits from six citizens of Somerset Co., sworn to before a Justice, each one of which corroborates Mr. Scott's declaration of fealty to the Colonies. One of these, Mr. James Geoghegan, swears that,

"After frequent converse with Mr. Scott on the subject of politics, and particularly of the Association, as an intimate friend, he always found the said John Scott exceedingly tenacious of American Freedom, and said nothing should hinder him from signing the Association but an opinion of his being comprehended amongst the Governour's household; and finding that his postponing to sign the Association was a check upon others, that he, notwithstanding his opinion of being of the Governour's household, as an encouragement of those of divided opinions to unite in the common cause, signed it himself within a very short time after it was introduced by the Committee, and verily believes that he has been as instrumental as any man in the county in procuring signatures to the same." (Force's Arch., S. 4, Vol. III., 1586–7.)

James Geoghegan appears to have been a man of character, as, on recommendation of Hon. Gustavus Scott, then a mem. of the Md. Conv., he was employed by

---

before Us subscribed the Articles and taken the Oaths which in this case are Required by Law to be Subscribed and taken.)

In witness whereof We have caused our Seal which We use in this Case to be hereto affixed. Dated, the Twenty-Fifth day March in the Year of our Lord 1769 and in the Fifth Year of our Translation.
                                        RIC. [Seal] London.

[Ordination of Rev. John Scott as Priest.]

By the tenor of these Presents, We Edmund by Divine permission Bishop of Chester do make it known unto all Men that on Sunday the Second Day of April in the year of our Lord one thousand seven hundred and sixty nine. We the Bishop aforenamed, solemnly administering Holy Orders, under the Protection of the Almighty in his Majesty's Chapel at White Hall, Did, at ye Request of & for our Right Rev'd Brother Richard by Divine permission Bishop of London admit into the Holy Order of Priests according to the Manner and Form prescribed and used by the Church of England our beloved in Christ, John Scott a Literate person, (of whose virtuous and pious life and conversation, and competent Learning and Knowledge in the Holy Scriptures, We were well assured) and him the said John Scott did then and there rightly and Canonically ordain a Priest. He having first in our Presence, taken the Oaths appointed by Law to be for and instead of the Oath of Supremacy; and he also having freely and voluntarily subscribed to the thirty-nine Articles of Religion, and the three Articles contained in the thirty Sixth Canon. IN WITNESS whereof WE have caused our Episcopal Seal to be hereunto affixed the Day and Year above written and in the Eighteenth year of our Consecration.
                                        EDM. [Seal] Chester.

the Council of Safety as Commissary for the troops in Somerset. (*v.* Letter to G. S., *id.* Vol. IV., 1167.) After the action of the Md. Convention, May 24, 1776, requiring Gov. Eden to leave the Province, against which action Gustavus S. voted in the negative (*id.*, V., 1595), Rev. Mr. S. again fell under the suspicion of the Council of Safety, through a memorial of Josiah Polke, Esq., of Somerset. Mr. S. gave bonds to appear before the Council in July following, Geo. Plater and John Hall bondsmen. On Monday, July 22, he appeared in Annapolis and wrote the Council of his presence. (*id.*, Vol. I., 491.) After waiting five days the Council examined the depositions presented by Polke and Scott, and ordered the latter to repair to Kent Co., to remain until the next Convention, giving him possession of the sloop Liberty, purchased by him of Peter Herbert, in which to remove his effects, and to appear at the next Conv. to "answer such matters as may be objected against him." The Council placed him under bonds for £500 cur., and allowed him to pass through Talbot Co. for his family, but ordered him to repair to Charlestown in eight days from date. (*id.*, 1343.)

When the Conv. met in 1776 Mr. S. appeared before it Aug. 19. A committee of six members was appointed to take his case into consideration (II., 91)—Mess. Sam'l Chase, J. T. Chase, Paca, Worthington, Ridgely and Chamberlane. On the 28th their report was read, and as it was represented that Mr. Scott was not desirous of being heard, but was ready to submit to the determination of the Conv., Mr. J. T. Chase moved that he be committed to the custody of the Sheriff of Fred'k Co. until further orders, and pay £500 towards the expenses of the war. This motion was negatived by a vote of 38 to 8. Mess. J. T. Chase and Ridgely of the Com. voting aye. It was then resolved,

"That the said Rev. John Scott is a disaffected person, who has a dangerous influence in Somerset Co., and that he is ordered to be removed to Fred'k Co. and give bond in £1,000 str. not to leave said county without permission of the Conv. or Council of Safety, nor correspond on public matters with any one whatsoever." (II., 96.) On the 29th he was "ordered to be discharged on giving his bond, and allowed a fortnight to settle his affairs and remove himself and family to Fred'k Co., but not to return to Somerset, nor hold any conversation or correspondence with any inhabitants thereof on public affairs during that time." Sept. 11, "he was allowed one week longer time." (*id.*, 109.)

This sentence was further mitigated, Oct. 12, 1776, when Mr. S. was

"Allowed, on giving good and sufficient security in the penalty of £1,000 str., conditioned that he will not go on the East'n Shore of Md. or Va., or correspond, &c., to reside in any part of the Western Shore of Va., or in Fred'k Co., Md., such bond making his bond of Aug. 29 void. He was allowed to visit Annapolis to give such new bond." (II., 123.)

This latter and final action in his case was brought about by the following letter, which, like his previous letter, is manly and dignified in its tone and language, consistent in its expressions with those recorded in his first protest, and shows that throughout this severe trial Mr. S. conducted himself as a brave man, with a "*mens conscia sibi recti.*" The time has passed in America when men suspected of disloyalty during the Revolutionary, or any other war, can be treated as devoid of that principle which constitutes true and courageous manhood. No one can read this letter without deep sympathy and esteem for the writer of it.

"George-Town, Frederick Co., Oct. 9, 1776.

"*Sir :* Permit me through you to address myself to your honourable House for permission to pass some time among my friends in Virginia; or, if the House can be induced so far to relax from their sentence, to permit me to remain there without any limitation of time, under the restraints which they have been pleased to lay me under, and which I have given bond with security to the President of the Council of Safety in the penalty of a thousand pounds sterling to observe. I beg, sir, that you will lay me with all humility before the House, with an assurance that I would have addressed them in the first instance either by petition or through you, but unacquainted as I am with bonds and the forfeitures of them, did not know but it might be going beyond the line of my engagements. My principal reasons for desiring to go to Virginia are, that I have many near and dear relations there. My fortune, little as it is, lays chiefly in that country, and having lost my living, which has hitherto been my chief support, I wish, by my industry, to do something for the subsistence of my family, which I cannot possibly do while confined to Frederick County. I have also, sir, the assurance of several gentlemen of no inconsiderable rank and weight in my native country, that my residence among them will not only give no offence, but that they will even solicit this House, if necessary, for my enlargement. That my situation is a most unhappy one, those acquainted with the human heart will readily conceive, and if my sufferings can be alleviated without any injury to the publick weal, I flatter myself humanity will plead powerfully in my favour. To be held up to the world as an enemy to my native land; to be deprived of my living, in which the laws of my country had taught me to believe I had a permanent estate, must sink deep into the heart of a man less attached to worldly affairs than I profess to be. But the voice of the Representatives of the State has pronounced the sentence, and I must submit to my fate, yet conscious as I am of having never harboured one thought injurious to the rights of mankind.

"I cannot but hope but your honourable House will remit my too vigorous sentence, and permit me to try my fate in some other land, where, if my inclinations lead me, which I call God to witness they never have done, it will be out of my power to hurt this country. If not for my own, for the sake of those innocents who have me alone to look up to for protection and support, I hope I may gain thus much at your hands, more especially as the common rights of mankind are yet preserved inviolate in the State of Maryland, give me some grounds for the hope.

"I have the honour to be, with the greatest respect, sir, your most obedient and most humble servant,   "JOHN SCOTT."

"To the Hon. Matthew Tilghman, Esq." (F., S. 5, III., 951.)

In this connexion Bishop Meade relates that when Mr. Scott was summoned before the Council at Annapolis to give account of his principles, he was examined by Hon. Robert Goodloe Harper, then a young man, and "who afterward spoke of Mr. S. as the most talented man with whom he had ever engaged in controversy." (II., 211.) On his removal to Va. Mr. S. abstained from clerical work until 1782, when he became Rector of Dettingen Parish, Pr. Wm. Co., which position he resigned on account of his health, 1784, and was succeeded by Rev. Spence Grayson. At his death in 1784 he was buried under the pulpit in the old church in Winchester, Va.

I am permitted to give several letters that passed between Mr. Scott and his wife, 1767-1783, which present a charming picture of their character.

"St. Andrews [Scotland] 31st September 1767.

"*My dearest Betsy*: I am in a great deal of pain and anxiety upon your account. I returned here yesterday evening full of the hopes of hearing from you. Is it possible that your Papa can have forbid your writing to me? What would I not give to know what has past between you & him since the receipt of my last; for sure you must have received the the letters that I sent you eight days ago. You cannot conceive how uneasy I am at not hearing from you in Course (that is, by yesterday's post) as you must be sensible how impatient I would be to hear how your Papa received my letter, especially as I beged of you so earnestly to lose no time in writing me, I persuaded myself it must be owing to something more than ordinary that you neglect me, and thus I torment myself with the fear of your Papa's being displeased at my late Declaration to him, and having treated you unkindly upon that account. I am perfectly stupid for want of sleep, but if I happen to close my Eyes my troubled imagination was continually haunted with the most melancholly dreams about yourself. I thought I saw you overwhelmed with grief, and tears, while your Papa loaded you with the most bitter reproaches and I was unable to afford relief. In short my present situation of suffering is unenviable. If I dont hear from you by to-morrow's post I shall certainly be buried before the next arrives. For God's sake never lose a post in writing to me again. When you know how impatient of neglect I am how can you tempt me? What mighty business can you ever have more than I to hinder you from writing me in course, at least a few lines. Upon my honour I had rather we should entirely drop all litterary Core-

spondence than that you should disappoint me so often. Yet nothing would make me so easy at present as to be assured that my not hearing from you yesterday was owing wholly to your own neglect, as my suspicions with regard to your Papa would then be removed. I did not receive your short letter of Tuesday evening till Saturday. I cannot now give you more of my reasons for taking my letters from you but what you suspect was really one of them. They shall live till you consent to their destruction. I received a packet from the family at Westwood four days ago, which consisted of only 3 letters from my father, mother and a little sister all of which were wrote before my last to them had come to hand. My father was in perfect good humour with me, and expressed his highest satisfaction at my conduct since I came to Scotland. He leaves it entirely to my own choice either to stay in Britian till I take orders, or to return without them, and at the same time assures me that I may depend upon receiving a better parish than his own as soon as I am in condition to receive it. I believe this (My father's) good opinion of me is owing in a great measure to the flattering accounts transmitted to him, by very partial Relations in this Country. I saw Nelly Ogilvie as I expected upon Saturday last when it gave me an illnatured pleasure to find that I was not the only Person who suffered your neglect. She is far from being in good humour with you, tho' she was very sparing in expressing her thoughts. I really think she deserved to be taken more notice of and that if you have not done it already you should lose no time in appologising for your long silence to her. Tho' I sometimes speak differently of her for my divertion, I really think her a very deserving girl and your sincere friend. This letter is so rough and inaccurate that I must insist upon your burning it as soon as you have read it. Adieu, I ought not to let you know how much I am your truly affectionate Lover
"JOHN SCOTT.

"(Address) To be forwarded to the old town on thursday evening.
"To | Miss Betty Gordon | at | Old Aberdeen."

"OLD ABERDEEN (Scotland), March 24th, 1769.

"My dear Mr. Scott: You cannot imagine what a fright the first part of your last letter to Papa put me in;—& assure you it was some time before I could recover myself enough to get to the end of it, when I was a good deal eas'd with your accounts of succeeding with the Governour. What a disapointment it has been! & at your first setting out too;—however I hope that all will be well now. They have it in Aberd'n that you are provided in a living of 300 a year in England, & are gone up in order to take possession of it, but I hope your prospects are better than even that, which is not amiss either. I did not tell you in my last that Blackhills brought a packet for you, and had stupidly mislaid it as I was afraid that your certificates might be in it, & you might be uneasy about it; It may yet cast up, & Mr Crombie promises to send it to me by the first post. But how comes it that your friends have sent you no title? & what would have been the case if you had not been introduced to the Governour? Providence has been very kind to us! You dont mention Lord & Lady Errols letters having reached the Governour & Miss Eden yet. I hope they are not lost. Mr & Mrs Boyd & Miss Charlotte together with Mrs Ogilvie, a visitor of theirs and an acquaintance of Papas, & Capt'n Livingston dined here to-day They are gone only a little while ago; I could not help looking upon them with particular complacency after reading your letter; Pray take the earliest opportunity of thanking Mr. Boyd tho' you should enclose it to me, I hope you will not forget Papa's postscript to my last letter;—It seems Capt'n Boyd is an invalide at present and lives at Spring Gardens for his health, they expect him down to Scotland soon, but in the meantime are anxious to hear about him. Dont delay executing my commissions waiting for Mary Forbes, for she is not sure of leaving this for a fortnight yet. As you talk of being here early in Aprile, I am afraid I shall not have an opportunity of writing you again. How do you intend to travel? by land or water? I have been a constant attendant upon publick prayers this week, both on account of my soul and body. I am not strong enough only to go as far as the Chapple & cannot go as far as my Aunt's house. I have been frequently at Mrs Dallas' of late, they are really excellent girls & have been particularly obliging to me;—they all desired their best comp^ts to you; by the bye they are greatly mortified at the thought of your getting a wig, & beg'd me to advise you against it: tho' I am afraid it will end in that at last, as it will be very troublesome to keep your hair in good order now that it is cropped—poor head!

"Papa ask'd me if there were any secrets in your letter, I said I would read every thing material in it to him, which I did, after that, he beg'd a sight of what I had read—so I turned over one page, & desired him to read the rest, which I am sure gave him great pleasure, as I had not done justice to your account of your Father's & mother's letters. I hope your next will bring an account of the time being settled for your ordination & consequently of your leaving the great city. I will not tell you how much I long to see you again, as I am sure you will need no inducement to make your absence as short as possible;—you can easily form a guess by yourself. As you don't mention your cold, I hope you have got free of it;—pray take care of yourself as you love me. If you come by sea I wish you could catch Bomstead, who sails for Abd'n in about a week, he has the best accommodation for passengers as is very lucky. Good night my dearest;—I have been interrupted and it now pretty late;—That Heaven may preserve you & send you safe home, is the constant prayer of your truly affectionate wife. ''ELISA SCOTT.''

"My Papa & sisters beg to be remembered to you.   Friday night 11 o'clock.

"(Address) To | Mr. John Scott | To the care of Mr. Speediman | near St. Clement's Church, Strand | London.

"LONDON, 1st of April, 1769.

"*My dearest Betsy:* I received yours yesterday forenoon but have for once omitted to answer you in Course. You must not however conclude that I have done this through neglect. It was because I had the prospect of sending you agreeable news to-day. The young West Indian I mentioned to you in my last had prevailed with the Bishop of Chester to promise to admit him to priest's orders to-morrow, and I had found means to be taken in by the bye.

"This day was appointed for our examination, I therefore thought proper to defer writing to you till it was fairly over. It is now past and we are ordered to attend at White Hall Chapple in order to receive priest's orders at ten o'clock to-morrow. I waited on Governour Eden on Thursday when I found him very busily imployed packing np for his departure to Maryland. He had only time to desire that I might lose no time in following him. The affair of his chaplaincy is now secured. I am perfectly sure or it, and I would not take four hundred pounds per an. in Britain for my prospect in consequence of it, You will expect now to hear with more certainty about the time of my leaving London. I cannot receive the £20 bounty from the Treasury till Wednesday next. I have also invi * * McKennon to spend the next week with me in London, it is therefore" * * * *

[The rest of this is lost.]

"25th August, 1776, Saturday, 12 o'clock.

"*My dearest:* Nothing adds more to the uneasiness I feel at the thought of being detained here 'till Monday or Tuesday next than the assurance that you will be all this evening & to-morrow looking out for me with anxious solicitude. But we who are condemned to dance attendance must submit to our fate. The Committee for examining into my affair will not bring in their report 'till Monday, 3 o'clock, after which it is expected I shall be soon discharged and upon pretty easy terms. Whether you will receive this intelligence before I come over to you myself is uncertain, for as I have lately lived so do I now write merely upon the hope of what may happen. I have endeavoured to make this week pass away like the rest in outside cheerfulness in spite of inward anguish, but whether it is that the hot weather has been too hard for me or the struggle too great to be so long supported I know not but I have for two nights past been feverish and out of order and have hardly thro' the day been able to support myself in company. I have just now made shift to walk as far as my brother's lodging (* * Frs.) where the odd Figures that in various forms present themselves under the name and title of Convention men have given me barely spirits enough to hold the pen. While in the sincerity of my heart I assure you that if I were to be deprived of your company for ten days longer I should become the most wretched creature that ever existed. If I had never known my dearest Betsie, I think I could set the world and all its persecutions at defiance, but the thought of being torn from all that I hold dear to me unmans me at once and makes me almost ready to sacrifice my conscience, my judgment and everything else to the times. In the course of my present banishment I have often endeavoured to reason myself out of my extravagant attachment to your company and I have frequently asked myself why it happens that the conversation of other women is so exceedingly insipid in your absence. Is it because love has made me blind that I can behold nothing pleasing but in her who first taught me to feel the tender passion? or is it that habit—that powerful law-giver—has made your presence necessary for my happiness? Shall I tell you my answer. Will it not be putting myself too much in your power to let you know my weakness? Heaven is my witness that I never yet have thought so, or ever wished in any one instance of my life to conceal myself from you. Hear then the effusions of a fond heart and believe your enamoured husband. It is because seven years experience has proved you the most excellent of women and the sweetest companion that ever man engaged to carry with him about the world. To be possessed of you even in banishment and obscurity is to be happy beyond the reach of accident. I have hated to draw characters because I could not flatter even when I have been paid for it, but I love to bear testimony to the truth, and to encourage the good and virtuous. So take the outlines of yours, as follows—which if you do not already you must learn to deserve.

"Along with a cultivated understanding naturally good, and a firmness of mind raises you above your sex, you possess that sweet pliability of temper which qualifies you for passing quietly thro' the world. Happy in the power of adding yourself to every conversation you are at once modest and sensible, sprightly and elegant; and never yet did I know your vivacity or your wit, altho' when in spirits you possess a large share of both, outstrip the bounds of strict propriety. During ten happy years that I have been so blessed as to call you mine I have uniformly found you affable to all men free with no man and only kind to me. Often cheerful, sometimes gay, always pleased—but when I am angry—then sorry but not sullen. Public amusements etc: you have occasionally complied with, but have always found that when you have been at liberty to consult your own inclinations that your diversions and your pleasures have centred entirely at home. Add to this that you are beautiful as an angel and have ever used the most unwearied diligence to please your husband. And now ask yourself my dear charmer, if I can be blamed for loving you to adoration. As Lord Dunmore—who has rose from the dead before the general resurrection,—and his fine fleet have left the Bay; and my Somerset friends will not have it in their power to swear treason against me; I shall venture down to Eversham as soon as I am permitted and wait a little longer before I come to a final resolution. If I can conform to public measures, I am offered a subscription of £500 a year by the church people, when the establishment shall be no more. I spent last evening with Richard Henry Lee on his way to Congress, from whom along with many other important truths, I learn than henceforth every one goes to Heaven in his own way in Virginia. It gave me a great deal of concern to hear by young —— Edmonson that Mr. Hayward was ill. Why dont you find means to let me hear from you. Every thing conspires to plague me—or in the language of our worthy friend Duff, Providence is against me.

"Best compliments to all friends who remember me. "JOHN SCOTT."

Ripponlodge Monday 12 o'Clock 22d September 1783

My dearest: After riding as far as Mr. Fitzhugh's on Saturday last I found myself so much fatigued as to decline proceeding further 'till Sunday being resolved if possible rather to better myself than to be worsted by the Journey which I have accordingly accomplished. Yesterday I dined at Alexandria and spent the evening at Westwood having been made easy on the score of our dear little Girl who has been very ill but is now able to laugh talk and work and will get home along with me in the course of the week in our baggage waggon or some other means of conveyance that I will contrive for her, but if I should be detained 'till after Sunday you must not allow yourself to be uneasy on that account as Betsy is at present I thank heaven perfectly well and myself in a very happy way of being so also; my Lax being almost wholly gone as well as my fevers and my appetite much mended. The Lady at Westwood is very low, but thinks herself out of all danger, which is, in my own opinion, as far from the truth of her case that without a miracle she cannot last many months, so very ill is her Breast complaint which allows her no rest, but is in danger of suffocating her every moment. Our excellent and amiable friend the Colonel is in a Condition which must wound the feelings of all who know him. Before I came here to-day he had just swollowed ninety Drops of Laudanum in spite of which I found him in such pain as has made me entirely forget the pleasure of finding poor little Betsy in health. On Wednesday next Doctor Brown and others meet here in order to extract the ball which they mean to do by cutting in to the opposite side of the thigh. There being as they say a large cavity now formed by the ragged bullet filled with matter to the quantity as they calculate of near half a pint, which will readily lead them to it altho' they have not yet been able to feel it. The interest I feel in the Colonels recovery will keep me here 'till this dangerous and most painful operation is performed, which must in a great measure determine the fate of this unfortunate and most valuable man whom to know is to love and whom if I were to lose this Corner would from that moment be insupportable to me.* My brother Will by moping at Westwood and nursing the Good Lady there has in a great measure deprived himself of that stock of health which he layed in at the Springs and if he is not relieved will soon reduce himself to his old Condition. Col. Alexander is ill of the ague and fever and much reduced but talks and thinks as much as ever of Georgia. But I am this day informed that General Green lately from the Southward, and now confined by sickness at Alexandria says that Land speculations cannot yet be made there with any degree of certainty, which will probably throw cold water on that business, and postpone our trip 'till the Spring. There is a vague report here that D. Constable is in this river with a cargo of Goods, if so we shall be sure of news from Aberdeen. Campbell's ship will sail about a month hence—Gibson passenger—Campbell to stay in the Country and the ship to return as soon as possible, perhaps we may think it advisable for me to take this opportunity to * * trip Solus to that quarter but of * * not

---

* This was Col. Thomas Blackburn, No. 7, p. 602, wounded at Germantown.

thought a single moment * * I return to Fauquier. Tell John White that Jack was detained here 'till this evening. Tell him also to cut no Tobacco 'till it is ripe but to push his fodder with all possible expedition. God bless you and your dear little Charge.

"Adieu. JOHN SCOTT."

"(Address) Mrs. Scott | Gordon's Dale | Fauquier County.
"By | Negro | Jack"

Children† :

+ 36.   i.   ROBERT EDEN,[4] b. Apr. 13, 1769; d. s. p. Jan. 14, 1811; m. Mar. —, 1797, Rachel Forbes-Mitchell.

  37.   ii.   JAMES, b. "Westwood," Va., June 4, 1770; d. Jan. 26, 1772.

  38.   iii.   ELIZABETH BROWN, b. Md., Aug. 10, 1773; d. —; m. June 9, 1796, Chandler Peyton. (PEYTON 87, p. 538.)

  39.   iv.   THOMAS GORDON, b. June 4, 1775; d. Aug. 12, 1775.

  40.   v.   MARGARET ANN, b. — 26, 1779; d. Sep. 28, 1779.

+ 41.   vi.   JOHN, b. Feb. 3, 1781; d. Jan. 17, 1850; m. ——, Elizabeth Pickett.

  42.   vii.   MARGARET CHRISTIAN, b. Dumfries, Va., Jan. 30, 1783; d. Oct. 11, 1843; m. (I.) —, Yelverton Peyton; (II.) July 19, 1809, Hon. Charles Lee (PEYTON 88, p. 540—543); (III.) June 27, 1821, John Glassell. (GLASSELL 8, p. 8.)

EXCURSUS—GORDON

OF ABERDEEN, SCOTLAND.

The following records of this family give presumptive evidence of descent from the ancient line of Gordon which goes back to the time of Edward I.

Mrs. Chandler Peyton left, in manuscript, the following traditions of the family of Professor Thomas Gordon, received from her mother, Mrs. Eliza Gordon Scott, the daughter of Prof. Thomas G. Coming from this source they are entitled to a place here.

"There resided on the border of the Hielands of Scotland a certain Laird of the House of Gordon. His family consisted of his wife, a son, and daughter. His son was educated at King's College, Old Aberdeen, and while there displayed a peculiar talent for acquiring different languages. He was master of thirteen different languages when he graduated, and he returned home the joy and pride of his parents, who invited his friends to visit him and form shooting parties. His sister was handsome and much admired by the youths of the neighborhood. One morning she entered the room where her brother and his friends were making ready for the chase, and expressed great alarm at seeing them loading their pieces in doors. Her brother laughingly said he intended to punish her for her cruelty to her admirers. She cried out "Do not shoot Laddie! do not shoot!" but he not heeding her the gun accidentally went off and she fell. The shock was so great to her brother that he instantly left his Parents, and all search for him proved vain; in this discousolate situation they remained for two years. At that time the Duke of Marlborough was on the Continent, in the Netherlands, with the victorious army. Thither young Gordon fled, and joined the Army of Marlborough as a common soldier. His conduct was such as to render him a favorite with men and officers. It so happened at a large dinner, given by the General officers, Gordon and some others were selected to stand guard before the tent. While at table there arose a dispute among the officers respecting the pronounciation of a Greek word. While they were discussing the matter one of them remarked the attention of Gordon to the dispute, and observing him smile enquired the cause, and he replied, 'The subject of your discussion.' They then asked if he knew anything of the Greek. Gordon replied that he did. 'Which of us is right?' enquired the officer. 'Neither,' answered Gordon. He then displayed so much learning in discussing the point their curiosity was excited to know who and what he was. He related his misfortune which greatly excited their sympathies. His story reached the ear of the Duke, who sent for him and recommended him to return to his mourning Parents, remarking it was a sufficient misfortune to lose one child, and the evil was doubled by the loss of both. He accordingly returned and was soon after elected Professor of Ancient and Modern languages, in the College of Old Aberdeen. He married and had a family. His eldest son succeeded him in the Professorship, and was the father of my Grandfather Gordon, who, in a like manner, was elected to fill his father's place."

This tradition refers pro. to Prof. George Gordon, 1673-1730, who was Prof. Oriental Lang., K. Coll., 1698-1730, and the accident pro. occurred while Marlborough was in the

---

†This list of the Children of Mr. S. is taken from a copy of Cruden's Concordance in which he recorded the names and dates.

Netherlands, 1692. He was, however, son of Patrick Gordon, Prof., 1640–96, and brother of Alexander Gordon, Prof., 1696–1739.

"My Grandfather Gordon married a lady of the name of Forbes, and the history of her Parents has somewhat of romance. Her father (of the name of Forbes) possessed a handsome estate, and married, very early in life, a lady remarkable for her beauty. He became giddy and extravagant, neglected his affairs; and his wife, finding she could not reclaim him, separated from him, after which they did not see each other for 20 years. They then accidentally met at the house of a mutual friend. He did not recognize his wife, but was charmed with her beauty, and after she had left her friend's house Mr. Forbes spoke in raptures of her and lamented his hard fate that he was not at liberty to offer himself. The lady of the house smiling, asked him if he had no recollection of seeing that lady before. He replied "None." She then informed him that lady was his *wedded wife.* He then implored her to bring about a reconciliation and she promised to do her best, on condition he could convince her he was a changed man. After the preliminaries were settled they were reunited, and my Grandmother, the first wife of Professor Thomas Gordon, was born after their second union. Their eldest daughter was married to Professor Thomas Gordon's older brother, and my mother has told me there was twenty-five years between the two sisters. My Grandmother was delicate and died leaving three daughters, the eldest of whom was my mother (Elizabeth Gordon) who was only in her fifteenth year when she had charge of her father's household. . I have heard her say she was her mother's chief nurse for five weeks preceding her decease. The evening of her decease she took from her finger a ruby ring, in the form of a heart set with diamond sparks and gave it to my mother, who never suffered that ring to be taken from her finger during her life."

These were pro. Forbes of Thainston, as the annuity from the lands of Thainston came into the hands of Prof. Thos. Gordon at his brother's death.

Through Miss A. L. Peyton (PEYTON 267, p. 540) I have been able to procure a search into the family history of this line of Gordons by the Lyon Office at Edinburgh. The late George Burnett, LL. D., the Lyon Herald, wrote me under date of Nov. 22, 1889, thus:

"I can supplement your information about the Gordons to some extent. I send a copy of a note in the handwriting of Thomas Gordon of Aberdeen, 1714–1796, showing that he could not go very far back. But the pedigree is an interesting one, and I have been enabled to carry it two generations beyond the first Professor and give you a few interesting collaterals. Theodore Gordon, minister of Kinnethmont, brother of your Thomas, wrote a MSS. history of the Gordons, mostly taken from other and older MS. histories, but adding what he calls the 'Gordons of Kethok's Mills.' I have copied the extract from this MS. pedigree relating to them. It comes after the descendants of Thomas Gordon of Daach, suggesting a traditional belief that that was the source from which his people sprung. I have got extracts from the Aberdeen Burgh Records, &c., throwing further light on the Professional family of Gordons, and showing an earlier connexion with Virginia than is alluded to in your notes. I believe more could be got by a thorough search of all the local records of Aberdeen, as to marriages and children of the various professors, &c., but I would require to send an experienced searcher there, as no one on the spot could be relied on to do it exhaustively, and the cost might be considerable."

Dr. Burnett, in his published history of the family of Charles Gordon, Marquess and Earl of Huntly (Burke Peerage, Huntly), gives the origin of the Gordons thus:

"The Gordon family take their name from the lairds of Berwickshire in the end of the 12th century. Sir Adam Gordon was justiciary of Lothian 1305, under Edward I., and sat in the English Council at Westminster as one of the representatives of Scotland. Tardily joining Bruce, he had a grant of the great northern lordship of Strathbogie, forfeited by the Earl of Athole. His younger son, William, was ancestor of the Gordons of Lochinvar, and Viscounts Kenmure. His elder son, Adam Gordon of that ilk, was father of John Gordon of that ilk, who, taken prisoner at Durham in 1346, was released 1357, had a confirmation charter of Strathbogie in 1376 as great grandson of Sir Adam, and was, through two sons, John Gordon of Scudargue, and Thomas Gordon of Ruthven or Daach, ancestor of a wide circle of Gordons in Mar, Buchan and Strathbogie."

Dr. Burnett also wrote me thus:

"These two brothers, John and Thomas, popularly known as 'Jock' and 'Tam,' have been contended for by many genealogists, as uncles of the heiress Elizabeth Gordon, who, in 1408, m. Alex'r Seton, who was made Lord Gordon 1437, and whose son, Alexander Seton, Lord Gordon made Earl of Huntly 1445, took the name of Gordon. Others have represented them as brothers of the heiress."

"The Gordons of Pitlurg, the senior representative of 'Jock,' have always regarded themselves as the chiefs of the Gordon family, regarding the Huntly family as excluded from that position as being Setons. The Gordons of Pitlurg have given birth to several people of distinction. They are still a flourishing family, and have sent off various offshoots.

"The Gordons of Lessmoir spring from William, 2d. son of 'Jock;' acquired large property, and founded an influential branch, on whom a Baronetcy was bestowed in 1625.

"The Earls of Aberdeen also descend from 'Jock'—one of whose younger sons acquired Methlick with an heiress named Harper. His son, Patrick Gordon of M., fell under the Earl of Huntly at Arbwath, 1445. Haddo was acquired by Patrick's grandson, and his descendant, Sir John Gordon of Haddo, made Baronet 1642, was the 1st royalist who suffered death by judicial sentence, being beheaded by the Covenanters 1644. His son, Sir George Gordon of Haddo, Lord Chancellor and President of the Court of Session, was raised to the peerage as Earl of Aberdeen 1682. His great grandson George, 4th Earl of Aberdeen, one of the greatest statesman of the last generation, is the most famous member of the family since the 1st Earl. Of the descendants of Thomas Gordon of Daach, or 'Tam,' the best known are the Gordons of Hallhead, who acquired Easlemont from the Cheynes, and whose heiress m. 1856, Henry Wobrige, who took her name. It is from some one of the descendants of Thomas Gordon of Daach that the Professors Gordon seem to have been supposed to descend. The 'Tams' have not been nearly so thoroughly genealogyzed as the 'Jocks.' "

From a MS. "Genealogy of the name of Gordon with the branches and cadets thereof, conform to the preceding histories of Stralock and Ferrerius, and likeways to an old MS. written by George Gordon of Prony, and other unexceptionable authorities." (By Theodore Gordon, minister of Kinnethmont, son of Mr. George Gordon, professor of Oriental Languages in King's College, Aberdeen.) The parenthetic words were added by Dr. Burnett.

"The Gordons of Kettokismill. This family has given five professors to the University of the Kingis College of Aberdeen, and one to the University of Glasgow. 1. To the former, Mr. Patrick G., Humanity Professor. He had the lands of Boghole (since called Rosehall.) 2. Mr. Alexander G., who suc'd him. 3. Mr. George G., Prof. of Oriental Languages, who was suc'd by 4, Mr. George, his son. 5. Mr. Thomas G., Prof. of Humanity, son to the 1st George. And to Glasgow, Mr. Thomas, son of Mr. Patrick, a Prof. of Philosophy." (v. under No. 12.)

1. ALEXANDER GORDON, in Kethoksmill, b. cir. 1550; m. ——. Child.—2. *Alexander.*

2. ALEXANDER GORDON in Kethocksmill, b. cir. 1575; m. Isabel Hervie, dau. of Andrew Hervie of Denstoun, or Mr. George Hervie of Kinermeit and his wife Jean Forbes. "1602, Dec. 20, Sasine proceedings in charter of sale, by Andrew Hervie of Denstoun, in favour of Alexander Gordon, younger, at Kethaksmilne, and Isabella Hervie, his spouse, in conjuct fee and life rent, and to the heirs begotten or to be begotten between them, whom failing, to the heirs whatsoever of the said Alexander, of ten oxgates of the lands of Monycabok, in the barony thereof, parish of St. Machar, and shire of Aberdeen, under revision, and redeemable for £1000." This charter is dated at Aberdeen, 3d Nov., 1602, and Sasine is given on 23d of same month. (*id.* II., Fol. 136.)

The term "oxgate" I do not find, but "plough gate," which is used below, and "ox gang," means as much land as an ox can plough in a season, about 40 Scotch acres, which is equal to about 70 English acres.

"1607, July 29, Sasine on Charter by Thomas Forbes, (not designed) in favour of Alexander Gordon, younger, residing at Kethocksmilne, his heirs, etc., of one plough of land of the western half of Monycabok, redeemable for 1100 Merkes and £43.6.8 in terms of contract between said Thomas Forbes and Andrew Hervie of date, 11 Aug., 1598." (*id.* VI., Fol. 194.) Monycabok was known as New Machan or Maunleuch. Child.—3. *Thomas.* 4. *Patrick.*

3. THOMAS GORDON, in Kethocksmill, named in charter, *Supra*, 1605; an elder in the church. He m. ——. Child.—5. Margaret, buried July 26, 1686; m. Jan. 17, 1643, Rev. Alexander Middleton, M. A., buried Aberdeen, Dec. 7, 1686; son of Robert Middleton of Caldhorne, of John Killhill, of John Middleton of Middleton, ancestor of the Earls of Middleton, and who was son of Malcolm, son of Kenneth, who got a charter from King William conferring a donation to him, by King Duncan, of the lands of Middleton. (Douglas 749.) He was Minister of Rayne, then of Old Aberdeen. In 1634 he was Regent; then 1641 Prof. Philos. King's Coll. and Sub-principal; Principal 1662, resigning to his son Geo., 1684. "In his time the College flourished, as he caused good order to be kept therein" His marriage caused much comment, as prior thereto the Regents and Masters of the Aberdeen Coll. had voluntarily practiced celibacy. From Spalding it is learned that "Anno 1643, Tuesday 17th Janur Mr Alexander Middletoun subprincipall is marriet with Gordoun dochter to Mr Thomas Gordone at Kethoksmilne forbidding mareage to ony of the invard membris ser-

ving thairin. Thair was sundrie giftis tassis and cungzeit gold given to sindrie sitteris at this brydell, and sum gave ringis; but cungzeit gold was not in use to be given heir in Abirdene at frie brydellis * * * ." Mr. Middleton was turned out by the Cromwellian party in 1651, but restored. He had by Eliz'h Gordon—i. George, B. Feb. 25, 1645; Min. of Glammis, Regent King's Coll., 1671; Sub-principal 1679–1684; Principal 1684–1717; buried Aberdeen, May 28, 1726; m. Jane, dau. of James Gordon of Seaton; B. Mar. 28, 1652; buried Jan. 17, 1753, aged 101 ! They had many chidren, all of whom are in Douglas' Peerage. Their 12th child, Robert, had Charles, created a peer 1805, title Lord Barham.

4. PATRICK GORDON, 2d son, b. cir. 1613; d. 1706; 1640, Regent of King's Coll., Aberdeen; 1661, Civilist; 1669, Humanist; 1696, succeeded by his son Alexander. He m. twice, but the names of the wives are not preserved.

"Upone Sonday; the 29th of October [1643] oure covenant agane red out of oure pulpit in Old Abirdene be Mr Williame Strathanchia, minister. He exponet the same, not to be agnes the King, but against the malignant prelatis and papistis in England. He first himself sweir and subscrivit the same to be lauchfull and just with God, his reider richt sae; syne Doctor Goold, principall; Mr Alexander Middletoun, subprincipall Mr Alexander Gairdin, Mr Patrick Gordoun and Mr George Middletoun, regentis, cam down fra the loft whair they war sitting to ane tabill set before the pulpit of purpoiss and sweir and subscrivit the covenant. John Forbes." "Mr William Rait, and Mr John Lundie, Oldtoun ballies, cam nixt, with elderis and deacones, as they were callit upone, came in, for the most part sweir and subscrivit except William Gordoun of Gordonismill and Mr Thomas Gordone at Kethokismilne, who tuke to be advysit. At last they, on another day, came in, sweir and subscrivit * * * " "Upon the 16th of Nov, thair cam to Aberdene ane ballie of Edinbrugh, with ane deacon, who causit publish ane edict at the Kirk dur of Old Abirdene upon Sonday the 19th of Nov, summoning oure elderis and parochineris to compeir befoor the committee of the assemblee at Edinbrugh the sixt day of December next, to heir and sic Mr William Strathanchin, oure minister transplanted fra this Kirk to Edinbrugh to serve in the ministrie thair * * *. Quhaerupone Mr Thomas Gordoun at Kethokismilne, ane eldir, and Mr James Sandylandis, commoun procuratour for the Kingis college, wes send south to the committee of the said assemblie at Edinburgh, with ane ampill commissioun subscrivit be the parochia and memberis of the college, and labourit so as our minister gat libertie to byde at home, to the contentment of himself and of his flock."

Child., 1st mar.—6. Rev. John, d. cir. 1705; "Minister of Willmington Parish, James City Co., Virginia." Bishop Meade and Neill fail to notice him as having ministered in Va. Dashiell gives him, without designation, 1697. Dr. Slaughter wrote me that he was in Va. as late as 1700.* The following extract from the Burgh Records of Aberdeen was sent me by the late Dr. Burnett, Lyon Herald :

"At Aberdein 16th Feb. 1705 in presence of Alexander Patton of Kinaldie, provost of Aberdeen, and Robert Cumming, one of the balies of the said burgh: Compeared Doctor George Middleton, principall of King's Colledge of Aberdeen and James Gordon of Seaton, and being solemnly sworne, deposed that Mr. Patrick Gordon, rector of Aberley in the countey of Worchester in England, is the immediate younger brother german of Mr. John Gordon late minister of Willmingtoun parish in St. James' City county in Virginia, deceased, and that Mr. Alexander Gordon, professor of humanity in the King's Colledge of Aberdeen, Mr. George Gordon, professor of the orientall languages in the said colledge, Mary Gordon their sister, and Helen Gordon, also their sister, spous to William Baxter, balie in Old Aberdein, are brothers and sisters german to the deceast Mr. John Gordon, and only neirest of kinn to them, ther being no other brothers and sisters alyve but these five above named, and this is the truth as they shall answer to God. Mr. John Gordon, civilist in the said King's Colledge, deponed ut supra."

7. Rev. Patrick Gordon, Rector of Abberley, Co. Worcester, Eng. The present Rector writes me that John Goodwin, Rector of A., signed his name in the Register down to Jan. 16, 1699–1700. Patrick Gordon signed his name for the first time Mar. 24, 1699–1700, and for the last time Mar. 24, 1722–3. He was suc. by Rev. D. Payne as Rector. 8. Alexander, M. A., b. Oct. 27, 1665; Prof. of Humanity, King's Coll., 1696–1739. 9. *George*, M. A., "the Elder," b. May 23, 1673; Prof. of Oriental Lang., King's Coll., 1698–1730; suc. by his son George, "the Younger." 10. Thomas, M. A., Prof. of Philosophy and Regent Univ. Glasgow 1682. From the Maitland Club Pub. I gather this data :

"Demission by Mr. Thomas Gordon of his office of Profession of the Orientall Languages : 'De it known to all men by thir presentis, me, Mr. Thomas Gordon, Professor of the Orientall

---

* Rev. Thomas Gordon of Va. was involved in Bacon's Rebellion, 1676–7. (Hen., II., 370–8, 557) Rev. John Gordon, D. D., of Scotland, was ord. 1745, and ministered in Md. (Allen's Md. Clergy, p. 9.)

Languages in the University of Glasgow, for certain onerouse causes and important considertiones me moveing to, have dimittit and overgiven my said place and office of profession of the saids Orientall Languages in the said University, with the haill fees, caiswalities and emoluments thereto belonging, to the effect the saids Masters may dispose thereon as they shall see fit. In witness quhair of thir presents, written be Robert Robertson wryter in Glasgow, are subscryvit att Glasgow the twenty day of December j m v j c fourscore ten yeirs (1690) Befor thir witnesses Mr. William Blair of Auchinvoill and the said Robert Robertsonne. —Tho. Gordon.—W. Blair, witness. Robert Robertson, witness.' "

They were the days of political changes and persecutions. Prof. G. appeared as Regent 1682. In 1689 a "processe was intented and entred upon against Mr. Thomas Gordon, one of the Regents, for a scandall. He appeilled from the Facultie to the Lords of the Session, who assoiled [absolved] him from the scandall." He gave up his office to a personal friend, and the Faculty elected George Sinclair to fill his place. But Prof. G. appealed to the King, who appointed him Professor of Oriental Languages, at 600 marks yearly, 1687. Dec. 20, 1690, the Faculty compromised with him for 1000 marks, and he retired as above.

11. Mary. 12. Helen, m. Wm. Baxter, Bailie of Old Aberdeen in 1706.

9. GEORGE GORDON, M. A., "the Elder," b. May 23, 1673; d. 1730 (?); m. ——; was Prof. Oriental Languages, King's Coll., 1698-1730, when he was suc. by his son, "George the younger." Child.—13. *Theodore* or *Anne.* 14. *George.* 15. *Thomas.*

13. REV. THEODORE GORDON, M. A., b. —; d. Aug. 29, 1779; m. —, Anne Gordon. He grad. M. A., King's Coll., 1722; Minister of Cabrack 1731 to 1739. In 1736 he publicly expressed his repentance before the Presbytery "for having been present at a rope dancing." (Pres. and Synod Rec.) He settled at Kennethmont, June 20, 1739, where he d. Aug. 29, 1779. A tablet to his memory in the church there bears this record:

"Sacred to the memory of the late | Rev. Theodore Gordon, A. M. | who was Minister of the parish of Kennethmont during a period | of Forty One Years | and who departed this life 29th Aug., 1779. | He was no less distinguished for his exemplary conduct as a clergyman | And his learning & taste as a scholar | Than he was esteemed for his liberal mind & generous disposition | to his parishioners and all his numerous friends. | This monument was erected by | His Grandson Theodore Gordon of Overhall | as a small memorial of that warm affection | & sincere veneration with which his memory has never ceased | to be cherished by all his Grandchildren and in testimony | of that deep feeling of regret and affectionate regard | in which it continues to be held by the Heritors of the Parish | where he lived respected & died lamented by all." |

He was author of the MS. Account of the Gordons referred to *supra.* In 1772 he became an heir of the lands of Thainston through Mrs. George Gordon, as appears from Prof. Thos. Gordon's letters.

A tablet to the memory of his wife is still preserved in the parish church of Kennethmont, bearing this inscription:

"M. S. | ANNÆ GORDON | M. GEORGIJ GORDON O. L. P. | IN ACAD REGIA ABERDONENSI | FILIÆ NATU MAXUMÆ | M THEODORI GORDON V. D. M. | CONJUGIS OPTUMÆ CHARISSIME | QUAM RAPUIT MORS EHEU! PRÆMATURA | ANNO MDCCXLII ÆTATIS SUÆ XXXIV | VIVENS AC MŒRENS M MARIIUS | D. S. P."

It will be noticed that a singular conflict of authorities occurs here. Dr. George Burnett, the Lyon Herald, gave me Theodore Gordon as son of George Gordon, Prof. Oriental Lang., while the monumental tablet erected to Anne Gordon, doubtless by her husband, makes her the eldest daughter of Prof. George Gordon. Dr. J. Balfour Paul, present Lyon Herald, wrote me Jan. 9, 1891, that "Dr. Hew Scott, in his Fasti Ecclesiæ Scoticanæ, gives Theodore as the son of Professor George. This is probably the authority on which Dr. Burnett relied, and as Dr. Scott took much pains in verifying his information, I should be inclined to credit him rather than the monument, testimony of the latter class being always more or less open to suspicion. I may say that Dr. Scott quotes the Degrees of King's College, Aberdeen, the Records of the Presbytery of Seford, and the Moray Register of Wills, for the information he gives regarding Theodore Gordon."

Prof. Thomas Gordon's letters speak of him frequently, but not so as to indicate whether he was his brother or brother-in-law.

Children:

i. Rev'd Algernon, M. A., b. —; d. 1796. Prof. Thos. G. wrote, July 16, 1796, "Noony Gordon at Keith is dead." He then gives a record of his sons. He m. ——, who d. April, 1784. He was the minister at Keith. Child.—1. Dr. Theodore of Overhall, eldest; studied medicine; entered the army as Surgeon's mate, Sep., 1788; served in Barbadoes. In 1796 he became Surgeon General of the British forces in Jamaica at £600 per ann. and his regular practice. 2. Thomas, a coppersmith, who settled in Jamaica and had a profitable business. 3. John. In 1796 had "good offices in Dominica." 4. Peter, a millwright; in 1786 attending a store at Vienna in Mr. Bowie's Parish, Maryland, Great Choptank Par., Dorchester Co. In 1796 he was a merchant in Cambridge or Baltimore, Md. 5-6. Jane and her sister, living in Aberdeen 1796.

ii. Forbes, d. Sep. or Oct., 1801 ; buried at her request in "Gordon's Isle."
iii. Margaret, or Peggy, d. before 1788 on the eve of marriage.
iv. Kitty, or Catharine (?), m. "a worthy, amiable farmer of Auchlyne," and had two sons and one daughter, Forbes, who always lived with her aunt Forbes until her death, when she went South to Mrs. Brown (Anne Gordon). Prof. G. says "she is a beautiful girl."

14. GEORGE GORDON, M. A., b. Dec. 23, 1711 ; d. cir. 1767 ; m. —— Forbes, who d. s. p. Oct. 8, 1772, leaving an unsigned will, but her estate was equally divided among her six heirs—Dr. Farquherson, Mrs. Dalgetie, Mrs. Brown, Mrs. R. E. Scott, Peggy Gordon, Annie Gordon. It does not appear who Mrs. George Gordon was, but her Executors were Prof. Thomas G. and Wm. Thom. The tradition that she was the sister of Prof. Thos. Gordon's first wife is sustained by the latter's account as executor, in which he records "to cash received as the half of the annuity due out of the lands of Thairnstoun to Prof. (Thos.) Gordon in right of his brother, Mar. 8, 1774, £4.6.11. To a year's annuity due the defunct by Col. Farquhar's heirs settled £10 to avoid a dispute." At 19 years of age George G. was Prof. Oriental Lang., King's Coll., 1730 ; suc. 1767 by John Ross. Rev. Alex'r Keith, in a MS. history of the "Diocese of Aberdeen, 1732," now in the Advocate's Library, Aberdeen, states under the Parish of Monycabok: "Mamewlach is now possessed by one Mr. Gordon, literarum orientalium professor in the King's College, and before him by the Harveys."

15. THOMAS GORDON, M. A., b. Aug. 14, 1713 ; d. Aberdeen, May 10, 1797, æ 84 ; m. (I.) Lillias Forbes (?), d. Oct. 12, 1772 ; est. adm'd Mar. 8, 1774 ; (II.) ——, Eliza ——, b. 1717 ; d. Feb. 20, 1799, of asthma, æ 82. He was Prof. of Humanity, King's Coll., 1739 ; Regent 1765 ; Prof. of Greek, 1796. He was the Agent of Lord Gordon and in intimate relations with him ; also of Miss Inniss, Mrs. Gordon Crombie, Mrs. Geo. Gordon, &c., &c.

Principal W. D. Geddes, LL. D., of Aberdeen Univ., writes that no Arms or Crest appear on the Gordon tombs in Aberdeen. If the line of Prof. Thos. Gordon descends from Thomas Gordon of Daach, doubtless those of Gordon of Hallhead would be his proper Arms.

"*Az.,a fess betw. three boars' heads couped or.*" Crest—"*A hart's head ppr.*" Motto—"*Bydand.*"

The Crest and Motto are those of Gordon of Newry, Ireland. (*v.* Col. James Gordon, CONWAY 16, p. 248.)

" In the present enumeration of eminent and learned men particular notice should be taken of the late Mr. Thomas Gordon, an alumnus who d. 1797, having been professor of humanity and latterly of philosophy in this University for no less a period than 61 years. He continued to fulfill the duties of his office till the time of his death in the 83d year of his age. His attainments in the sciences, in polite literature, his ability as a scholar, his suavity of manner, his social disposition are all well known and will be long remembered." (Prof. John Kerr's Donaides, Edinburgh, 1725.)

A monumental tablet of white marble, oval shape, size 2 ft. x 2 ft. 5 in., placed near the W. end of the wall, S. aisle, Cathedral Church of St. Macham, Aberdeen, bears this conjunct inscription :

" In sepulchreto Gordoniensi jacent reliquiæ, Thomæ Gordon Armigeri. Qui Philosophiam In Regio Collegio et Universitate Aberdonensi per sexaginta annos, Professus, ex hac vita migravit, Decimo die Martii Anno Domini 1797, ætatis 84to.

ITEM.—Nepotis Roberti Eden Scott Armigeri Qui in eadem Universitate Per annos quindecim Philosophiæ docendæ incubuit Die Januarii decimo quarto A. D. 1811 aetat 42do mortales exuvias deposuit Vidua moestissima Dma Rachel Forbes Observantiæ in Professorem Gordon, Amoris in clarrissimum Maritum debita persolvens hæce monumentum extruendum Familiæque Gordoniæ sepulchretum pariete cingendum curavit."

Children, 1st marriage (Prof. T. G.) :

i. Elizabeth, b. —; m. June 10, 1768, Rev. John Scott, A. M. (SCOTT, p. .)
ii. Margaret, d. s.
iii. Annie, d. Aug., 1800 ; m. Dec. 13, 1788, Rev. Andrew Brown. He was tutor to John Buchan, and chaplain of the 21st Royal Regiment during the American War, and probably surrendered with Burgoyne at Saratoga. On his return to Scotland he became minister of Falkland, 1784-1802 ; then of Tranent.

SCOTT FAMILY.

Rev. Jno. Barrach, Minister of Falkland, Fife, has kindly sent me this transcript from the Records of his Church:

"June 10, 1784. The Rev. Andrew Broun, Chaplain of the 21st Reg't was admitted Minister of this Parish." "Apr. 25, 1802. To Collection Dr. Broun's farewell, 15s. 11d." "Sep. 28, 1802. This day Mr. George Buist was ordained Minister of this Parish, vacant by the translation of Dr. Broun to the Parish of Tranent."

"Mrs. Broun was a great authority on our old Scottish melodies, and she was very much commended for her varied and correct knowledge on this subject in one of our Magazines, not long ago."

In Sir Walter Scott's "Minstrelsy of the Scottish Border," Baudry's ed., Paris, 1838, vol. 1, p. 63, appears the following from the pen of Sir Walter. Writing of what he calls the Romantic Ballads, he quotes Mr. Tytler, son of Wm. Tytler, Esq., author of a "Dissertation upon Scottish Music," thus:

" My father got the following songs from an old friend, Mr. Thomas Gordon, Professor of Philosophy, in King's Coll., Aberdeen. The following extract of a letter of the Prof. to me explains how he came by them. An aunt of my children, Mrs. Farquhar, now dead, who was m. to the proprietor of a small estate near the sources of the Dee, in Braemar, a good old woman, who had spent the best part of her life among flocks and herds, resided in her latter days in the town of Aberdeen. She was possessed of a most tenacious memory, which retained all the songs she had heard from nurses and country women in that sequestered part of the country. Being naturally fond of my children, when young, she had them much about her, and delighted them with her songs and tales of chivalry. My youngest daughter, Mrs. Brown, at Falkland, is blest with a memory as good as her aunt, and has almost the whole of her songs by heart. In conversation I mentioned them to your father, at whose request my grandson, Mr. Scott, wrote down a parcel of them as his aunt sung them. Being then but a mere novice in music, he added, in the copy, such musical notes as he supposed might give your father some notion of the airs, or rather lilts, to which they were sung."

Sir Walter Scott adds: "The MSS. are cited under the name of Mrs. Brown, of Falkland, the ingenious lady to whose taste and memory the world is indebted for the preservation of the tales which they contain."

Jamieson, in his Ballads, thus refers to Mrs. Brown:

"In the groundwork of this collection, and for the greater and more valuable part of the popular and romantic tales which it contains, the public are indebted to Mrs. Brown of Falkland. Besides the large supply of ballads taken down from her own recitation many years ago by Professor Scott of Aberdeen, in 1800, I paid an unexpected visit to Mrs. Brown at Dysart, where she then happened to be for health, and wrote down from her unpremeditated repetition, about a dozen pieces more, most of which will be found in my work. Several others, which I had not time to take down, were afterwards transmitted to me by Mrs. Brown herself and by her late highly respectable and worthy husband, the Rev. Dr. Brown. Every person who peruses the following sheets, will see how much I owe to Mrs. Brown, and to her nephew, my much esteemed friend Professor Scott; and it rests with me to feel that I owe them much more for the zeal and spirit which they have manifested, than even for the valuable communications which they have made. As to the *authenticity* of the pieces themselves, they are as authentic as traditionary poetry can be expected to be, and their being more entire than most other such pieces are found to be, may be easily accounted for, from the circumstances that there are few persons of Mrs. Brown's abilities and education that repeat popular ballads from memory. She learnt most of them before she was twelve years old, from old women and maid servants. What she once learnt she never forgot, and such was her curiosity and industry, that she was not contented with merely knowing the story, according to one way of telling, but studied to acquire all varieties of the same tale which she could meet with."

From. Prof. Thomas Gordon's papers I derive these notes:

Mr. Forbes, his father-in-law, had three daughters, if not more; one m. Prof. Geo. Gordon, one m. Prof. Thos. Gordon, and one m. Joseph Farquhar, or Farquharson, a small landed proprietor at the source of the Dee in Braemar. His children, with Prof. Gordon's three daughters, were heirs of Mrs. George Gordon. He had—i. Dr. —— Farquharson of Old Aberdeen, a loyalist in South Carolina, 1775-6, not named by Sabine, who rec'd a pension of £200 per ann. from the British Gov't and £50 per ann. from his nephew Jack Brown. ii. Mrs. Dalgetie. iii. Lillias, m. John Brown, engaged in a mercantile house in London. She d. of palsy Feb., 1787. He d. London, Jan., 1787. They had Betty, b. 1770; d. of fever April, 1787. John (Jack), b. 1773, at 14 employed where his father had been employed, and at 18 able to pay his uncle, Dr. F., an annuity of £50. He was also an heir to his grandmother, Lady Balbethan. These were all cousins of Prof. Thos. Gordon's children. The Farquharsons of Braemar were of the Invercauld line.

Margaret Gordon (Peggy), Oct 20, 1784, writes of the mar. at that time of Jack Forbes Blackford to Miss Ann Gregory of Edinburgh, sister of Dr. Gregory.

Mrs. R. E. Scott writes, Feb. 14, 1807: "My favourite Forbes is just going to join his regiment at the Cape of Good Hope. Though but 15 he is a sensible, well informed young
man, and is your (Mrs. Eliza Scott) cousin, and nephew of the famous Dr. Gregory of
Edinburgh."

Prof. Thos. G., Mar. 30, 1789, names Miss Nancy Innes, Mrs. Gordon's niece, who lets
lodgings in Edinburgh. In 1775 names Fannie Innes of Glasgow, Mrs. Gordon's niece,
who m. Andrew Buchanan, a merchant of that city. In 1772 he named in letter to his
daughter, Mrs. Eliza Scott, "your cousins George Wilson, also John Wilson, your cousin
Mrs. Strahan, George Wilson's aunt, Miss Peggy Forbes of Kennithmont, and Mrs. Wilson's daughter, and your cousin Mary Forbes, who d. 1772."

These notes indicate that the Forbes family into which the Professors Gordon and Scott
married were branches of the ancient house of Forbes.

John Gregory, M. D., F. R. S., Prof. Univ. of Edinburgh, m. 1752, Elizabeth Forbes, b.
Jan. 5, 1730, d. 1761, dau. of Sir John, 13th Lord Forbes, and the 3d Bart. of Monymusk.
Douglass' Peerage says he had Dr. James Gregory of Edinburgh, and Margaret (Miss Peggy
Gordon says Ann), m. 1784, John Forbes of Blackford. It was her son Forbes to whom
Mrs. Scott referred in her letter of 1807. Mrs. Scott herself was a daughter of Forbes-
Mitchell of Thainston, and the wife of Prof. Geo. Gordon, and doubtless the 1st wife of Prof.
Thos. Gordon was a Forbes of Thainston. Anderson's Scottish Nation has interesting
sketches of these Drs. Gregory. Dr. John Gregory's arms, 1766, were "*Ar. a fir tree growing
out of a mount in base vert surmounted by a sword in bend, ensigned by a royal crown in
the dexter chief point all ppr.; in the sinister chief and dexter base a lion's head erased or.*"
Crest—"*A sphere ppr.*" Motto—"*Altius.*"

One letter from the correspondence of Prof. Thomas Gordon is given here, as it specially
treats of the Scotts. Others it is hoped will some day be published with Rev. James Scott's
correspondence.

KING'S COLLEGE, Sept'r 23, 1770.

My dear Sir : Your letter from Dumfries enclosing a letter from your Papa at Westwood
were anxiously longed for & joyfully received at Humanity Castle. I give you joy of your
American son & wish him health and prosperity. Tho' far from unconcerned about him, I
must indulge myself in a partiality for my Scots boy, who every day wins me more and
more. For some weeks past he has been under the eye of uncle Gustavus. I shall refer the
comparison therefore to his impartiality which cannot be called in question in this case.

We lost Professor Lumsden since I wrote last. Dr. Gerrard thinks our Divinity chair
worth quitting his own for. Dr. Campbell probably shall have the double office of Principal
& Professor of Divinity in the Marischal. We have had the pleasure of a visit of your Brother
Gustavus since their Law vacation commenced. Beginning of August I attended him in a
visit to friends in Murray who were all mighty happy to see him. They all agreed he was in
person much liker your Pappa than you are. Uncle Roby accompanied us to your friend,
Col. Grants. He is married to a mighty pretty spirited young girl of whom he is mighty
fond. The Col. was very civil to your brother & would not part with us under a visit of two
days, tho' we intended no more there than a dinner. He is putting up a handsome house hardly
a Gunshot from the old one, but so situated as to command the beautiful prospects that the
banks of the Spey afford in that neighborhood. At Elgin we visited Lady Innes and her
family, who expressed great satisfaction at being informed that you was agreeably situated.
Some days after we left that, your acquaintance Mr. Brander of Pitgavny was married to
Miss Dunbar of Thunderton. Mr. Gordon Achenreath & family enquired very kindly concerning you. I carried your brother next to Cullen-house, the politeness of which you are
acquainted with; in this part of the jaunt Uncle Roby also attended us. We went next
morning to Portsay, where we saw Mr. and Mrs. Robertson, Betty's Peterhead acquaintances
& Thom Steel who is by this time set out for Dort in Holland where he is called to be Scots
minister. Your Brother is so addicted to his Law studies, that he made his way from thence
to Humanity Castle leaving Mr. Theod. Gordon and I to prosecute a Ross shire jaunt. At
Ginnes, I learned that two of their sons have crossed the Atlantic in the merchants service.

---

* "Dr. William Gordon, Professor of Medicine in Old Aberdeen University, dyed Mar. 10, 1640, one of
the founded members of the college of Old Aberdeen, and common procurator thereof, departed this life in the
10th of March in his own house in Old Aberdeen, a godly, grave, learned man, and singular in common works
about the College, and putting up on the steeple thereof most glorious as ye see and staitly crown throwa
down be the myud before." (Spalding's History, I., 191.)

Dr. G. was a contributor to the Funeralls of Bishop Patrick Forbes, p. 347, 353. His son, James Gordon, parson of Bauchary, St. Devenick, was author of "The Reformed Bishop," &c. (Gordon's His. of
Scotch Affairs, III., 129. Also Peabody.) He was made Mediciner of K. C. 1632.

James McLeod is at Peterboro', James River Virginia & William some where in Maryland. If you find them out or they you I hope you will take notice of them & be of what service you can. I have done nothing about sending out a young man to Mr. Thercald as I have heard of no remittance for the passage. Meantime I saw Mr. Frazer, who will accept if you recommend it. I believe likewise that your friend Gray, will by this time be so wearied with threshing at a school, that he will embrace any good family that wanted a Tutor. John Davidson is with Col. Masson before now. God bless you, my dear Sir—I expect by your next to hear of your removal from your present parish & am happy that things turn out so well.

Yours sincerely,

Thos. Gordon.

To Reverend John Scott.

11. HON. GUSTAVUS[3] SCOTT (*James,*[2] *John,*[1]), of Montgomery county, Maryland, b. "Westwood," Prince William county, Va.,—, 1753; d. Washington, D. C.,—, 1801; will dat. Dec. 4, 1797;* m. Feb. 16, 1777, MARGARET HALL CAILE, b. —; d. —; daughter of Hall Caile, of Annapolis, Md., and his wife Miss Haskins.

Mr. Scott went with his brother John to Scotland, 1765, immediately after the Bullitt and Baylis duel. He studied at King's Coll., Aberdeen. In 1767 he entered No. 4, Essex Court, Middle Temple, London, where he completed his law studies, 1771. Prof. Gordon, in his letters, *supra* (p. 622), writes of having taken a "jaunt" with him into Scotland, 1770, during his vacation, after which Gustavus returned to his law studies. When he had completed his course he located in Somerset Co., Maryland, where he practiced his profession with eminent success.

Mr. Scott was a man of too much intelligence to be led into the use of honours to which he was not entitled. In his travels through Scotland among his various

---

*In the name of God, Amen. I, *Gustavus Scott*, of Montgomery County, Maryland, do make and ordain this my last will and testament.

Imprimis—I give and bequeath to my dear & much beloved wife, *Margaret Scott*, an annuity of One Thousand Dollars per annum charged upon all my estate real, personal, and mixed and to take place of all other Legacies or Bequests whatsoever; but the same to cease and become void on her second marriage. I give also to my said wife, provided she does not marry again, all my Plate, Household furniture, Carriage and Horses, and six of my house servants, at her election and also one Thousand Pounds current money, to be disposed of at her decease among her children as she may think they deserve. It is also my will and desire that whilst she continues single she shall have the entire management of my children & estate, and the direction of all their affairs, until the period at which I have directed their portions to be paid over to them, & that she shall not be accountable for any profits, confiding that she will apply them to their education and preferment in such manner as she knows best consists with my own ideas of what is proper and necessary for them.

and.—I give and bequeath to my son *John C. Scott* and the heirs of his body lawfully begotten, forever, all my lands called Strawberry Vale, and all such lands as I purchased contiguous and adjacent thereto; but in case of his death without such issue as aforesaid then to go to his next brother, entail general, and so to the next brother in priority of age so long as any remain, and failing such brothers and their lawful issue, then to be equally divided amongst my daughters and their legal representatives.

3d.—I give to my Son *Gustavus H. Scott* and the heirs of his body lawfully begotten, forever, all the residue of my lands in Fairfax County, and also all my lands in Stafford County Virginia, and failing in him such issue then to pass to his next brother *Wm. B. Scott*, entail general, with remainder as in the devise preceding, and failing issue in all my sons to be divided amongst my daughters equally as before directed.

4th.—I give and devise to my son *Wm. Bushrod Scott*, and the heirs of his body lawfully begotten, forever, all my lands in the Counties of Fauquier & Loudoun, in Virginia, and failing issue in him then to my youngest son *Robert Scott*, entail General, with like remainder and contingencies as in the next preceding clause.

5th.—I give and bequeath to my youngest son *Robert Scott* and the heirs of his body lawfully begotten, forever, all my lands in Alleghany County, Maryland, My lands in Kentucky, all my others lands in the Commonwealth of Virginia, and my lands in Montgomery County, Maryland, bought of General Forrest, some of which lands are not yet conveyed, though they are intended by me to pass by this my will, and in case of his death without issue remainder to my son *John C. Scott* and the heirs of his body lawfully begotten forever, with remainder to my other sons in like manner according to priority of birth and failing issue in all my said sons then to be divided equally as mentioned in the second clause of this my will. And I hereby further declare that in case I myself or my Executrix by my derection should make sale of the said lands, or any of them, I charge my said estate real and personal to make good to my said son the amount of such sale.

6th.—I give and bequeath to my four daughters and each and every one of them Six thousand Dollars each to be paid to them at the age of Eighteen, or marriage with the consent of their mother if she be single, or of my other Executors if she be married, or a majority of such as may be living & have thought proper to accept of the trust and my wish is that their said legacies as soon the exigencies of my affairs will permit, shall be invested in Bank Stock of Columbia or such other as may be thought advisable or placed in the name of a trustee for their separate and entire use and to be out of the power of any husband except as to the interest. I give also to my said daughters an equal share of all my remaining personal estate together with their broth-

relatives he doubtless obtained authentic knowledge of his family connexions. It is therefore highly probable that the Arms which he had engraved in Scotland, and used throughout his life, on his book plate, &c., were those borne by his family in Scotland. These differ somewhat from those engraved on the tomb of Rev. Alexander Scott, for which difference the marble cutter may have been responsible. The Arms of Gustavus Scott were as follows:

"*Or, on a bend az., a bezant between two crescents of the field. In a bordure arg., eight bezants or.*" Crest—"*A dove with an olive branch in its beak.*" Motto—"*Gaudia Magna Nuncio.*" Burke gives the arms of Scott of Scotstarvit, Co. Fife, thus: "*Or., on a bend a star between two crescents of the field, a bordure engr. gu.*" And those of Scott, Sheriff Clerk of Edinburgh, 1672, "*same as Scotstarvit, the bordure charged with eight bezants.*" The arms of Scott of Elie are: "*Or., on a bend az., a mullet betw. two crescents of the field, a bordure gu. charged with bezants.*" Scott of East India Service, 1811: "*Or. on a bend engr. az. a star between two crescents of the field, in sinister chief a dove with an olive branch in its beak ppr.*" Crest—"*A dove as in the arms.*" Motto—"*Eureka*" and "*Arno.*"

When the Revolutionary war opened Mr. Scott took an active part in all the patriotic measures of Md. He was elected a deputy from Somerset Co. to the Md. Conv. of June 22, 1774, and Dec. 7, 1775. He was also a mem. of the Md. Association, 1775. The Conv. of 1775 elected him a mem. of a committee "to prepare a draught of instructions for the deputies representing this Province in Congress." He was also elected one of the four delegates from Somerset to the Md. Conv. of Aug., 1776, which formed the State Constitution. He removed to Dorchester Co., Md., after the adoption of the State government, and represented that county in the Assembly of 1780 and 1784. The State appointed him one of her Conferees

---

ers and of the surplus which shall remain after the payment of my just debts of such lands as I shall direct to be sold, hereby expressly declaring that I mean and intend such surplus to be equally divided among all my children.

7th.—I give and bequeath to my housekeeper, *Margaret Bullock*, Forty Dollars per annum during her life and charge the same on my estate both real and personal.

8th.—My Will and desire is that all my real estate during the minority of my sons whom I now declare not to be of age to receive their estates until they respectively arrive at the age of twenty two years shall remain under the entire care and management of their mother whilst single and that after they respectively arrive at 22 years of age if she still continues single so much shall remain under her care as shall be sufficient to secure the payment of her said annuity and that she shall be secured therein to her entire satisfaction before she delivers up the possession of such real estate, the same being taxed equally on all the said real estate so far as a deficiency of the personal estate after payment of my daughters fortunes may render necessary. I give to my oldest son my gold watch, his late Grandmother's my gold kneebuckles and sleeve buttons as monuments of the great affection I bear him, hoping they will be received and remembered as the tokens of a fond and affectionate Father's remembrance of his dear son to whom he looks as to a protector of his younger brothers and sisters.

I will and desire that all my shares in the Potomac Company, Potomac bridge Company, and all my shares in the North America land company and all other companies whatsoever be considered as personal estate and as such to be sold by my Executrix or Exec'rs for the payment of my just debts. I also hereby authorize my Executrix and eventually Executors hereinafter named to sell my place called Rock Hill or any other of my lands in the State of Maryland for the payment of my debts, leaving to their discretion as circumstances may arise which shall be sold, the surplus of such sales whether of lands or shares as before mentioned to be considered as personal estate and divided as before mentioned.

It is my express will and desire & solemnly handed down to my sons, that as soon as their educations are completed they industriously devote themselves, to some Profession or business & do not altogether rely on the little pittance my professional industry has raised for their good education and advancement, hoping their own good sense will soon convince them that there exists no real independence to the man who cannot support his own existence by the operations of his own mind or body.

I hereby nominate and appoint my wife, during her remaining single, whole and sole guardian of my children and Executrix of my last will and testament; and in case of her death or marriage prior to my eldest sons arrival at the age of 22 years, I then nominate and appoint *Thomas J. Bullett, Nathaniel Crawford* and *Uriah Forrest* Guardians of my children and Executors of my will, until my said son shall arrive at the age of 22 years, at which period I appoint him Executor of my Will and Guardian of my infant children fully confiding he will then Execute with honor and integrity the sacred trust confided to him. In testimony whereof, I hereto, this 4th day of December in the year 1797 set my hand and seal in presence of the then subscribing witnesses who attest the same in my presence at my request & in the presence of each other.

GUSTAVUS SCOTT.

Witnesses: Cath. Brown, Sarah Scott Brown, Catherine Brown, Aatze Hortulanio. [This will was sent me by Dr. G. S. F.]

to meet those of Va. at Annapolis, Dec. 22, 1784, to devise some action towards the improvement of the Potomac. This conference resulted in the origination of the "Potomac Company," which later on became the "Chesapeake and Ohio Canal Co." He was elected a del. from Md. to the Continental Congress from 1784–1785. He was one of the Md. legislative com. which reported in favour of James Rumsey the inventor of the steamboat, who claimed the exclusive privilege of making and selling his boats in Md. Force's Archives give many records of Mr. Scott's work in the Conventions of Md. He was a member of the Com. on Prizes, Aug. 11, 1776, of the Com. to prepare instructions for recruiting sergeants, the Com. on the Potomac Ferry, &c., &c., &c.

In all the actions of the Conv. relative to his bro., Rev. John Scott, he refrained from voting. Mr. Scott moved to Annapolis in ——, where he built a brick dwelling which still stands, and about 1794 he moved to his Montgomery Co. estate, near Georgetown, where he built a fine mansion which he named " Rock Hill." This he sold afterwards to Joel Barlow. In 1793 he was appointed, with others, on the Com. of Health of Baltimore to take precautions against the yellow fever, which had just then broken out in that city. In 1795 Mr. Scott, William Thornton and Alexander White were appointed Commissioners of Washington City, to succeed Messrs. Johnson, Carroll and Stuart, in superintending the erection of the public buildings in that city. This responsible position he filled for several years. The reports of the Commission will be found in Ex. Docs., 4th Cong., 2d Sess., 5th Cong., 2d Sess., and 6th Cong., 1st Sess., the last report being dated Dec. 5, 1799. It appears from the first report, Dec. 21, 1796, that the Commission memorialized Congress on the institution of a national university ; on the cession by proprietors of lands adjacent to the site of the seat of Government of territory for the purpose, and recommended the authorization of persons to receive pecuniary donations, &c., for the use of the intended establishment, but nothing was done by Congress. The 11th Cong., 1811, decided that Congress had no power to endow a university, but the 42d Cong., 1873, recommended a bill for the establishment of a national university !

Mr. Scott's influence as one of the Commissioners was of great assistance to the President. When the act of Congress locating the Federal Capital on the Potomac R. was passed in 1790, the State of Va. made a donation of $120,000, and Maryland $72,000, for the erection of the public buildings. But in 1796 this am't was found insufficient to meet the cost of the buildings. The Commissioners failed to borrow money on the credit of the Government either in Europe or the States United. In 1796 Washington made a personal appeal to the State of Md. for a loan of $150,000. To this appeal the Legislature responded promptly by a loan of $100,000, and by eulogistic resolutions about the President. But such was the low state of the U. S. credit that the loan was granted only on the personal security of Gustavus Scott and his two associates. The following letter from Gen. Washington to Mr. Scott has been published in Varnum's "Seat of Government," &c., 2d ed., 1854, p. 42, but it is also appropriate here :

PHILAD'A, 26 December, 1796.

To GUSTAVUS SCOTT, ESQ.:

Sir : Your favor of the 13th inst. was not received until the 22d. To what the delay is to be ascribed I know not.

The voice of Maryland, as expressed by its Legislature in the Resolutions which you enclosed, is flattering indeed as it respects myself, personally; and highly pleasing as it relates to their federal sentiments. I thank you for sending them.

From what you have said of the disposition of the Senate of that State, the presumption is that the loan of $100,000 for the use of the Federal City, must 'ere this have passed through all the requisite forms. The necessity of the case justified the obtaining of it on almost any terms, and the zeal of the Commissioners (if they, in their individual capacities, which they surely may do without hazarding any thing) in making themselves liable for the amount, as it could not be had without, cannot fail of approbation. At the same time I must confess that the request has a very singular appearance, and will not, I should suppose, be very grateful to the feelings of Congress. With very great esteem, &c., GEO. WASHINGTON.

Mr. Scott, and one other of the Commissioners, resided in Georgetown, The President thought the immediate growth of the new Capital demanded their residence in or near the site of the Federal buildings. As Mr. Scott was at that time erecting his mansion of "Rock Hill," a lengthy correspondence on the subject resulted between himself and the President. Two of Washington's letters to Mr. Scott at this time have been kindly sent me, and are here presented; four others are locked up in the archives of the Government. This correspondence does not seem to have impaired the friendly relations which always existed between the correspondents. It is not known that Mr. Scott ever resided in Washington.

PHILAD'A, 25 May, 1796.

To GUST'S SCOTT, ESQ.:

Sir: Your favor of the 20th inst. came to hand yesterday. I have neither received nor heard of an address from the proprietors of the Federal City, nor do I know any more of Mr. Law's sentiments relative to the concerns of it than I do of Tippo Saib's. [Those] conveyed in my last to the Commissioners (dated the 22d) are not of recent adoption. They are as old as the change which took place in the establishment of the Commissioners, and were the cause of that change. A combination of causes have brought them more actively and pointedly into view than heretofore. Among which, and not the least to be regarded, are the remarks which were made during the discussion of the Guarantee Bill, even by its friends (not so much in as out of the House)—the indispensable necessity for close attention and great exertion in all those to whom the business is entrusted, with an eye to the strictest economy under the best system that can be formed.

You cannot, I am persuaded, be entirely unacquainted with the remarks which have been made on the want of economy, and due attendance to the operations which are carrying on, by those who are entrusted with the management of them. Nor, acquainted as *you are* with the jealousies and contracted views of the proprietors, can the utmost circumspection, and the minutest attentions in the Commiss'rs to all the wheels that are in motion, and to all the persons who move them, appear unimportant. Consequently, wherever the scene of business is, there also should be the principal actors; and until this happens, the jealousies between the upper and lower end of the City will not subside, nor will the injurious consequences flowing from them cease. Nor indeed will it be believed, be the fact as it may, that while the Commiss'rs, or the major part of them (with the subordinate agents), reside in George Town, that the concerns of the City will be conducted uninfluenced and to the best advantage. We may despise public opinion and these kind of reports as we please, but they are not less injurious on that account. The time is very short in which a great deal for the reception of Congress is to be done, and no means or exertion should be wanting to accomplish it. It would be ineligible and highly impolitic to bring any new proposition before Congress before the Government is fixed there.

I do not precisely know what the late Secretary of State may have written with respect to the alternative allowed the Commissioners to reside in the City or *George Town*. But it is a fact known to every one who ever heard me express a sentiment on the subject, that it has been decidedly in favor of the former, and that nothing but necessity, arising from the want of accomodation, could justify the latter. Nay more, it is known to the first Commissioners that I not only coincided in opinion with them, that a house situated between the two principal buildings should be built for their accommodation, but actually approved a plan for the purpose. Why it was laid aside, unless their going out of office or the want of funds was the cause, I am unable to say.

I have been thus particular that you may see what my opinion *uniformly* has been; that it has not proceeded from any recent movements in the City (which were unkown to me before your letter came to hand), and that it has appeared more necessary and has been more pointedly mentioned since I find that the *friends* of the City, and I presume the community at large, conceive (as I have always done) that the measures which have been suggested are useful and proper. With esteem and regard, &c., GEO. WASHINGTON.

SCOTT FAMILY.

MOUNT VERNON, 4th July, 1796.

Sir : If the public dispatches which I receive, and am obliged to answer by every Post, would permit, I would go more into detail and explanation of the subject of your last (separate) letter, than it is possible for me to do at present. I will not, however, let it pass without some further expression of my ideas; and the understanding I always had of your entrance into the office you now hold, in the Federal City.

That the Secretary of State's letter to you (which I have not by me at this place to resort to,) may have been so worded as to leave the alternative of residing in the City, or in George Town, is not necessary, if it was justifiable, to deny; because a change of circumstances would certainly authorize a change of measures. But independent of this, it must not be forgotten, that at the time the letter above alluded to was written, such an alternative was indispensable, for as much as there were no *convenient* accommodations for the Commissioners *in the City*, and because houses could not be erected in a moment, under the circumstances which then existed. In addition to this, let it be remembered, also, that the first Commissioners, sensible of the propriety and advantages which would result therefrom, had resolved to build a house for their own accommodation at or near the spot where the Hotel now stands; and were diverted from it (if my memory serves me,) partly by two causes :—first, from a doubt of the propriety of such an application of public money; and 2ndly, from an opinion that they could be accommodated in the Hotel, when built,— which, it was expected, would have happened long since.

I mention these things to show there has been no inconsistency in any sentiments or conduct ;—and that to enable the Commissioners to comply with the views of government, and to devote their time to its service, the present compensation was resolved on.

Your other allegation is of a more serious nature; and if deception withdrew you from what you deemed a permanent establishment at Baltimore, it cannot be justified. But be assured, Sir, this is a new view of the subject; and that the proposal to you, to become a Commissioner, originated in assurances, confidently given to me, that you had resolved to remove to the Federal City, or to George Town; and because I knew you had a considerable interest in the vicinity of them. Was not the first application to you predicated on this information ?

But I must be explicit in declaring, that not only to obviate the suspicions and jealousies which proceed from a residence of the Commissioners without the City, or in a remote corner of it, not only that they may be where the busy and important scenes are transacting, that they may judge of the conduct of others not from *reports only*, but from occular proof, as the surest guide to economy and dispatch ;—independent, I say, of these considerations, which are momentous of themselves, I should view the residence of the Commissioners of the City, and their officers of different grades, in some central part of it as a nest egg (pardon the expression,) which will attract others, and prove the *surest* means of accomplishing the great object which all have in view—the removal of Congress at the appointed time—without which, everything will become stagnant, and your sanguine hopes blasted.

To be frank, I must give it to you as *my* opinion, that in relation to the concerns of the City, the Commissioners stand precisely in the same light (if not in a stronger one,) that each does to any interesting matter in a train of execution for himself.—Would you, then, notwithstanding you may have an architect to carry on your buildings on Rock Hill, and a man to superintend your attending laborers, trust to their proceeding without your minute inspection of their conduct ? I think, and am sure, you will answer, no. I do not mean by this question to exhibit a charge, for I do as truly tell you, that I do not know, or ever heard, how often you visit your own concerns there. It is upon general principles I argue. A man of industry and exertion will not, on his own account, have a work of that sort on hand without giving close attention to it. And certain it is, the obligation (because of the responsibility) is at least equally great when entrusted by the Public.

After all, as the season is now far advanced, houses, in the situation I have described as most eligible, may not be to be rented. I am not unwilling that the removal of the *Commissioners*, if they find much inconvenience in doing it, may be suspended until the commencement of the operations of next Spring, when it will certainly be expected, and if known, I have *no* doubt but that houses will be prepared for their accomodation by that time.

You, will, from the length of this letter, with difficulty, give credit to my assertion in the beginning of it; but as a proof, not only of its verity, but of the friendship and candor with which it is written, it shall go to you in its present rough garb; and with all its imperfections, accompanied with assurances of the esteem and regard with which

I am, Sir, your Obd't and H'ble Serv't, GEO. WASHINGTON.

GUSTAVUS SCOTT, Esq'r.

VIRGINIA GENEALOGIES.

In 1796 Mr. Scott's health beginning to fail, he resigned his office on the Commission in the following letter, but his resignation was not accepted :

WASHINGTON, 7th July, 1766.

Sir : My physicians having recommended to me to try the waters of the Sweet Springs in the western frontier of Virginia, for the restoration of my health, I am about setting out for that country. During the period that I have been honored with a seat at the board of commissioners my time has been entirely devoted to the duties of my station, and I believe no member of a public board has been less absent. Whilst I continue in office I do not consider myself as authorized to quit the duties of it without giving the necessary information to you. I accepted the appointment because I would not refuse to serve under a government I loved, or any appointment to which the constituted authorities thought proper to call me. The same principles now induce me to say that if it is thought that the public service will suffer by my absence, which may probably continue 5 or 6 weeks, that I shall readily vacate my seat by sending in my resignation. I do not know that any important business can occur in the city during my absence, or that any great injury can arise from the boards having no more than two members present. Every measure for the summers operations being settled, there seems to be nothing left to do but to push them forward.

I have the honor to be, with sentiments of perfect respect,

To Presd. U. S.   Dr. Sir, yr. mo. obd. servant,   GUSTAVUS SCOTT.

The *National Intelligencer* some years ago published the following, of "Rock Hill."

"This beautiful, romantic and extensive suburban seat was originally founded by Gustavus Scott, Esq., a lawyer of distinction and great wealth, who came here from Cambridge, on the Eastern Shore, Maryland, and built an elegant home shortly after the Capital was here located. In 1797, when the money furnished by Virginia and Maryland for erecting the Capital buildings had been exhausted, Mr. Scott was one of the Maryland commissioners appointed to aid in securing a loan. Washington applied to him to give his private name as collateral security, as the Holland bankers were not satisfied with the State securities. The letter is preserved in the history of the loan. The request was granted. This shows the weight of Mr. Scott's name at that time. There was a blood relationship as well as a warm friendship between Washington and this Scott family, and the former is known to have contributed his advice in the selection of Rock Hill, as Kalorama was originally named by its proprietor.

The Rock Hill mansion—which burnt a year or two ago during its occupation as a small pox hospital, now stands with blackened and tumbling walls— was built of imported brick, in the very best style of that period, at a cost of more than thirty thousand dollars. The corner-stone was laid with great ceremonies, after the customs of the period, about 1798. Washington, prevented from filling his engagement to be present on the occasion, addressed Mr. Scott a long letter, regretting the disappointment, and covering nearly three pages of large foolscap, in a close, plain hand, giving particular advice as to the location of the mansion, which was adopted. That letter is preserved by the family. Under the corner-stone, among the articles usually selected for such purpose, including gold and silver English and American coins of the period, was deposited a small silver waiter, bearing sculptured upon it the family coat-of-arms, consisting of a dove bearing an olive branch, with "Pax" beneath. The mansion, with its front facing the south, consisted of two distinct, spacious, two-storied, porticoed structures, with eighteen-inch solid walls, with a long story-and-a-half building running east and west, connecting the two main portions with a hall and dormitories. There was erected also a fine, spacious brick stable on the southern declivity of the hill, which, however, was some years ago, burnt, the lower portion of it only remaining to mark the outlines of the original. Washington and his family often visited the Rock Hill Mansion, and there subsisted marked familiarity between the Rock Hill and Mount Vernon people. Major William Bushrod Scott, of the Marine Corps, and who, in the latter part of his life was for twelve years navy agent in this city, was a son of the proprietor of Rock Hill, and used to vividly describe the visits of Washington to his father's house. On one occasion he found him in one of the large trees on the hillside, looking for the nests of the birds. When he landed hastily at the foot of the tree, Washington, chiding him as in naughty work, touched his heels with the whip as they flew towards the house, a circumstance which ever afterwards put the youngster out of sight when Washington was on the premises. Major Scott's family still reside in this city. At the death of the Rock Hill proprietor, which occurred more than half a century ago, the executors of the estate sold the Rock Hill property for $16,000 to Joel Barlow, the famous poet and politician, who gave it the name of Kalorama."

"Mr. John C. Bullett, of Philadelphia, representing a number of capitalists of that city, purchased in 1886 an undivided four fifths of the property known as Kalorama heights near Washington, for the sum of $400,000."

Children (from will; all minors 1797):

+ 43.   i.   JOHN CAILE,[4] b. —, 1782; d. Mar. 14, 1840; m. Nov. 21, 1802, Ann Love-
+ 44.   ii.   GUSTAVUS HALL, b. —; d. —; m. July 1, 1806, Elizabeth Douglas Marshall.
   45.   iii.   WILLIAM BUSHROD, U. S. M. C., b. —; d. —; m. —, Ann Holton; appt'd
          2d Lieut., U. S. Marine Corps, July 4, 1809; resigned May 13, 1810. He
          resided in Washington. Is called Major S. in the account of Rock Hill,
          supra.

Children :

      i. Rebecca, m. —— Henriques, Washington, D. C.
      ii. Margaret. iii. Gustavus. iv. Mary.
      v. James. vi. Ann, m. —— Young. vii. Eliza.

+ 46.   iv.   ROBERT JAMES, b. 1798; d. 1834; m. —, 1818, Mary Ann Lewis.
   47.   v.   ELIZABETH CAILE, b. —; d. —; m. Dec. 10, 1801, Capt. Robert Rankin, U.
          S. M. C., b. —; d. —; 2d Lieut. U. S. Marine Corps, Sep. 2, 1795; 1st
          Lieut., Mar. 2, 1799; Captain, Jan. 16, 1808; resigned Jan. 1, 1809.
          (Hamersly.)

Children :

      i. Thompson. ii. Margaret. Both d. s.

   48.   vi.   JULIANA B., b. —; d. —; m. —, Capt. Robert DeWar Wainwright, U. S. M.
          C.; comm'd 2d Lt. U. S. Marine Corps, Feb. 15, 1807; 1st. Lt., Jan. 23,
          1809; Capt., Sep. 29, 1812; Bvt. Major, Mar. 3, 1823; Bvt. Lt. Col.,
          Mar. 3, 1827; Lieut. Colonel, July 1, 1834; d. Oct. 5, 1841. (Ham-
          ersly.)

   49.   vii.   CHRISTIAN, b. —; d. —, m. June 9, 1808, Charles Tyler.
   50.   viii.   MARY, d. s.

EXCURSUS—CAILE,—HARRISON.

The name Caile is not found, so spelled, in Burke's Gen. Armory. He gives Cayle or Cayly, Kayle, Keyle, doubtless the same name, and pronounced "Kyle."

1. MR. CAILE of ——, had—2. *Hall.* 3. John, m. Rebecca Ennals, for whose issue see Hanson's "Old Kent, Md." 4. *Mary.*

2. HALL CAILE, m. —— Haskins; had—5. Margaret, m. Gustavus Scott, *supra.* 6. Mary, m. (I.) John Caile Harrison, her 1st. cos., No. 7; (II.) Judge Thomas J. Bullitt. (SCOTT 14.)

4. MARY CAILE, m. Christopher Harrison of Appleby, Eng., who came to Easton, Md., *cir.* 1760; had—7. *John Caile.*

7. JOHN CAILE HARRISON, m. his. cos. Mary Caile, No. 6, *sup.;* had—8. Hall, m. Elizabeth Gault of Ireland; had—9. Rev. Hugh Thompson Harrison, M. A., b. 1810; d. Balto.' June 21, 1872; m. June 3, 1834, Eliza Catherine, dau. of Craven Peyton Thompson, Alex'a' Va.; grad. A. B., Yale, 1831; A. M. 1839; classmate of Bishops Kip and Clarke; grad. Va' Theo. Sem., 1832; ord. Deacon by Bishop Stone Dec. 2, 1832; Priest do., 1833; was Rector of Queen Caroline and St. John's Par., Howard Co., Md., 1833–1866, resigned the 1st par. 1839, and retained the 2d until 1866, when he removed to Balto., Md. He had—i. Rev. Hall Harrison, S. T. D., b. St. John's Par., Nov. 11, 1837; grad. A. B., St. James Coll., Md., 1854; M. A. 1857; instructor there 1854–63; ord. Deacon by Bishop Chase, N. H., May 25, 1865; Priest, 1866; appointed Asst. Master St. Paul's School, Concord, N. H. In 1879 became Rector St. John's Parish, Howard Co., Md., where his father had ministered 33 years. P. O., Ellicotts City, Md. He m. Agnes Spottiswoode Kennedy, dau. of Hon. Anthony and Sarah (Dandridge) Kennedy of Md. (*v.* Campbell's Spotswood Gen.) Dr. H. stands justly high as an author. He has edited "Hugh Davey Evans on the Christian Doctrine of Marriage," N. Y., 1870, and published a "Memoir of Hugh Davey Evans," Hartford, 1870, and a charming "Life of the Rt. Rev. J. B. Kerfoot, D.D., LL.D., 1st Bishop of Pittsburgh;" 2 vols., N. Y., 1886; also "William Pinkney, Fifth Bishop of Maryland;" Balto., 1891. He rec'd hon. deg. of S. T. D., Trin. Coll., Conn., 1889. He has contributed many valuable articles to the Church papers. ii. R. S. Steuart Harrison of Balto., Md., b. 1840; m. Sally Dorsey Pue. iii. William Gilpin, M. D., b. 1843.

21. ALEXANDER⁴ SCOTT (*James,³ James,² John¹*), b. "Clermont," 1762 (?); d. "Seven Islands," June 29, 1819; m. (I.) —1786, FRANCES WHITING, b. —; d. Feb. 16, 1807; daughter of Henry and Humphrey Ann Frances (Toy) Whiting (BROWN, p. 178, note*); (II.) July 13, 1813, SARAH BUTLER (HENRY) CAMPBELL; b Jan. 4, 1780; d. Dec. 10, 1856; daughter of Gov. Patrick and Dorothea (Dandridge) Henry, and widow of Robert Campbell of Scotland, brother of Thomas Campbell, the poet. (S. M. P., p. 190.)

An Alexander Scott served as private in the Continental line, Revolutionary War, from Va. His heirs rec'd 200 a. land in 1834 for his services; the warrant was issued to Alexander Scott. (Rep. Sec. Treas., 1834.)

Children, first marriage :

    51. i. JAMES,⁶ b. —. 52. ii. SARAH SCOTT, b. —.
    53. iii. ALEXANDER, b. —; d. —; m. (I.) —, Elizabeth Dixon, d. s. p. (II.) Mary Jane Dixon.

        Children, second marriage :

        i. Turner Dixon, C. S. A. ii. Robert. iii. William, C. S. A. iv. Mary Anna, m. Salem, Fauq'r, Co., May 10, 1853, George S. Hamilton. Had i. Annie Berry, b. June 4, 1854. ii. Mary Welby, b. Sep. 21, 1856. iii. Alexander Scott, b. Jan. 18, 1858. iv. Janet, b. Jan. 8, 1860. v. William Scott, b. Mar. 23, 1862. vi. Lilias Ritchie, b. Oct. 30, 1864. vii. Alice Turner, b. Sep. 15, 1866. viii. Harriet Glassell, b. Oct. 24, 1869.

  + 54. iv. FRANCES TOY, b. —; d. —; m. —, 1813, Edward Carter.
    55. v. HARRIET, b. —; d. —, 1880; m. Oct. 19, 1883, William Erasmus Glassell. (GLASSELL 15, p. 15.)
    56. vi. CHRISTIANA B.

Second marriage :

  + 57. vii. PATRICK HENRY, b. June 4, 1815; d. Jan. 9, 1865; m. Nov. 17, 1852, Mary C. Yancey.
    58. viii. HENRIETTA DANDRIDGE, b. "Seven Islands," Oct. 24, 1817; d. —; m. Sept. 24, 1835, Gen. Wm. H. Bailey of La.
    59. ix. KITTY HENRY, b. do., Aug. 18, 1819; d. Dec. 8, 1845; m. April 19, 1843, Dr. Robert W. Scott.

25. ELIZABETH⁴ SCOTT (*James,³ James,² John¹*), b. "Clermont," Fauquier county, Va., July 17, 1771; d. May 16, 1858, æ 87; m. April 15, 1788, MAJOR LAWRENCE ASHTON, b. —; d. —; son of John and Mary (Watts) Ashton, of Charles. (EXCURSUS—ASHTON, 16.)

Major Ashton settled in Fauq'r Co., 1786. "Mrs. A. was noted for intelligence, beauty, vivacity, wit, courtly manners and dignity, and in later years for exemplary piety." (Mrs. Whiting.)

Children (ASHTON) :

    60. i. JOHN JAMES,⁵ b. —; d. s. cir. 1809; grad. A. B., Washington Coll,, Va., 1807; farmer, King George Co., Va.
    61. ii. LAWRENCE, b. —, 1790; d. s. Oct. 6, 1859, at Mr. John Glassell's; bur. Warrenton.

*See also Excursus.—Whiting p. 479.

62. iii. HENRY WASHINGTON, b. "Clermont," May 6, 1794; d. "North Wales," Mar. 4, 1796; m. Mar. 25, 1822, Anne Allason Rose, b. —; d. Feb., 1876, a few days before her husband. She was dau. of Capt. Robert and Mary Seymour (Hooe) Rose, "North Wales." (WALLACE 36; HOOE 61.)

> Children:
>
> i. Arthur, b. —; d. —; m. at "The Manse," P. W. Co., Dec. 15, 1857, Anne Carter Balch, dau. of Rev. Thomas B. Balch, my valued friend, in whose company I have passed many charming hours. Had—i. Charles. ii. Courtland, d. Apr. 11, 1873, æ 10.
> ii. Henry, C. S. A., Sergt. Major Poague's Artillery, Batt. A. N. Va.
> iii. Rosina, b. —; d. —; m. "Ashley," Sep. 22, 1847, Lucius Dixon, son of Turner Dixon, of "Vermont," Fauq'r Co.; had—i. Anna Ashton, m. Aug. 16, 1866, "North Wales," Col. L. W. Russell, U. S. A., 1861-5, of Salem, N. Y., and had Solomon Dixon, Anna Ashton, Rosina, Alice Fitzhugh, Zada, Mary Seymour, Sarah Helen.
> iv. Ellen, b. —; d. Aug. 22, 1876; m. "N. W.," Aug. 22, 1865, Robert Little Horner. (BROWN 202, p. 197.)
> v. Anna Rose. vi. Mary Katherine.

63. iv. SARAH SCOTT, b. —, 1797; d. Jan. 8, 1869; m. Nov. 20, 1845, John Glassell. (GLASSELL 8, p. 8.)

64. v. RICHARD WATTS, U. S. M. Corps, b. 1799; d. Sept., 1853; m. Aug. 4, 1835, Mary Devereux, dau. of Patrick and Katherine (Kane) Devereux, Wexford, Ireland. He was in the war of 1812 at 14; was afterwards Cadet at West Point; was commis'd 2d Lieut., U. S. Marine Corps, Jan. 28, 1817; resigned Jan. 22, 1821.

> Children:
>
> i. John Devereux, C. S. A., b. June 26, 1836; d. Apr., 1888; lawyer; entered C. S. Army as private Apr., 1861, Co. D, 2d Ga. Reg., Army No. Va.; 1862, Capt. in a Ga. Reg.; wounded and made prisoner; at Johnson's Is. nearly 2 years; never recovered from the exposure in the prison there; m. 1859, Sarah Roberts of Ga.; had—i. Julia, b. Oct., 1867; m. Capt. James White, Athens, Ga. ii. John Devereux, b. Apr., 1869; lawyer.
> ii. William Whetcraft, M. D., C. S. A., b. Sep. 26, 1837; m. —, Mrs. Holland, s. p.; practicing physician in 1861; entered C. S. Army as priv. Co. D, 2d. Ga. Reg.; transferred 1862 to Co. D, 2d La. Reg., the Co. of his brother James, and made 2d Sergt.; wounded at 2d Manassas, Chancellorsville and Spots. C. H.; captured 1862; surrendered at Appomattox C. H. Is practicing Alexandria, La.
> iii. James Scott, C. S. A., b. Nov. 13, 1838; d. Sep. 27, 1873; m. (I.) —, 1869, Mattie Maples of La. She d. s. p. a few months after marriage. (II.) Sep. 3, 1873, Sallie Land, dau. of Judge Thos. T. Land, Supreme Ct. La.
>
> > I knew Maj. A. personally, a handsome man of attractive manners, high-toned, chivalrous, and of generous impulses. Ed. Va. Mil. Inst.; in 1858 he went to La. and taught school; enlisted 1861 in the Pelican Rifles, 2d La. Inf., C. S. A. He was elected 2d Lt., and his brother Richard 1st Lt. In 1862 he was promoted Captain; lost an arm at 2d Manassas; rejoined his command before recovery, and took part in the battle of Chancellorsville, where he was again wounded. Broken in health, he was, on recommendation of Gen'l R. E. Lee, promoted Major and assigned to duty in the Enrollment Bureau, Trans-Miss. Dep., where he remained until the war closed. Studied law and began practice in Shreveport, La. Elected 1866 District Att'y; re-elected 1868. The Shreveport *Times* says that "in the discharge of his duties he won the admiration and respect of the public, and to his great personal popularity added a reputation for a fine conception of the spirit of the law, a fearless discharge of duty, a logical reasoner, and an impressive speaker."

iv. Richard Watts, C. S. A., b. Nov. 13, 1840; killed at "Malvern Hill," July 2, 1862; buried Hollywood, Richmond; ed. Culpeper Mil. Inst.; removed to Mansfield, La., and read law; enlisted, 1861, Pelican Rifles, 2d La. Reg., C. S. A., and was elected 1st Lt. Appointed Adjutant of his regiment, he soon rose to the rank of Major, which office he held when killed. Of this gallant soldier Gen. Magruder says, in his Official Report of the "Seven Days Battles," June, 1862:

"I cannot speak too highly of the conduct of * * * * Major R. W. Ashton, 2d La. Reg., who fell heroically bearing the colours of his regiment to the front."

Gen'l Howell Cobb speaks of him in his report of the battle of Malvern Hill:

"It was at this point of the battle that Col. Norwood, of the 2d. La., while gallantly leading his regiment, fell severely, but not mortally, wounded. Major Ashton, of the same regiment, had seized the colours of the regiment after three brave men had been shot down in the act of bearing them forward, and was bravely cheering on his men and rallying them to their standard, when, pierced by several balls, he fell and died instantly." (Off. Rec. U. and C. S. A., XI., 672, 749.)

v. Julia Devereux, b. —; m. —, Wilmer Shields, U. S. N., b. N. O., La., —; d. N. O. —; (son of Thomas Shields, Purser U. S. N., 1812, who d. May 22, 1827); Midshipman U. S. N., Oct. 19, 1835; passed Mid., June 22, 1841; Master, Oct. 23, 1847; Lieut., Sep. 14, 1848; resigned Apr. 6, 1852. Had—i. William Mercer, d. inf. ii. Wilmer. iii. Devereux. iv. Agnes. v. Julia. vi. Ashton. vii. Clifton.

vi. Lee, d. inf. vii. Taylor, d. inf.

65. vi. Thomas Scott b. —, 1803; d. Apr. 4, 1873, æ 70; m. —, Mary Willis Lee. Had 11 children.

66–69. vii. Christian Elizabeth, b. —, 1867; d. s. "Cottage Farms," 1826.

EXCURSUS—ASHTON, No. 2.

Additional to Excursus on p. 489.

From the *Gentleman's Magazine*, Nov. and Dec., 1854, through the kindness of Mr. Stanard, I have this data, viz: "Edmund Ashton or Assheton, 2d son of Sir John Ashton (see Assheton of Middleton, Burke's Extinct Baronetage), married 32d Henry VI. (1455), Joan Radcliffe of Chadderton, Lancashire. At the partition of Sir John Radcliffe's Est., May 6, 35th Henry VI. one-third of the manor of Chadderton passed to the said Joan." Edward Ashton of Chatterton, Lancaster, Esq., was one of the landed gentry of Eng, 1673. Sir Ralph Ashton of Middleton, Lancaster, Bart., was one of the nobility of that shire 1673. It will be remembered that Col. Peter Ashton named his estate on the Potomac "Chatterton." (*v.* p. 489.)

The Visitation of Lincolnshire, Eng., 1634, now in press, is said to contain pedigrees of John and Peter Ashton of Va.

A deed from Henry Ashton, West'd Co., Va., gent., and his wife Elizabeth, dau. and *sole heiress* of William Hardidge, West'd Co., gent., to Burdett and Charles Ashton of same, gent., and dated 1711, is on record in West'd Co. It shows that the Elizabeth Hardidge named in will of Gerrard Peyton, p. 488, was his half sister. It is pro. therefore that Gerrard P. d. unm. This Henry Ashton had a gr. dau. Elizabeth, who m. Wm. Booth, Cople Par., West'd Co., gent., and held 500 a. land by entail from Henry, which entail was broken Feb., 1772. (Hen., VIII., 640.) See will of Henry A., p. 489, *note.*

1. Charles Ashton, K. G. Co., Va.; will dat. 1778; pro. K. G. Co., 1783; had—2. *Burdett.* 3. *John.* 4. Lawrence.

2. Burdett Ashton, "Chestnut Hill," K. G.; alive 1791; had—5. Charles Augustine of K. G., who d. 1800, leaving his estate to his father, Burdett. 6. Sarah. 7. Burdett. S. >nn.

3. JOHN ASHTON, "Lebanon," West'd Co.; will dat. and pro. K. G. Co., 1788; m. (I.) Mary, dau. of Richard Watts, West'd Co.; (II.) Hannah, dau. of Col. John and Margaret (Terrett) West. (Critic, III., 47.) In 1768 he deeded land left by Richard Watts of West'd to Mary, wife of said John A. His will names bros. Burdett and Lawrence. Had—9. Mary Watts. 10. Sarah, m. Henry Washington. 11. Margaret (Peggy). 12. Hannah. 13. Charles, "who at my death will enter into a very valuable estate in land by inheritance from his mother." 14. Henry. 15. Richard Watts. 16. Lawrence, b. cir. 1765; d. Fauq'r Co., 1811; m. Apr. 15, 1788, ELIZABETH SCOTT, *supra.* 17. Burdett, mem. Va. Conv., 1788; del., 1799-1800; Justice, 1803; m. Anne, dau. of Augustine Washington, p. 489. 18. West. 19. John.

Henry Ashton, who m. 1748, Jane, dau. of Philip Alexander (Excursus—Alexander, No. 11, p. 192), pro. had Henry Alexander A., who, 1784, deeded land to his sister Sarah Dade. Hannah Butler A., m. George Hunter Terrett. Dr. Henry D. A. had Lola Ruggles; m. Dec., 1869, Frank C. Fitzhugh of K. G. John Washington A. was del., Fairfax, 1818. John. M. A. m. D. C., 1847, Mary Stuart, formerly of Va. Louisa C. A. of D. C. m. 1847, Dr. J. H. Robins, K. W. Co., Va. Ensign John A., Jr., served in Capt. Bernard's Co., 5th Va. Reg., May 22, 1776. (Va. His. Soc. Coll., VI., 175.) Lieut. Charles A., Jr., do. (p. 182). John A. petitioned the U. S. Cong., 2d to 28th, for compensation for Revolutionary services; a bill was reported in his favor 1834.

Colonel Henry Ashton, Marshal of the City of Washington, b. Va. —; d. D. C. cir. Mar. 1, 1834; was Inspector Penitentiary D. C.; made claim on the 23d U. S. Cong. for services as Marshal. He had—1. Sarah B., m. 1841, John M. Todd, I. of W. Co., Va. 2. Caroline Henry, m. 1833, C. R. Ramsey, Raleigh, N. C.

Elizabeth Dent Ashton, K. G. Co., m. John Henry Peyton. (PEYTON 104, p. 517.) John B. A., Sgt. Capt. Stuart's Co., 25th Va. Reg., 1813-14. Lawrence and Charles H. A. were privates do. (Pay Rolls 413.)

80. CAPTAIN RICHARD SCOTT[4] BLACKBURN, U. S. A.

(*Christian,*[3] *James,*[2] *John*[1]), b. pro. 1760; d. —, 1804-5, as Mar. 2, 1805, Thomas Blackburn, adm'r of his est., rendered his account. (I. 147); m. (I) —, JUDITH BALL, b. —; d. —; daughter of John and Mary (Ball) Ball. (BALL 107, p. 167.) (II.) —, ANN BLAUSE, b. —, d. s. p. —.

Capt. Blackburn was comm'd Captain U. S. A., June 2, 1794, and retained in the re-organization of the Army in 1802. Hamersley, in the Reg. U. S. A., p. 50, adds under Capt. B.'s name, "Revolutionary Army." The Court of P. W. Co., Sep., 1790, ordered Philip Fitzhugh, John Brown, *Scott Blackburn* and others, gentlemen, to be recommended to the Gov'r as proper persons to be appt'd Justices for the Co. (C. P., V. 280.) This was pro. No. 30, as no other of the name appears in the pedigree. He was Mem. Va. Leg. 1790-91. Mrs. J. B. A. says "Judith Ball was a beautiful woman, neat and graceful, and a Bible Christian."

Children (BLACKBURN):

70.   i. JANE CHARLOTTE,[5] b. —; d. Aug. 1856; m. —, 1814, John Augustine Washington, b. —, 1792; d. June, 1832; son of Corbin and Hannah (Lee) Washington, and nephew of Hon. Bushrod Washington. (John A.,[6] Corbin,[5] John A.,[4] Augustine[3], Lawrence,[2] John[1].)
            Children, b. "Blakeley," W. Va.:
      i. George, b. —, 1815; d. yng.
      ii. Anna Maria, b. —, 1817; d. Mar. 29, 1850; m. May 15, 1834, William Fontaine Alexander, M. D. (BROWN 100, p. 181.)
      iii. John Augustine, C. S. A., b. May 3, 1820; killed at Cheat Mountain, W. Va., Sep. 13, 1861; m. "Exeter," Loudoun Co., Feb. 1842, Eleanor Love Selden. (SCOTT 43, *note.*) *See below.* Child.—i. Louisa Fontaine, b. Feb. 19, 1844; m. Col. R. P. Chew, C. S. A. ii. Jane Charlotte, b. May 26, 1846; m. Nathaniel H. Williss. iii. Eliza Selden, b. July 17, 1848. iv. Anne Maria, b. Nov. 17, 1851; m. July 22, 1873, Rev. Bever-

ley Dandridge Tucker, C. S. A., son of Nathaniel Beverely[4] and Jane (Ellis) Tucker of Henry St. George,[3] St. George,[2] Henry[1] of Bermuda. He was ed. Vervay, Switzerland; grad. Theo. Sem., Va., 1873; Ord. Deacon, 1873; Priest 1874; Rector, St. John's Par., Warsaw, Va., 1874-1883; St. Paul's, Norfolk, 1883; author of various hymns of high merit; had Henry St. George, b. July 16, 1874. Emily Selden, b. Nov. 1, 1875. v. Lawrence, b. Jan. 14, 1854; m. June 14, 1876, Fannie Lackland, dau. of Thomas of Charlestown, W. Va. vi. Eleanor Love, b. Mar. 14, 1856; m. May 5, 1880 (S. C.) Julian Howard, Richmond, Va. vii. George, b. July 22, 1858; ed. Univ. Va. 1876.

iv. Richard Blackburn, b. Nov. 12, 1822; m. Nov. 20, 1844, Christine Maria Washington, dau. of Samuel Walter Washington of "Harewood," Va., and his wife Louisa Clemson of Phila., Pa. Child.—i. Elizabeth Clemson, b. Aug. 21, 1845. ii. John Augustine, b. May 27, 1847. iii. Ann M. F. Blackburn, b. Nov. 1, 1849. iv. Louisa Clemson, b. Nov. 17, 1851. v. Samuel Walter, b. Nov. 1, 1853. vi. Richard Blackburn, b. Mar. 21, 1856. vii. Christine Maria, b. June 13, 1858. viii. George Steptoe, b. June 7, 1860. ix. William de Hertburn, b. Feb. 14, 1864. (From Welles Washington.)

v. a daughter, d. inf.

71.   ii. ANNA MARIA THOMASINA, b. —; d. Nov. 1850; m. 1810, Bushrod Corbin Washington, bro. of John A., 70, *supra*; b. —, 1790; d. Jefferson Co., W. Va., July 28, 1851. He m. (II.) 1835, Maria Powell Harrison, dau. of Matthew Harrison. (PEYTON, p. 513.)

Children, first marriage:
i. Hannah Lee, b. "Ripon Lodge," May 19, 1811, William P. Alexander.
ii. Thomas Blackburn, b. 1813; d. Aug., 1854; m. 1840(?) Rebecca Janet Cunningham, b. 1820; d. London, Eng., Sep. 5, 1890. (Obit. S. C., 10, 16, '90.); was raised at Mt. Vernon. (BROWN 45, p. 165.)

72.   iii. CHRISTIAN SCOTT, b. —; d. s.

73-75.   iv. JUDITH BALL, b. Oct. 12, 1796; d. Apr. 18, 1866 (S. C.); m. —, Gustavus Brown Alexander of "Caledonia," b. 1800; d. Sep. 22, 1868. (BROWN 102, p. 181.)

COLONEL JOHN AUGUSTINE WASHINGTON, C. S. A., was ed. W. Va., 1838-40; farmer; inherited "Mount Vernon," the estate of General W., by the will of Hon. Bushrod Washington. Here he lived until, in 1860, he sold the estate to the "Mount Vernon Ladies Association," and removed to "Waveland," an estate he had bought in Fauq'r Co. When the War between the States commenced he at once offered his services to the Gov. of Va. Gen. R. E. Lee offered him the position of Aid de Camp on his staff with the rank of Lt. Col., which he accepted. Gen'l W. H. F. Lee, who was by his side when he was killed, thus related the particulars of his fall. (Univ. Va., Mem. 57.)

"Col. W. was with my command on a scout near the enemy in W. Va., during the advance of Loring's army from its position on Cheat Mt. He had long been anxious to accompany me in some of our expeditions. On this occasion he brought me orders from headquarters, and his face beamed with delight as he told me that he was to accompany us * * It was with difficulty that I could restrain him. In one skirmish with the enemy's cavalry he charged with the leading files. We had come within sight of the enemy's camp and I gave the order to retire. "Oh no," said Col. W. "let us ride down and capture that fellow on the gray horse." After some hesitation I assented, and, leaving our main force, we took only two men and proceeded to capture the fellow on the gray horse. Our road lay through a narrow defile in the mountain, some half mile in length, at the end of which the fellow on the gray horse was awaiting, very quietly, our approach. We had hardly proceeded 300 yds. when fire was opened on us from an ambuscade in the side of the mountain. At the first volley Col. W. fell from his horse, pierced with balls, myself and escort wheeled and spurred back, running the gauntlet of their musketry * * How we escaped was one of the mysteries of the war. My horse was shot in 3 or 4 places, the other two killed. Col. W's horse came out with us, bringing his sword which was tied to the saddle. His body was sent to Gen. Lee on the next day, under a flag of truce, and sent by Gen. L. to his family.

"Thus fell Col. John A. Washington, an early victim in that deadly struggle in which so many noble lives were lost. It is not groundless conjecture when we say that, if he had lived, he would have earned and *honoured* the highest rank in the gift of his country. His courage, his knowledge of men, his resolution, his inflexibility of purpose, and the lofty ambition with which he was inspired, all of these were of too high a type for him to have come through such a war without enrolling his name among the noblest which its annals contained. In private life he shone with all the virtues which should characterize the husband, father, son, and brother. In his friendship he never faltered, and his noble, generous heart prompted him to seek out and aid the distressed. To a stranger this language may seem mere panegyric; by those who knew him it will be thought to fall far short of describing the actual virtues of the man."

President Davis thus speaks of him in his "Rise and Fall of the Confederate Gov't," I. 436. "The loss of this valuable and accomplished officer was much regretted by his General and all others who knew him."

31. THOMAS⁴ BLACKBURN (*Christian,³ John,² John¹*), b. cir. 1765; d. —; m. cir. 1805, ELIZABETH SINCLAIR, b. —, 1776; d. —, 1840; daughter of John and Margaret (Zwill) Sinclair,* Jefferson county, West Va. She m. (II.) Dr. Samuel Taylor, Delaware, and had Charles Sinclair Taylor.

Children:

76.   i.   SARAH JANE,⁵ b. —, 1807; d. —, 1871; m. —, 1843, Col. Treadwell Smith, Berryville, Va.

77.   ii.   RICHARD SCOTT, M. D., b. —, 1809; m. Nov. 13, 1833, Sarah Ann Ellen Thomas, dau. of Col. John Thomas.

      Children:
      i. Thomas. ii. Eliza S. Smith
      iii. John, m. Sue Taylor. iv. Catherine Thomas.
      v. Jane Moran. vi. Ellen Washington.
      vii. Sarah Frances. viii. Major Scott.
      ix. Grace. x. Richard T., d. yng.

78.   iii.   JOHN SINCLAIR, b. July 28, 1811; d. —, 1838, Vicksburg, Miss.

79.   iv.   ELIZABETH SINCLAIR b. Aug. 20, 1813; m. Sep. 6, 1843, Dr. Randolph Kownslar, Berryville, Va., b. June 3, 1809; d. Feb. 26, 1865; grad. M. D., Univ. Pa.; 1831. He was son of Conrad and Elizabeth (Bayard) Kownslar.

      Children:
      i. Randolph, b. July 18, 1850; m. Sep. 23. 1873, Alice Maude, b. July 17, 1854, dau. of John W. and Ann (McCormick) Stribling. Had—i. Alice Maude, b. Aug. 14, 1874; d. Dec. 25, 1879. ii. Randolph, b. July 3, 1876. iii. Ellen Jett, b. Sep. 19, 1878. iv. Elizabeth Sinclair, b. Dec. 5, 1879; d. Feb. 10, 1884. v. Conrad, b. Aug. 11, 1886.

      ii. Conrad, b. Sep. 28, 1851.

      iii. Sarah Jane Blackburn, b. June 11, 1853; m. Sep. 25, 1879, Rev. Wm. Byrd Lee, b. Mar. 21, 1851, son of Col. Richard Henry and Evelyn (Byrd) Lee; grad. Va. Theo. Sem. 1878; ord. Deacon 1878; Priest, 1879. Is Rector Abingdon Par., Glouc'r Co., Va. Had—i. Elizabeth Sinclair Blackburn, b. July 26, 1879. ii. Richard Henry, b. Sep. 20, 1880; d. Sep. 26, 1881. (S. C.) iii. and iv. Evelyn Byrd and Mary Page, twins, b. Sep. 23, 1881. v. Ellen Moore, b. June 11, 1884. vi. Wm. Byrd, b. Feb. 1, 1888.

* John Sinclair of Scotland came to North'd Co., Va., about 1775; m. Margaret Zwill. Driven to the interior by the British, he located Fauq'r Co., thence to Jefferson Co. He had—i. Elizabeth, *supra*. ii. William Zwill, d. s.

iv. Elizabeth Sinclair, b. Nov. 11, 1854; d. May 26, 1888; m. June 30, 1880, William Ludwell Baldwin, Fred'k Co., Va., son of Dr. Robert and Portia (Hopkins) Baldwin. (S. C.) Had—i. William, b. Apr. 3, 1881. ii. Portia Lee, b. Oct., 1882.
v. Lydia Kownslar, b. May 22, 1856; m. Jan. 11, 1883, Edward McCormick Stribling, b. June 1, 1859, bro. of Alice M. S., *supra.* Had—i. Randolph Kownslar, b. Oct., 1883. ii. Edward McCormick, b. June 5, 1885. iii. and iv. John W. and Annie Maude, twins, b. Apr. 5, 1887.*

32, JULIA ANN[4] BLACKBURN (*Christian,[3] James,[2] John[1]*), b. 1768; d. s. p. Nov. 9, 1829; m. —, 1785, HON. BUSHROD WASHINGTON, LL. D., b. Westmoreland county, Va., June 5, 1762; d. Philadelphia, Pa., Nov. 26, 1829; son of John Augustine and Hannah (Bushrod†) Washington, and the favourite nephew of General George Washington·

Bushrod Washington entered W. and M. Coll. 1775-6; grad. A. B. 1778; was an original mem. of the Phi Beta Kappa Society organized Dec. 15, 1776. He received the Hon. degree of LL. D. from Princeton, 1803, Univ. Pennsylvania 1815, and Harvard Univ. 1827; studied law with James Wilson, LL. D., Philadelphia, and practiced in his native county. He served as private in the Virginia Line at Yorktown; was mem. Virginia Leg., 1787–8, and Va. Constitutional Conv., 1788. During his residence in Richmond, whither he moved cir. 1790, he received many students into his law office, among whom were Hon. Henry Clay, General Walter Jones, Professor Robert Eden Scott. He was Pres. Va. Colonization Soc., 1790, and was made by Prest. Washington Associate Justice U. S. Supreme Court, 1798. He was author of " Reports Va. Court of Appeals," 1790-6 and 1798–9, 4 vols; also " Reports 3d Circuit U. S. Court," 1803–29, 4 vols. As Washington's favourite nephew he was one of his principal legatees, and one of the ex'rs of his will. Like all the Washingtons of his day, he was a Churchman, confirmed by Bishop White, a lay dep. to the Dio. Council of Va., 1815, from Christ Church, Alex'a, and a punctual member for many years of the Standing Committee of the Diocese. His name appears on the title page of Marshall's " Life of Washington," where the author credits him with having given his supervision to that valuable work. Hon. Horace Binney published privately a "Life of Bushrod Washington," Phila., 1858. (*v.* also a sketch of Judge W. in Mr. Justice Story's "Miscellaneous Writings," Phila., 1852. Also App. Cyc. Am. Biog.)

* Dr. Kownslar had by a former mar.—i. Ellen, b. Nov. 16, 1837; d. Mar. 17, 1888: m. Feb. 16, 1858, Samuel S. G. Moore, b. June 29, 1826. (Obit. S. C.)

† RICHARD BUSHROD rec'd 2,000 a. land West'd Co., Va., Oct. 15, 1660 (L. Bk., IV., 450); 2,000 a. same county, Apr. 10, 1665. (V., 14.) Richard and Thomas Bushrod and John Ingram rec'd 300 a. North'd Co., 1665. (V., 15.) At Bushfield, West'd Co., the tomb of John Bushrod bore this inscription: "Here lies the body of John Bushrod, gentleman, son of Richard Bushrod, gentleman, by Apphia his wife. He was born in Gloucester Co., Va., the 30th of Jan'y, 1663. He took for his wife Hannah, the daughter of William Keene of Northumberland, and Elizabeth his wife, and by her left two sons and four daughters, and died the 6th of Feb'y, 1719, in the 56th year of his age." (M., II., 151.)
Mr. S. says that Col. Thomas Bushrod, b. 1604; d. York Co., 1651; m. Elizabeth, the wid. of Capt. Thomas Hill. She d. 1679, and names in her will dau. Lydia, wife of Thomas Harwood, and Elizabeth, wife of Col. John Scarsbrook. Mr. Thomas B. was Burgess, York Co., Mar., 1658-9. (Hen., I., 506.)
1. RICHARD BUSHROD and Apphia, his wife, Glouc'r, had—2. *John.* 3. Thomas, b. —; d. cir. 1709; will dat. Sep. 1, 1697; had Richard, pro. Capt. R., 1740, and Anne, m. John Bushrod.
2. JOHN BUSHROD, b. Glouc'r Co., Jan. 30, 1663; d. Feb. 6, 1719, *supra:* m. Hannah, dau. of Wm. and Elizabeth Keene, North'd Co.; had—4. John, m. Anne, dau. of Thomas Bushrod, and pro. had Col. John, Burgess West'd, 1748-1755; m. Jenny, dau. of Col. Gawin Corbin, and had Hannah, m. John Augustine Washington, and had Hon. Bushrod W. 5. a son 6. Apphia, m. 1712 (?), Wm. Fauntleroy, &c., &c. (Va His. Mag., I., 14.)

33.   CATHERINE⁴ BLACKBURN (*Christian,³ James,² John¹*), b. cir. 1770; d. —; m. —, 1796, HENRY SMITH TURNER ; b. —, 1770 ; d. "Wheatlands," Jefferson county, —; son of Col. Thomas Turner, "Smith's Mount," Westmoreland county, Va., 1751–1787, and his wife Jane, daughter of Col. William Fauntleroy, Naylor's Hole, Richmond county, Va., and his wife, Miss Murdoch.*   Henry S. Turner, m. (II.) Lucy Lyons, b. —; d. s. p.

Children (TURNER) :

80.   i.   MARY,⁵ b. —; d. s. p. —; m. —— Allibone, Phila., Pa.
81.   ii. JANE, b. —; d. —; m. —, Charles Byrd, M. D.
            Children :
            i. Lucy.   ii. Thomas.
82.   iii. GEORGE WASHINGTON, U. S. A., b. —; d. Oct. 18, 1859; grad. West Point Mil. Acad., 1831; Bvt. 2d Lt., 1st Artill., U. S., July 1, 1831; 2d Lieut. do., July 1, 1831 ; resigned June 30, 1836; murdered Oct. 18, 1859, at Harper's Ferry, by the fanatic, John Brown of Ossawattamie.
83.   iv. WILLIAM FAUNTLEROY, "Ripon Lodge," b. —; d. —; m. (I.) —, Ellen Beirne, Miss.; (II.) —, Sydney Patterson.
            Children, 1st marriage :
            i. Ellen, b. —; m. —, Col. John S. Saunders, U. S. A. and C. S. A., b. Va. —; Grad. West Point, 1858; Bvt. 2d Lt., 2d U. S. Artill., July 1, 1858; trans. to Ordnance Sep. 1, 1858; 2d Lt. Feb. 1, 1861; resigned Apr. 22, 1861. In Jan., 1861, before Va. had seceded from the Union, Lt. S. was sent to Pensacola, Fla., by the U. S. Sec. of War with despatches to Com. Armstrong, U. S. N., where he was arrested by the State troops, his despatches seized and himself paroled. (O. R., S. I., Vol. I., 353–5.) When Va. seceded he resigned his rank in the U. S. A. and entered the C. S. Army as Captain of Volunteers. He was later appointed Major, and Chief of Artill., Anderson's Div., C. S. A. Before the war ended he became Colonel of Artillery.
            2d marriage :
            ii. Sydney, b. —; m. —, Mr. Swann. (S. A. E. B.)
84.   v.   THOMAS BLACKBURN, b. —; d. —; m. (I.) 1838, Mary Fenton Wallace, b. —; d. 1844 ; dau. of Gustavus Brown and Frances (Lurty) Wallace (WALLACE 69) ; (II.) —— Brockenbrough.
            Children :
            i. Charlotte Washington, b. —; m. 1858, Jeremiah Morton, Culp'r Co.   Had 10 children.
            ii. Frances Byrd, b. —; m. Lucian Dade, K. G. Co.; had—i. Lucia. (WALLACE 138, Dade.)
85.   vi. CHRISTINE, b. "Wheatlands," July 22, 1815 ; d. —; m. —, Dr. Lewis O'Conner Cordell, Charlestown, Jeff'n Co., W. Va., b. Nov. 15, 1803, son of Presley and Amelia (Orme) Cordell; (see Excursus—Cordell); grad. M.D., Univ. Md., 1825.
            Children :
            i. Christine, b. —; m. Gen. James Harding, C. S. A.
            ii. Henry Smith, C. S. A.; b. —.
            iii. George Edward, C. S. A., b. 1839; d. Mar. 4, 1876. In Mosby's command; captured and imprisoned at Camp Chase.
            iv. Kate, b. —; d. yng.

---

* THOMAS TURNER of Walsingham, K. G. Co., Va., Clerk, 1723–1742, Justice, &c., was the first of this line known in Va.   He m. 1711, Martha, dau. of Richard Taliaferro, Richmond Co., and had Harry Turner of K. G., who m. —, Elizabeth, dau. and heiress of Col. Nicholas Smith of "Smith's Mount," K. G. Co. and had Col. Thomas Turner, *supra.*   Harry Turner was also Clerk of K. G. Co , 1742–1752. Mr. Stanard will publish a pedigree of this family in Wallace's Virginia Historical Magazine, 1892.

v. Eugene Fauntleroy, M. D., C. S. A., b. —; m. Sep. 17, 1873, Balto., M. D., Louisa Tazewell Southall, b. Smithville, Va., Mar. 15, 1856, dau. of Dr. James and Martha (Tazewell) Southall; ed. Va. High School, which he left 1861 to enter the C. S. Army. Being only 17, parental care withdrew him from the field and entered him at the Va. Mil. Inst., June 14, '61. July 4, '61, he left Lexington and joined the command of Gen. Henry A. Wise; was assigned to duty as Drill Master in Co. E, 3d Reg. (60th Va. Inf.), Wise Legion; Nov. 1, 1861, appointed Sgt. Maj. of the Reg. and Acting Adjutant. In the battles of Gaines' Mills and Frazer's Farm he commanded Capt. Dew's Co., at the request of the Capt., and led them into action. Of his conduct during the Seven Days Battles, June and July, 1862, Col. Starke of the 60th Reg. says in his Off. Rept.: "I would be doing injustice to Sergeant Major Cordell, a mere youth, were I to omit calling especial attention to the coolness and soldierly bearing that marked his conduct throughout. He is a young officer of great promise." (Off. Rec. Union and Confed. Armies, S. I., Vol. XI., Pt. II., p. 851.) In August, 1862, he was promoted to 2d Lieut. Co. C, same Reg't, and Jan'y 26, 1863, Provost Marshal and Commander of Post at Narrows of New River, W. Va. May 28, 1864, promoted Acting Asst. Adjt. Gen. of the Brigade, then commanded by Col. Fosburg, 51st Va. Reg. He took part in the action at "New Hope," Valley of Va., in the spring of 1864. Of his conduct at this time Col. B. H. Jones, then commanding the First Brigade, Army of the Valley, wrote: "I feel that distinctions are invidious where so many, both officers and men, did their whole duty so long as resistance held out the faintest prospect of success; yet I cannot omit noticing the intelligence and calm courage of A. A. Gen'l Eugene F. Cordell, as displayed throughout the engagement." (Southern Opinion, Sep. 14, 1867.) He was severely wounded twice in the battle of Winchester, Sep., 1864, but returned to duty in two weeks before his wounds had healed; was captured with Early's Command, by Sheridan, at Waynesburg, March, '65, and confined in Fort Delaware until discharged, June 23, 1865. He was captured once before, but made his escape. Dr. C.'s reminiscences of his army life are full of interest, but too long to be inserted in full here. Dr. C. grad. M. D., Univ. Md., 1868; is a practicing physician, Balto., Md. Child.—i. James Southall, b. June 9, 1874. ii. Eugene Fauntleroy, b. Nov. 22, 1875.

86. vii. CATHERINE BLACKBURN, b. —; d. —; m. —, John S. Wright, Chicago, Ill.
Children:
  i. Augustine. ii. Charles. iii. Maria.

87-89. viii. BUSHROD, b. —; d. yng. on Gulf of Mexico.

EXCURSUS—CORDELL.

1. REV. JOHN CORDELL and wife Eliz. Edwards of Wiltshire, Eng., 1720, had—.2 *George Edwards,* b. Feb. 17, 1742. They em. to America, 1743. George E. m., Oct. 4, 1768, Catherine Basye, b. May 20, 1752; d. 1839, and had—3. *Presley,* b. Mar. 5, 1779; d. 1849; m. Sep. 1, 1802, Amelia O'Connor, dau. Richard and Mary (Orme) O'Connor, son of Thomas O'Connor who em. from Ireland to the U. S. with his two sons Richard and Thomas. Richard O'Connor had also Levi Orme and Arrete who m. Mr. Musgrave of Md. Mary Orme was dau. Rev. Jno. Orme, b. Wiltshire, Eng.; em. to Pr. Geo. Co., Md. and m. Ruth Edmonson, niece of Col. Geo. Beale of Georgetown, and had John, m. (I.) Eliz'h Collet, whose dau. m. Thos. Beale of Georgetown. (II.) Lucy Beale (wid) and had twin daus., one of whom m. George C. Washington, and one Maj. Peter of Naletown, they had Lewis Washington, and Colin Peter. *Presley Cordell* had 1 Levi O'Connor, b. Nov. 15, 1803; d. Nov. 14, 1870. 2. Catherine Basye, b. Oct. 28, 1805; d. Jan. 17, 1808. 3. Enos Basye, b. Sep. 6, 1807. 4. Asa, b. Sep. 29, 1809; d. Mar. 3, 1839. 5. Presley, b. Oct. 29, 1811; d. Aug. 24, 1812. 6. Mary Ellen, b. Aug. 27, 1813; d. Jan. 1, 1864. 7.

Helen Arrete, b. Dec. 15, 1815; d. Dec. 20, 1865. 8. Richard Lewis, b. Mch. 23, 1818. 9. James Hervey, b. Apr. 5, 1820. 10. Henry Claggett, b. Apr. 18, 1822. 11. Virginia, b. Feb. 14, 1824. 12. Presley Thomas, b. Dec. 12, 1825; d. July 28, 1849; m. Keziah Wilson of Loudoun, Va., who d. of consumption soon after. Presley Cordell was a Magistrate, and a mem. of Va. Leg.

Rev'd John Cordell appears to have served in the Revolutionary Army as a Captain as well as a Chaplain. The muster rolls record him as apptd. Chaplain, 11th Va. Reg., Feb. 15, 1777. The Auditor of Va. certified, 1843, that he had settled his accounts with Va., Apr. 4, 1783, for services ending Jan. 1, 1779. Jan. 30, 1837, his heirs rec'd 6000 a. land for 3 years service. (Rep. 1063, 27th Cong., 2d Sess.) Va. State Doc., No. 31, 1835, says, he was Captain from Jan. 1, 1777 to Jan. 1, 1779, and Chaplain to Feb. 10, 1781. He then rec'd £4,000 advanced to him for the use of the Army. "He served upwards of 4 years and is entitled to bounty land for a service of 3 years as Chaplain." Rep. No. 457, 28th Cong., 1 Sess., says, "he was taken *prisoner* at Brandywine, and kept in captivity till the beginning of 1797, when he became a Supernumerary Officer," and as such his heirs rec'd bounty. Gen'l Dan'l Morgan certified, 1792, that Jno. Cordell was Chaplain to his Reg., Jan. 1, 1777, and so did Chief Justice Marshall.

36. ROBERT EDEN[4] SCOTT, M. A. (*John,*[3] *James,*[2] *John*[1]), b. Aberdeen, Scotland, Apr. 13, 1769; d. s. p. Aberdeen, January 14, 1811; m. Aberdeen, Mar., 1797, RACHEL FORBES-MITCHELL, dau. of Duncan Forbes-Mitchell, Esq., of Thainston, county Aberdeen, Scotland, b. —, 1757, and his wife Catherine Ann, dau. of William Fraser, Esq., of Fraserfield, Scotland. Duncan Forbes-Mitchell was 3d son of Sir Arthur Forbes, Bart. of Craigievar, county Aberdeen, Scotland, by his 2d wife Margaret Strachan.

The house of Forbes is now represented by Sir William Forbes, 8th Baronet. The family trace back to John de Forbes, who was a man of rank and importance, *temp.* King Richard the Lion Hearted. Duncan Forbes assumed, under deed of entail, executed by his father, Sir Arthur, 4th Bart., 1772, the arms and name of Mitchell of Thainston, in memory of Sir Andrew Mitchell, K. B., of Thainston, by whom the estates of Thainston and Easter Beltie were left to Sir Arthur. Wm. Fraser of Fraserfield was gr. s. of William, Baron of Saltoun, and his wife Lady Katherine, dau. of David, 9th Earl of Buchan. (*v.* Burke's Peerage for Forbes, and Landed Gentry for Forbes-Mitchell.) Arms—"*Quarterly 1st and 4th az. three bears heads, couped, arg. muzzled, sa.: in the center a cross pattée, fitchée, of the second.*" For *Forbes* of Craigievar: "*2d and 3d sa. a fesse, waved, betw. three mascles, or.*" for *Mitchell* of Thainston. (*v.* Mrs. Scott's letter, p. 642-3.)

Prof. Scott was grad. M. A., King's Coll., Aberdeen, Mar. 30, 1785. He became Tutor to Mr. Hay, 2d son of Lady Errol, Whitsunday, 1787. In Nov., 1788, when Prof. Leslie, of King's Coll., was unable, from severe illness, to fill his chair as Prof. of Greek, Mr. Scott was appointed to his chair until his health was restored. In 1789 he was Tutor in the family of Mr. Oswald. In 1791 he came to Virginia, then aged 22. As stated in Mrs. Lee's letter (p. 608), although 21 years had elapsed since his mother had left him an infant in Scotland, and no intimation was given her of his visit, she recognized him as soon as she saw him. At this time he had made no decision as to his future course of life.

A letter written by him to his mother from Old Aberdeen, Jan. 31, 1787, discusses this matter. It appears that while Prof. Gordon wished him to remain with him and be in the way of a Professorship in King's Coll. his mother desired him to study Law or Medicine in America. In the letter he states that his uncle Gustavus declined taking him into his office as clerk, to study law, and he himself declines to allow his mother to be at the expense of his studying. However a letter of Dec., 1791, states that he had that day matriculated at the Univ. Pa. to study medicine. Another of June, 1792, he wrote from Pt. Tobacco, where he had just become an apprentice to his uncle, Dr. Gustavus R. Brown. In 1793 he began the study of law with his kinsman, Hon. Bushrod Washington, in Richmond, Va. In one of his letters, written at the time, he mentions a fellow student who, it was understood, was that eminent lawyer, General Walter Jones. In Aug., 1794, Prof. Scott returned to Aberdeen, and in Nov., 1794, he was elected to assist his grandfather, Prof. Thomas Gordon of King's Coll. In May, 1796, he was made Regent of the Coll., and in 1800, full Professor of Philosophy to succeed Prof. Gordon. Thus ended his purpose to enter the legal profession. But his studies in Medicine and Law, during his sojourn in Va., fitted him more efficiently to fulfill the responsible position which he afterwards held until his death.

In 1801 Prof. Scott was elected Provost of Aberdeen. After his death his widow m. —— Masquirier, Esq. (*v.* Burke's Peerage.) Prof. S., it will be noticed, did not always sign his name Robert Eden Scott, as he was known in Va., but simply Robert Scott. In 1782 he is entered in the "Album Studiosorum," of King's Coll., as "Robertus Scott, Aberdonensis." The following description of this Christian and Scholar is taken from a funeral sermon preached at the time of his death, and entitled,

"The Consolations on the death of Friends arising from the Christians hope of immortality. A sermon occasioned by the death of Robert Eden Scott, M. A., Professor of Logic and Moral Philosophy, in the University of King's College, Old Aberdeen. Preached in the church of Old Aberdeen on Sunday, the 20th of January, 1811, A. D. By the Rev. Skene Ogilvie, D. D., Senior minister of Old Aberdeen. Published, with the permission of the Author, By the young gentlemen of Mr. Scott's class, & sent by his widow to his friends in America."

" * * As a man the conduct of Mr. Scott was dignified and correct. He neither assumed that austerity which sets others at a distance, nor descended to those frivolous levities which lead to unbecoming familiarities. Possessing, in an uncommon degree, a calm firmness of mind, by which he could control his feelings and adhere to his purposes, he was generally able to avoid the errors into which the unwary are led by the disorders of the passions, and to ensure the success of his undertakings by the caution with which they were commenced and the undeviating steadiness with which they were kept in view. In domestic life his character was amiable, the tears of his disconsolate widow can but feebly express her grief for a most worthy, indulgent husband, who rejoiced with her in prosperity, councilled her in her perplexity, and in affliction soothed and composed her by his kindly, constant, and sedulous attention. Her happiness or sorrow he felt as his own. Steady and warm in his attachments, his intimate friends will long recollect with mingled gratitude, and regret the readiness of his sound tho' unobtruded advice, the cheerfulness with which he endeavoured to promote their interest and the pleasure he felt when fortune fovoured their views. Unostentatious in his professions of regard, the sincerity of his professions was marked chiefly by the assiduity of his efforts to relieve their distress.

"His house was the seat of hospitality, affability and kindness. His door was opened with complacency to the stranger, and he was always pleased to see a companion or a friend. In company he neither anxiously sought nor affectedly shunned learned conversation, but was at all times willing, as far as propriety would admit, to adapt his discourse to the humor and inclination of his associates—to the young as well as to the old, to the gay as well as to the grave, to the man of the world as well as to the scholar. With an accurately discriminating eye he could perceive where and with whom he might safely unbend his mind, and when and how far it was expedient to use reserve. Wherever he was known his company was anxiously courted, and we admire the talent by which he could devote large portions of his time to the gratifications of social intercourse without suffering his ardour in literary pursuits to cool. Where he was accustomed to visit, often will the sigh be heard among those who feel the loss of the cheerful conversation with which he was wont to amuse, to please and to inform his associates. Long will his fellow citizens lament his death and recollect his virtues. Often will they mention his name with feelings of respect and esteem due to the memory of the man who, with high credit to himself and advantage to the place, discharged during several years the functions of Chief Magistrate of his native city, who in all the offices that he held among them successfully directed his undeviating efforts to their common good, and whose purse, without the ostentation of charity, was ever open to the poor. As a man of letters his attainments were truly great. Endowed with more than ordinary natural abilities, and availing himself of all the advantages of an excellent education, he directed his attention to literary pursuits with that ardour which marks the scientific mind. Nor did he fail to reap the fruits of industry, for his philosophical publications and his extensive and highly valued correspondence with learned men had procured him uncommon esteem in the literary world. The numerous compositions he left in an unfinished state serve now, alas! only to shew what might have been expected from his genius, knowledge and industry, had it pleased God to prolong his inestimable life. In his academical lectures he combined original observation with judicious selection, and accurate scientific arrangement with that simplicity and perspicuity and neatness of style which is the best and most captivating vehicle of instruction. Deeply conversant in all the writings both of ancient and modern Philosophy, he freely availed himself of all their information; while trusting modestly to his own powers, he had the courage to think and judge for himself; where reason tied him to differ from respectable authorities, cautiously avoiding that asperity of language which is often the disgrace of literary combatants, he stated the arguments on which he had founded his opinions with the manly firmness which becomes the advocate of truth.

"Perceiving the respectable deference due to distinguished learning and genius even while they err, his candid and unassuming manner never injured the memory of the dead or wounded the feelings of a living opponent. It was only against the sophists, whose pernicious tenets tend to sap the foundations of religion or to disturb the harmony of social life, that his indignation could be roused, and even then, while in terms of merited ridicule or contempt he exposed the fallacy, in pity he spared the man. Far from thinking that human science had yet attained perfection, he was constantly attentive to its progress. In his zeal for its improvement he was not misled by theories which fancy daily forms and which ingenuity and novelty alone support, but deliberately applying the test of reason to whatever the genious or learning of the age brought forward to his view, while he rejected what seemed frivolous or false, he carefully enriched his academical course with every new or important discovery. Such was the example which he gave to his pupils in his manner of investigating, illustrating and defending truth. Its happy influence appeared in the steadiness and dignity which commanded their respect, combined with the affability and kindness which won their hearts and in the pleasing address which he roused them to application by exciting in them a laudable emulation and animating them with the love of science. When the relation of pupil and teacher had ceased, young men of merit were sure to find in him the character of a father and a friend. By his loss science has lost a friend who bade fair to increase her stores, society one of its most respectable and agreeable members, and the University a professor of highly distinguished ability and usefulness.*

"But his abilities, his learning and the excellences of his manner of communicating knowledge are not the only important endowments for which the literary world and the public at large will long and deeply lament his untimely fate. Feeling in his heart the powerful influence of rational christianity, and sensible that the impressions of early life are lasting, the Philosophy which he taught was friendly to the best interests of religion and morals. In his writings, in his conversations, and in his school, scepticism and infidelity, with all their fallacies and fictions, were zealously opposed, while the sacred treasures of natural and revealed religion, which cherish whatever wisdom, virtue and affection value most, were supported with that force of argument which flows from the clearest understanding, and with that energy of manner which eminates from the heart that feels their power. These alone he knew could sooth the sensibility of a wounded spirit in those hours of sorrow when other consolations are of no avail—these alone he knew could ease the throbbing heart that mourns for departed worth, and these alone he knew could arm the dying man with fortitude, with resignation and with joy. Nor did his well-founded expectation terminate in disappointment. He showed on his death bed the magnanimity and hope which springs from the sound and rational principles

---

* "Mr. Robert Eden Scott died in the morning of the 14th of January, 1811. After having during several sessions of College held the position of assistant Professor, he held different chairs in the University nearly fifteen years, and taught with great reputation and success Greek, Mathematicks, Natural and Moral Philosophy and Logic. He was descended by his mother of the family of Gordons, who had been much and justly respected as Professors in the University of Aberdeen for almost two centuries."

which he had uniformly inculcated and by which he had regulated his conduct. During the progress of the fatal fever which deprived us of this truly worthy man, in every lucid interval he calmly viewed his approaching end. Observing a friend sitting by him and looking on him with anxious tenderness, he affectionately grasped his hand and with the noble confidence of a dying Christian he said, 'I know that I am going to another and a better world.' On the the evening preceding his death, and but a little time before he had entirely lost the power of speech, with the resignation and composure of a true disciple of Jesus, he recommended his departing spirit to his God through the merits and mediation of his Redeemer."*

Prof. Scott was the author of a work entitled "Present State of the British Constitution, Historically Illustrated by Britannicus.

——— "Servetur ad imum

Qualis ab incepto processerit et sibi constet!"—*Hor., A. P., 126*

8°. p. 182; London; printed for Longman, Hurst, Reese and Orme, Paternoster Row, 1807." In a MS. note on the fly leaf of the copy now in possession of Miss A. L. Peyton of Fauq'r, in the handwriting of and signed by Mrs. Rachel Scott, the following statement appears :

"This political tract was written in the year 1807 by the late Prof Scott, but never acknowledged by him ; he was a staunch Whig in principle, and as a member of the University did not deem it expedient to avow his sentiments at a time when party spirit ran so high in this country. In the various Reviews of the time it was highly praised, and by his pupils read as a short tho' excellent account of the Constitution of Briton. It was written at the time the Whig Ministry left their situation on account of the Catholic Emancipation, of which the author was a strenuous supporter. "RACHEL SCOTT."

He also wrote "The Angler," a poem, and "Scott's Enquiry," "Scott's Elements," and "Scott's Mental Philosophy." Col, John Scott, when visiting King's Coll., 1867, was shown in the Univ. Library these works of Prof S.; also unpublished manuscripts of both Professors Gordon and Scott. In Kennedy's History of Aberdeen honourable mention of both these professors is made. The portrait of Prof. S. is preserved in the Coll., and a copy of the same is owned by Mrs. Morson of Warrenton, Va.

The following letters, selected from many in the hands of the family, are given here as throwing much light upon the history of the writers and of the times.

[From Prof. R. E. Scott to his mother.]

"KING'S COLLEGE, Dec. 11th, 1797.

"*My Dear Madam :* Having an opportunity of conveying this letter to London to catch the first vessel for Virginia I take occasion to write you a few hurried lines. Your last letter informs me of your having received mine which contained the intelligence of the death of my worthy grandfather. Not two months after I had written that I had occasion to write you also of the death of my aunt Margaret, an event which a few week before was the most unlooked for, altho' at that time the cause of her dissolution was incurably fixed as it consisted in a deep seated imposthume in the lungs for which no alleviation could be found.

"In my last packet from Virginia you tell me that you are simply made acquainted with the news of my having become a married man, but are totally in the dark as to the person who has been the object of my choice. In case this letter should prove more fortunate in reaching you than that which I wrote for the express purpose of letting you into the whole matrimonial secret, I now inform you that I have become the happy husband of her who was Miss Rachel Forbes, eldest daughter of Mr. Forbes-Mitchell of Thainston—a lady who since the first moment I knew her & now in the tenth month after we have been married I continue to think the most amiable of her sex. She is in the twentieth year of her age, has had the best opportunities of education, company & improvement that Scotland & England can afford, & is nearly related to the most respectable families in this County—being niece on the father's side to Sir William Forbes of Craigievar, & and on the mothers to Mr. Fraser of Fraserfield. A mother may perhaps be anxious to know whether the wife of her son be handsome & that son thinks he may safely declare she is,—& with equal safety he may aver that she is possessed of the choicest gifts of the mind. Money was entirely out of view in this match &

---

* Professor Ogilvie was in his 80th year when he preached the above sermon.

could never have been thought of as the estate of the father was entailed. A match of attachment it undoubtedly is, & the husband has the consolation to believe that it is a match of attachment on both side.

"Several different times that I have written to you I have declared my readiness to transmit the £80 of legacy to my sister to which all impediment is now removed by the death of good old Mrs. Isobel Scott the last of my worthy old aunts in this country. None of my letters it would seem containing this notice have ever reached you or Dr. Peyton—luckily however the Dr. formed the resolution of drawing upon me for the money—his draught has arrived & has been duly honoured, so that this business is at length happily arranged.

"The Drs. new residence at Fauquier court house would I should think contribute much to your comfort—but what becomes of your abode at Middleburgh? I return my sister my hearty thanks for her letter of intelligence concerning herself & other folks. I give it as my opinion without flattering that she is a most agreeable correspondent. She claims a commencement of correspondent with my cara sposa—but [here the letter is so torn as to be undecipherable.]   Your dutiful son,   "ROBT. SCOTT."

Addressed, Mrs. Eliza Scott, care of Dr. Peyton, Fauquier by Dumfries, Virginia—Virg'a Coffee house.

Another letter from Prof. Scott to his mother, dated "King's College, March 3d, 1799," mentions the death, ten days before, of the widow of his grandfather, Prof. Thomas Gordon, at the age of 82. He mentions her estate as £200 per ann. settled on her for life by Mr. Walker, which returned to his relations, and £100 settled on her by Prof. Thomas Gordon, which returned to Mrs. Scott, Mrs. Brown and Margaret Gordon. "Margaret Gordon had bequeathed, at her death, all her portion to Mrs. Brown," showing that Margaret Gordon was dead in 1799. He speaks of his wife, "the daughter of Mr. Mitchell Thainston, now only 20 years of age and very handsome."

[From Mrs. Robt. E. Scott to Mrs. Eliz'h Scott.]

"Your kind letter of the 7 July my Dr Madam gave both Robt & I the sincerest pleasure, I congratulate you & your Daughters on the arrival of my nephews both of whom I trust are thriving. My Mother & family have lately sustained an irreparable loss by the death of my eldest Brother Arthur Forbes-Mitchell who fell by the hand of an Irish Villian of the name of Bellissis at Bombay last May, altho' but 21 he was in the very honourable & lucrative situation of Paymaster of the Company forces & a partner in one of the first mercantile houses there, he was one of the best Son's & dearest to me of any of my Brothers, there was but 11 months betwixt us, we were constantly together till 6 years ago when he went to India, we have however the consolation to reflect he died honourably & as the public papers bear testimony respected & beloved by all ranks in the Settlement. My Second Brother William Forbes has for four years been missing he left his Ship the Junt Frigate in the Danish island of St. Thomas in June '99 we have some idea if in life he is in America, he is now the heir of entail to the estate of Thainston at present about £700 pr ann, before he will be of age or a few years more it will be considerably advanced, he is 19 next august & was 6 years ago a handsome promising boy, Should you or any of your friends hear of him, may I bespeak your good offices in his behalf. Arthurs death has already been inserted in all the European newspapers & those of the West Indies. Might I take the liberty of requesting you would get inserted in your Provincial paper which Mr. S. thinks is published at Alexandria, the following Paragraph. Died at Bombay May the 3d 1801 Arthur Andrew Forbes Mitchell Esqr of Thainston in Aberdeenshire in the Honbl Company's Civil Service & a partner in the house of Forbes Smith and Co. This will be sufficient for poor Wm. if he is in life as he knows perfectly he is heir of entail. I can only plead as an excuse for this trouble the situation of my poor afflicted Mother who never will recover the loss of her favorite Son, her distress is considerably augmented by her anxiety about Wm whom I much fear is no more. On friday last died poor Forbes Gordon after a long & painful illness which she bore with great fortitude, two nights before her death she sent and gave me every direction about her funeral, of her wish to be buried in Gordon's Isle, her niece Auchlynes Daughter has always lived with her & is in the deepest distress; your Sister has expressed a wish that young Forbes would accept of her house as an asylum just before her Aunts death, She is a beautiful girl of 16 & is to remain with me 'till she goes South. Poor Forbes was highly gratified by your remembrance of her. Our session has commenced & the College very full. There are two young Cousins of yours in this house sons of Mr. Forbes Blackford's & Annie Gregory's:

their Grandfather you no doubt recollect, a little brother of mine is in the Greek Class, so you see I have plenty to do, we do not live in Humanity Castle Mr S got an excellent Modern house just opposite Powis gate it is by far the best College Manse Dr. Macpherson inhabits the old one, he is a young unmarried man & a Greek Professor. My Mothers name was *Kathairane* Ann Fraser about 2 years younger than Lady Buchan. (her sister H.) My Father's name was Duncan, the next to Sir William Your question which of my relations I resemble puzles me not a little, I am said to be like Sir Arthur & his Daughter by the first marriage, Nancy afterwards Mrs. Forbes Culloden, Some say I am like Miss May Burnet, but of neither I can be judge as both the Ladies had died before I was born, of my likeness to my Father I am sensible. Mrs. Carmichael desires me to say everything that is kind & affectionate to you, she has lost her Father & Mother & every near relation, but in point of pecuniary support is extremely comfortable, She is building a fine residence on the declivity beside Tilliedron, as is also Principal MacLeod, for a jointure house to his wife. Your Son is arrived at the *distinguished honour* of *being Provost of this ancient City* but to do him justice he *bears it meekly.* With the Character of Bushrod Washington every European is well acquainted, his life* has late been published in London & I must say it does honour to the name he bears. Your son and I often talk about the family at Rippon Lodge & of Dr. Browns family * * * * [several lines torn off] companion Mrs. Iod of Fochabers. I have hardly left room to say that I expect soon to hear from you | And that I ever am

"Your Affectionate Daughter "RACHEL SCOTT.

"Kings College, Dec, 13th 1801.

"Addressed Mrs Elizabeth Scott | care of Dr. Peyton | Gordon's Dale | by Dumfries | Virginia | To be left at the | Virginia Coffee house. | "

41. HON. JOHN[4] SCOTT (*John,[3] James,[2] John[1]*), b. "Gordons-dale," Fauquier county, Va., Feb. 3, 1781, "in the worst of times," as his father wrote in the family Bible; d. Richmond, January 17, 1850; m. —, ELIZABETH PICKETT, b. —; d. —; daughter of Colonel Martin Pickett, Fauquier county, and his wife, Ann Blackwell, daughter of Joseph Blackwell, Sr. (BLACKWELL Ex. 9, p. 266.) Col. P. was son of George Pickett, and grandson of William S. (Marshall, p. 54.†)

Judge Scott was ed. Dickinson Coll., Pa., but did not graduate. He studied law under Charles Marshall, Warrenton, Va.

"Admitted to the bar 1801, he at once gave promise of the eminence in the profession which he was destined to achieve. In a short time he was one of the leading lawyers of northern Va. No reputation is more transitory and fleeting than that of an advocate. That the memory of his forensic ability should still survive after the lapse of three quarters of a century is perhaps the most conclusive evidence that could be offered of the high esteem in which he was held by his contemporaries.

"He was deeply read in all the departments of the law, and these garnered stores of learning a retentive memory kept ever ready for efficient use, while a vivid imagination and an unrivaled command of elegant and exact English enabled him to present even ordinary subjects in a most attractive manner. In 1829–30, when in the meridian of life, he was sent as a member from Fauq'r to the Convention which met in Richmond, Va., to form a Constitution for the State. No more extraordinary body of men were ever assembled together. There were Marshall, Madison, Munroe, Leigh, Upshur, Randolph, Doddridge, Campbell, and a host of others eminent in the Councils of the State and nation, and among them the subject of this sketch not only sustained but added to the high reputation with which he entered the Convention. In 1832 he became one of the Judges of the Circuit Superior Court of Law and Chancery, and as such ex-officio member of the General Court of Va. As a Judge he was distinguished for a strong love of natural justice and an ardent desire to protect the poor, the weak and the oppressed. He had an exalted sense of the dignity and responsibility of his office, and ever brought to the discharge of its duties all the resources of his

---

* Mrs. S. confounds Bushrod Washington with his kinsman George, whose life by Marshall, "under the inspection of Hon. Bushrod Washington," was first published in London, 1801.

† Col. Martin Pickett was Tax Commissioner, Fauq'r Co., 1782; Coroner, 1783; Sheriff, 1785.

SCOTT FAMILY.

intellect. No one can read his opinions contained in the Reports of Leigh, Robinson and Grattan without being impressed with his learning, but still more with his force and vigour of mind; perhaps, however, that quality which most strikes the reader is the luminous order in which his ideas are arranged, and the precise, elegant and perspicuous language in which they are expressed. They stand now and will long remain as models of judicial excellence."

The Richmond *Whig*, of January, 1850, contained this notice of Judge Scott:

" He was a prominent member of the Senate of Va. during the sessions of 1811–12 and 1812–13. He distinguished himself by his services as a mem. of the Conv. of 1829, which formed the present Constitution of the State. His labors were especially directed to the preservation of the independence of the Judiciary. In the first session of the Ass'y under the new Constitution, 1830–31, he was appointed Judge of the 6th Circuit, third Judicial Dist., and a Judge of the Gen. Court. In the new construction of this last Court, and the establishment of the Special Court of Appeals, March, 1848, he was constituted one of the five members of those two Courts, and so remained until his death."

From the *True Index*, Warrenton, Aug. 6, 1889:

" It is related of Judge S. that when he first came to the bar, though a briefless barrister, he made it a rule to be present at every session of the court and attend strictly to the administration of justice in each case. A stranger in quest of a lawyer to take charge of his business in one of the courts, having observed the attentive young lawyer, took him into his service. He won the case, and this was the beginning of a professional career that led upward and onward. * * * He accepted the position of Judge with reluctance, but filled it with signal ability for two decades. On one occasion he rebuked an ill considered remark of one of his sons with this admonition: ' If you are so unfortunate as to entertain doubts of the divine authority of the Christian Scriptures, practice their precepts and you will believe.' His religious convictions did not desert him in the hour of death. As his end drew nigh, after naming each of his children and expressing regret at the parting, he said: ' I have had on the whole a prosperous life, for which I thank God. For twenty years have I administered justice between man and man to the best of my ability, impartially, and now I go before the Judge of Judges.' An interesting anecdote is told of him in connexion with the appearance in the heavens of a comet which created no little consternation in his section. The Judge had come to Warrenton, transacted his business with deliberation, and had approached his horse in order to return home. A citizen who had observed his calm demeanor remarked to him: 'You do not appear to partake of the anxiety about the comet, why is this, Judge?' 'I will answer you with an anecdote,' Judge S. replied. 'Many years ago I was travelling at night in a stage coach from Aquia Creek to Fredericksburg over the worst road in the United States, as was agreed by all who knew it. The coach was crowded with passengers, who were much troubled for their safety, and indeed I felt there was ground for uneasiness; but one man was composed in his manner. When we demanded the reason of this he answered, 'I know the driver;' and so I answer you about the comet. I know the driver.' "

Children (G. S. F.) :*

   90.   i.   ELIZABETH GORDON,⁵ b. 1805 ; d. s.
+ 91.   ii.   ROBERT EDEN, b. Apr. 22, 1808; d. May 3, 1862; m. (I.) Mar. 10, 1831, Elizabeth Taylor. (II.) Oct. 18, 1838, Ann Morson. (III.) Dec., 1849, Heningham Watkins Lyons.
   92.   iii.   ANNA, d. yng.
+ 93.   iv.   MARIA MARTIN, b. July, 1814; m. May 8, 1833, Arthur Alexander Morson.
   94.   v.   LUCY, d. yng.

---

* PICKETT.—The following data from Fauq'r Co. records differs from the Pickett Chart in the Marshall Family (pp. 53-56) :
William Pickett. Hamilton par., Fauq'r Co.; will dat. Sep 26, pro. Nov. 24, 1766 (Will Bk. 110); names wife Elizabeth and sons Martin and William ex'rs. Children—i. Reuben. ii. George. iii. John. iv. Martin. v. William. vi. Sarah. vii. Mary Ann Marshall.
William Pickett and Lucy his wife appear 1785.
William S. Pickett, will dat. Jan. 10, pro. Feb. 26, 1798 (102), names wife Martha. Children—i. William S. ii. James. iii. John S. iv. Sanford. v. Patty Fishback. vi. Sukey Brady. vii. Molly Jackson. viii. Sally Metcalf. ix. Anna. x. Libby Smith.
Colonel Martin Pickett, son of George, gr. son of William S. Pickett and his wife, Miss Cooke, had—i. George Steptoe. ii. Lucy, b. May 2, 1767; d. 1825; m. Sep. 13, 1787, Charles Marshall. iii. Elizabeth, m. Hon. John Scott, *supra*. She was aged 17 when her father died. iv. Ann, m. F. W. Brooke. v. Letitia, m. Johnson. (Marshall Fam , 53-4.)
William Pickett was awarded contract for building a prison for Fauq'r Co., July 26, 1764. Wm. P., Yelverton Peyton and John Ashley on the bond. It was pro. this William P. who was Shff., Fauq'r Co., 1788-9. Thomas Bronaugh was Shff. do. 1790. Both of these farmed out the office to John Blackwell as Deputy, according to custom.

95. vi. MARGARET GORDON, b. May, 1817; m. Oct. 9, 1835, Robert Eden Lee,
    b. Gordonsdale, Fauquier Co., Sep. 7, 1810; B. by Rev. Mr. Thompson;
    killed July 14, 1843. (Excursus—LEE, p. 543, vii.)
 96. vii. MILDRED, b. —, 1821; d. yng.
+ 97. viii. JOHN, b. Apr. 23, 1820; m. Nov. 14, 1850, Harriet Augusta Caskey.
 98. ix. MARTIN PICKETT, b. —, 1823; m. —, Caroline Pocahontas Bernard, Blacks-
    burg Coll., Va.
 99. x. CHARLES FRANCIS, b. —; d. s., V. M. Inst.

43. JOHN CAILE[4] SCOTT (*Gustavus*,[3] *James*,[2] *John*[1]), b. —,
1782; d. "Muhlenburg Farm," Pickaway county, Ohio, Mar. 14, 1840,
æ. 58; m. "Bush Hill," Nov. 21, 1802, ANN LOVE, b. —, 1780; d. "Keys
Farms," Ross county, Ohio, Oct. 15, 1832, æ. 52, daughter of Samuel
L ve, "Salisbury," Fairfax county, Va.[*]

  Mr. Scott lived at his seat "Western View," Culp'r Co., Va., until 1828, when,
becoming involved financially by having gone security for large sums of money,
he moved, with what was left of his large est. to Ross Co., O., where he is still
remembered as "an elegant, large hearted gentleman of the old Virginia School,
who delighted in hospitality." He was of medium size.
Children (F. B.):

100. i. MARGARET,[5] b. Rockville, Jan. 2, 1803; d. infant.
+ 101. ii. MARY ANN, b. Jan. 10, 1804; d. Oct. 23, 1842; m. Sep. 25, 1827, William
    Bussard Franklin.
102. iii. ELIZABETH CAILE, b. "Strawberry Vale," May 2, 1805; d. unm., Chillicothe,
    O., Nov., 1842.
+ 103. iv. JANE SELDEN, b. Oct. 16, 1806; d. Sep. 21, 1881; m. Oct. 20, 1825, William
    Ballard Brown.
+ 104. v. GUSTAVUS, b. Nov. 11, 1807; d. Jan. 25, 1867; m. Jan. 21, 1847, Elizabeth
    Danolds.
+ 105. vi. JOHN CAILE, b. July 17, 1809; d. Feb. 5, 1875; m. Oct. 18, 1832, Louisianna
    Eleanor Slesman.
+ 106. vii. HARRIET LOVE, b. Feb. 7, 1811; d. Feb. 18, 1865; m. (I.) Jan. 21, 1835,
    Asahel Renick. (II.) Mch. 5, 1844, Rev. Thomas Woodrow, D. D.
+ 107. viii. CHARLES LOVE, b. Sep. 20, 1812; d. Jan. 24, 1861; m. May 8, 1834, Eliza-
    beth Slesman.
108. ix. ROBERT RANKIN, b. Western View, Jan. 15, 1814; d. infant.
109. x. WILLIAM SCOTT, b. Oct. 10, 1815; d. Dec. 11, 1843; m. Jan. 16, 1839,
    Mary Nash Florence, b. July 6, 1820; dau. of Col. Elias Florence.
      Children:
    i. Elias Florence, U. S. A., b. Oct. 30, 1841; d. May 16, 1864;
      served in an Ohio Regt.; wounded at Resaca, Ga., May 14,
      1864.
    ii. William, b. Nov. 3, 1843; m. Oct. 25, 1866, Mary E. Steely, dau.
      of Lemuel Steely. Had—i. George Steely, b. Dec. 30, 1867;
      d. Aug. 8, 1870. ii. Mary Florence, b. Oct. 11, 1869. iii.
      Lizzie Bell, b. July 1, 1871. iv. Wm. Franklin, b. Jan. 1,
      1874. v. Nellie Gwynne, b. June 11, 1879. vi. Charles Love,
      b. Nov. 1, 1881. vii. Jennie Adams, b. Jan. 29, 1886.
+ 110. xi. ELLEN SELDEN, b. April 2, 1817; d. Feb. 26, 1857; m. Mar. 2, 1848,
    Philip Doddridge.
111. xii. RICHARD M., b. Nov. 28, 1818; d. Oct. 10, 1820.
112. xiii. ————, son; b. W. V., Sep. 20, 1820; d. inf.
112a.xiv. RICHARD M., 2d, b. W. V., Apr. 23, 1822; d. Mar. 2, 1827.

---

[*] LOVE. 1. Samuel Love, Salisbury, Fairfax Co., Va., m. Ann Jones of "Cleandrinking," Montg. Co.,
Md., who rec'd his est. from Queen Anne, 1736. He had—2. Nellie, m. — Selden and had—i. Wilson Cary,
m. Louisa Alexander. ii. Louisa, d. s. iii. Eleanor Love, m. Feb., 1842, John A. Washington. (SCOTT 7v,
p. 633.) 3. Mary, m. R M. Scott. 4. James, m. — Forrest, had ch. 5. Elizabeth, m. — Watson. 6.
Harriet, d. s. p.; m. — Simmes. 7. Ann, m. John Caile Scott, *supra*. 8. Charles, m. Dixon, ch. in
Nashville, Tenn. 9. Richard, m. — Lee, in So. Ca.

44. GUSTAVUS HALL[4] SCOTT (*Gustavus,[3] James,[2] John[1]*), b. —; d. —; m. "Bush Hill," Fairfax county, Va., July 1, 1806, ELIZABETH DOUGLAS MARSHALL, b. Oct., 1786; d. Crawfordsville, Ind., — 8, 1876; 2d dau. of Thomas Douglas Marshall, of "Black Friars,"* Charles county, Md., and his wife Sarah (Ford) Maddox, b. —; d. 1791.

Mr. Scott grad. A. B., Coll. N. J., 1805. "He was a warm personal friend of Henry Clay, and, while that distinguished gentleman was Sec. of State under Jno. Quincy Adams, was elected to bear important despatches from our Government to Bolivia, at Bogota, in So. America. Soon after his return from this mission Mr. S. removed his family to Indiana and purchased a farm near Cherry Grove, 6 miles N. of Crawfordsville. Mrs. Scott was for more than half a century a member of the Episcopal Church, and walked worthy of her calling." (Obit. of Mrs. S.) Mrs. S. had an older sister, Mary Scott Marshall. Their mother d. when they were 7 and 5 years. They were reared by their father's relative in Va., Richard M. Scott of "Bush Hill."

Mrs. Snyder, from whom the records of her family were received, writes:

"My father and mother were married at 'Bush Hill,' the residence of *her* cousin and guardian, Rich'd M. Scott. It is 3 m. from Alexandria, and when I visited it a few years ago found it unchanged, the same old furniture and pictures that I remember seeing in my childhood. Our own home was called 'Mulberry Hill,' and was 5 or 6 m. from Fairfax C. H. We were all born there. My father bought land in Montgomery Co., Ind., and in 1837 we moved there. It was a long and tiresome journey in that day. Father was much disappointed in the country, and was making preparation to go south, when he d. suddenly the following year. He left no will, and mother divided the property among us, she having an income of her own. In the spring of 1820 my father made the trip from our Va. home to Ashland, Tenn., to visit his friend Henry Clay. He went on horseback, leading another horse on which was strapped his portmanteau containing necessary clothing. He was absent several months, and while there put in a lawyer's hands certain papers regarding several thousand acres of Ky. land which had been entered by *his* father and had been neglected by the administrator, some of it having then been sold for taxes. A few years later this lawyer died, leaving no account of these papers, and the expense was too great at that time to carry on the search. But at the time of father's death he was preparing again to look up this land. With his death the matter ended, as his brothers were unwilling to undertake it. When Henry Clay was Sec. State and Southard Sec. Navy I went with my father and mother to visit them in Washington, and though very young the visit made a lasting impression on my mind. I also went with them to Mt. Vernon. John Washington lived there then, and his wife was a Blackburn, a cousin of my father."

Children b. "Mulberry Hill," Fairfax Co., Va.:

113. i. RICHARD MARSHALL,[5] b. May 11, 1807; d. s. p. Sep. 21, 1847; m. —, 1830, Eliza Alexander, Fredericksburg. He is buried in "Dipple" graveyard.
114. ii. JOHN THOMAS, b. June, 1809; m. —, 1839, Helen Somerville. Had six children, of whom i. Mary and ii. Helen, survive.
+ 115. iii. GUSTAVUS HALL, b. July 13, 1812; d. Mar. 23, 1882; m. May 3, 1843, Julia Todd.
116. iv. MARY LOVE, b. July 29, 1815; d. Apr. 13, 1889; m. Crawfordsville, Ind., Mar. 4, 1844, George Snyder, Phila, Pa., later of Crawfordsville.
Children:
    i. Anna Love, b. Sep. 22, 1846.
    ii. George E., b. Oct. 1, 1848; m. Oct. 1, 1874, Carrie Louisa Granger, Hardwick, Mass. Had—i. Scott Leslie, b. Dec. 21, 1875. ii. Corydon Granger, b. Feb. 24, 1874.

---

* "Black Friars" is a beautiful old place in the lower part of Charles Co., Md., that has been handed down frm father to son, from generation to generation, for over two hundred years. The homestead is a large brick building, but old, in every respect; stands on an eminence and commands an extensive view of the lovely Wycomico River." (Letter of Mrs. Annie L. Frobel, gr. dau. of Mary Scott Marshall, June 13, 1886.)

    iii. Julia Marshall, b. Phila., Pa., May 5, 1850; m. Sep. 29, 1870, Bertrand Rockwell of Warsaw, Ill. Had, b. Junction City, Ks.—
        i. Florence, b. Feb. 5, 1872. ii. Bertha, b. Aug. 17, 1874.
        iii. Mary, b. Sep. 8, 1877. iv. Catherine, b. Feb. 5, 1881.
    iv. James Evans, b. LaFayette, Ind., July 28, 1853; m. Feb. 19, 1885, Edia L. King, Corry, Pa.; s. p.

117. v. ELIZABETH DOUGLAS, b. July —, 1818; m. LaFayette, Ind., 1842, Weston D. Snyder, Phila., Pa., and Crawfordsville, Ind.

        Children :
    i. Elinore Frances, b. July 4, 1847; m. July, 1879, Frank McGauley, Ohio; s. p.
    ii. Weston Donaldson, b. Phila., Oct., 1850.

118. vi. DAVID WILSON, b. Aug. —, 1820; d. s. p.; m. —, 1864, Carrie Wilson, St. Mary's, Kas.

119. vii. ANNA, b. May —, 1823; d. s. —, 1840.

46. MAJOR ROBERT JAMES[4] SCOTT, U. S. A. (*Gustavus,*[3] *James,*[2] *John*[1]), b. Va., —, 1798; d. —, 1834; m. cir. 1818, MARY ANN LEWIS, b. —; d. June, 1879; daughter of Judge Lewis, Hagerstown, Md.

    "Major Scott was ed. U. S. Military Acad., West Point, May 8, 1813, to Mar. 2, 1815, when he grad. and was promoted in the U. S. Army to 3d Lt. Corps Artill., Mar. 2, 1815; served in garrison at Ft. Mifflin, Pa., 1815-16, and on leave of absence; 2d. Lt., Corps Artill., June 15, 1817-1818; resigned, Nov. 4, 1818; Sutler at Fort Washington, Md., 1826-31, and Fortress Monroe, 1831-34; d. May, 1834, at Fort Monroe, Va., æ 36." (McCallum.)

Children :
  120. i. ANN ELIZA,[5] b. —. P. O. Erie Pa.
  121. ii. HENRY LEWIS, b. —, 1822; d. Miss. —, 1851.
  122. iii. ROBERT WAINWRIGHT, U. S. N., b. —, 1827; d. s. Jan. 5, 1866; midshipman, U. S. N., Sep. 9, 1841; passed, Aug. 10, 1847; Master, Sep. 15, 1855; Lieut., Sep. 16, 1855; Lieut. Commander, July 16, 1852; d. at Acapulco, Mex., while in command of the U. S. Ship, Saginaw.
+ 123. iv. WILLIAM LAWRENCE, b. July 2, 1828; d. Sep. 19, 1891; m. Sep. 19, 1853, Mary Matilda Tracy.
  124. v. GEORGE RICHARDS, b. —; d. inf.
  125. vi. BARCLAY, b. —; d. yng.
126-129. vii. JOHN H. EATON, b. —; d. i4.

54. FRANCES TOY[5] SCOTT (*Alexander,*[4] *James,*[3] *James,*[2] *John*[1]), b. —; d. —, m. —, 1813, EDWARD[5] CARTER, Fauquier county, Va., b. —, 1784; d. —; son of John Carter[4] of "Sudley," Prince William county, and his wife, Janet Hamilton, grandson of Landon[3] and Maria (Byrd) Carter, Sabine Hall, of Robert,[2] John,[1] of Corotoman, 1649.

Children (CARTER) :
  130. i. WILLIAM FITZHUGH,[6] b. —; d. —.
  131. ii. RICHARD HENRY, C. S. A., of "Glen Welby," near Salem; Fauq'r Co., b. —; m. —, Mary Welby DeButts. He was Capt. 8th Va. Reg. and Major Qr. Mr. Dep., C. S. A.

Children :
i. Frances Scott, b. July 4, 1838; m. May 25, 1858, Major Robert
    Taylor Scott, C. S. A. (SCOTT 143.)
ii. Sophia DeButts, b. —; m. 1865-6, her cos., Lt. Col. Richard Welby
    Carter, C. S. A., Lt. Col. 1st Va. Cav. Had i. Mary M. ii.
    Frances. iii. Sophie.
iii. Edward, C. S. A., b. —; m. —, Jane Turner; Capt. 8th Va. Inf.,
    C. S. A. Had—i. Rebecca Welby. ii. Sarah. iii. Mary De
    Butts. iv. Selina.
iv. Selina Dulany, b. —; m. —, John Henry Washington, b. 1822,
    son of John Perrin and Hannah (Fairfax) Washington.
v. J. Alexander, b. —; m. —, Mary Henley, K. W. Co.
vi. DeButts, b. —; unm.
vii. Mary Welby, b. —, m. —, Wm. Beverley.
viii. Richardetta, b. —; m. —, Robert Beverley.
ix. Ann, b. —; m. —, Edward C. Turner, Jr.
x. Richard Henry, b. —; unm.

132. iii. JOSIAH T., C. S. A., b. —, m. Isabella Wilson.

Children :
i. Eva. ii. Elizabeth. iii. Francis. iv. Emily.
v. Henderson. vi. George Magill. vii. Isabel.

133. iv. WINSTON L., C. S. A., b. —; killed at battle of Williamsburg, May 5, 1862;
    m. —; Maria Louisa Nelson, dau. of Dr. Nelson and his wife, Seigniora
    Brown. (BROWN 95, p. 178.) He was 2d Lieut. Co. F, Prince William
    Rifles, 17th Va. Inf., C. S. A. "He was killed early in the day, cheering
    his men on. He was a steady, determined soldier and one of the most
    beloved officers in the Reg't." (Wise's His. 17th Reg.)

Children :
i. James. ii. Seigniora, m. John White.
iii. Frances, m. John Bleight.
iv. Stuart. v. Christian. vi. Earnest.

134. v. MARY LANDONIA, b. —; m. —, Robert Lawlor.

Children :
i. Winston.

135. vi. VIRGINIA. 135a. vii. ELIZA.
136. viii. CHRISTIAN, d. s. 136a. ix. ROBERT, d. s.

57. PATRICK HENRY[6] SCOTT (*Alexander,[4] James,[3] James,[2]
John[1]*), b. "Meadow Grove," Fauquier county, Va., June 4, 1815; d.
"Seven Islands," Jan. 9, 1865; m. Nov. 17, 1852, MARY CARRINGTON
YANCEY, b. —.

Children (H. W. S.) :

137. i. FRANCIS ALEXANDER,[6] b. Nov. 1, 1855; m. Dec. 12, 1877, Mary Carrington
    Pleasants, Providence Church, Va.

Children :
i. Elizabeth Baker, b. Jan. 12, 1879.
ii. Mary Catherine, b. Apr. 18, 1880.
iii. Annie Thweat, b. Oct. 12, 1881.
iv. Clara Yancey, b. Jan. 16, 1883.
v. Georgia Cabell, b. Feb. 25, 1884.

138. ii. CABELL CARRINGTON, b. July 24, 1857.
139. iii. WILLIAM BAILEY, b. Dec. 27, 1858.
140. iv. CHARLES YANCEY, b. May 9, 1860; m. Dec. 6, 1883, Nina Stuart Burke.

Children :
i. Jessie, b. Oct. 3, 1884.

141. v. SARAH BUTLER, b. Oct. 12, 1861; m. Apr. 1, 1885, Fletcher Yuille.
142. vi. HARRIETT WASHINGTON, b. Aug. 13, 1863.

91. HON. ROBERT EDEN[5] SCOTT (*John,[4] John,[3] James,[2]
John[1]*), b. April 22, 1808; d. May 3, 1862; killed by U. S. deserters;
m. (I.) Mar. 10, 1831, ELIZABETH TAYLOR, b. 1815; d. Mar. 11, 1834;
daughter of Robert Johnston Taylor, of Alexandria and his wife Mary
Elizabeth Berry, Berry Plains, K. G. county, and gr. dau. of Jesse and
Elizabeth (Johnston) Taylor of Ireland, 1778. (II.) Oct. 18, 1838,
ANN MORSON, b. Aug. 3, 1813; d. Oct. 2, 1846; daughter of Alexander and Anne Casson (Alexander) Morson, "Hollywood," Stafford
county. (III.) Dec. —, 1849, HENINGHAM WATKINS LYONS, b. Nov.,
1827; d. Richmond, April 27, 1886, æ 58 (Obit. S. C., 5, 8, '86);
dau. of Hon James. and Heningham (Watkins) Lyons of Richmond,
son of Dr. James Lyons of R., and gr. son of Judge Peter Lyons of
"Studley," Hanover Co., and his wife, a dau. of James Power, K. W.
Co. (Excursus—Morson, No. 12, p. 654. R. S., 3, 5, '81 and 1, 28, '82.)

Robert E. Scott was ed. Univ. Va., 1825-1827. He studied law and was
admitted to the bar, Warrentown, Va., 1829. He was elected Commonwealth's
Atty., and for years served in the Va., Leg. He was a mem. of the Const. Conv.
of 1850, and of the Conv. of 1861 that passed the ordinance of Secession, in which
Conv. he supported the Union until Va. seceded. He was a mem. Provisional
Congress of the Confederate States, July, 1861. In Sep., 1861, he was a candidate
for the C. S. Congress. The N. Y. Herald of May, 1862, stated at the time of
Judge Scott's murder, "Robert E. Scott, who was murdered the other day, was
offered the position of Secretary of the Navy under the present administration.
Mr. Seward wrote the letter conveying the tender."

The following sketch of Mr. Scott is taken from the 3d chapter of "Self
Government in America: An Inside View of the Great Republic," by Col. John
Scott, his brother.

"I will now bring into the domain of history a fact which belongs to the subject and the
era of which I am writing, and to the acquaintance of the foreign reader a man whom great
talents, and integrity and singular firmness of character, had qualified for the highest employ-
ments of State. A noble countenance and figure indicated the greatness of his mind and
character. In 1861 Honorable Robert Eden Scott was an eminent lawyer of Virginia, and
an opulent slaveholder, and extensive planter of Fauquier County. He had shunned federal
life and for many consecutive years had represented the voters of the county with distin--
guished reputation in the Legislature of the State, and in 1850 had been one of two delegates
to a convention charged with the responsible duty of amending the State Constitution. In
politics, with undeviating step he had trod the path of Whigism, and with warmth had opposed the Democratic party in its endeavour to obtain a federal control, because its tendency
was, he thought, to excess, latterly to disunion. When secession stepped into the arena and
sounded a fierce blast on his trumpet, he supported the side of the Union with all his strength,
and all the resources of his popularity and influence.

"In that period of anxiety and terror, he spoke memorably in Warrenton, the county
seat of Fauquier, and depicted in colors, not too dark, what, in the event of war between the
Sections, would be the wretched condition of Virginia—to be made a cock-pit for the North
and South and a prey to the vile banditti recruited from the outcast population of Northern
cities—a speech which will not be forgotten by any man who heard it. Nevertheless Mr.
Scott had been brought to appreciate the condition to which the southern republics had been
reduced by a fraudulent working of the collossal power, with its head at Washington but em-
bracing the entire slave section in its dreadful coil; yet he could not be persuaded that a
republic, reposing on the ground work of slavery, would redress the evils complained of and
would not rather plunge the unhappy South into a vortex of ruin. Therefore, in the new

division of parties, he was a warm and decided, indeed a vehement advocate of the Union, and had been elected by a great majority of the voters to the sovereign convention to be charged with the interests of Virginia in that imminent crisis. His colleague chosen for that great business was Honorable John Quincy Marr, afterwards captain in General Beauregard's army, an accomplished officer, and the first soldier who was killed in the civil war.

"Such was the attitude of affairs when Mr. Scott received at Oakwood, his country seat, a message from the Premier of Mr. Lincoln's Administration, inviting him to a consultation in respect to the public disorders. Mr. Scott repaired to the federal city hoping that something might be done by the new Administration to reunite the States or preserve the general peace. Though the strong bias of his character was towards conservatism in government yet he recognized the fact that the Union had worked off its centre and that the balance of sections would have to be restored as a condition of permanent settlement. Therefore when invited by Mr. Seward to state his opinion as to the policy which ought to be pursued to recall the detached States, he answered:

"'Justice, Mr. Seward, justice! Do the South justice, and I will engage that every State will return to the Union and abide with you forever.'

"'If justice be all that the South demands she will assuredly receive that at our hands.'

"Mr. Scott was a direct man, he was a matter of fact man, and not at all given to the fence of words, so he said to Mr. Seward:

"'The kind and measure of justice which the South now demands from you is not such justice as is contained in promises or paper guarantees. She must have a substantial guarantee. She demands to be admitted to equal power with the free soil section in every department of the government—in the legislature, in the judiciary, in the presidential office. The South must have equality in the Union as the condition of its restoration.'

"This brought the conversation to an abrupt termination, for the Premier responded promptly and with emphasis:

"'That cannot be. The North will never consent to part with its supremacy in the Union.'

"The conference had not been productive of compromise, but it had thrown on the sectional controversy a very strong light, and had convinced Mr. Scott that the North, notwithstanding sentimental professions, did not desire the Union, except as a means of governing a rich, dependent, and spoliated province. He was satisfied too that the claims of the South, if ever conceded, would have to be wrung from the North by a hand of greater strength than negotiation. With this impression graven on his mind he returned to Virginia and repaired to the sovereign convention where that consideration was brought directly to his attention."

The following account of the murder of Mr. S. is from the *National Intelligencer*, Washington, May 20, 1862:

"Hon. Robert E. Scott of Fauquier Co., Va., was killed on Saturday, the 3d inst., at Frank Smith's, near Salem, Fauquier Co. A couple of Geary's or Blenker's men, supposed to be deserters, having committed many depredations through the country, among other things violating a woman, Robert E. Scott, with Winter Paine and others, some ten or twelve, made an attempt to capture them at Smith's. On approaching the house Mr. Scott and his overseer, Delaney, were shot dead by the deserters; the others ran, and Scott's double barrel gun was afterwards broken over him by the villains. The deserters escaped. One account says Mr. S. went to the Provost Marshall at Warrenton to have a detail of soldiers to arrest the marauders, and that these soldiers were the persons who accompanied Mr. S. to their place of rendezvous when he was shot. The event gives the deepest pain in Washington to all classes, and particularly to the administration, as Mr. Scott was one of the noblest of Virginia's sons, and was seeking the return of his State to the Union."

The murder of Mr. Scott was brought before the U. S. Cong., where immediate action was taken by the passage of a resolution in the House, May 8, 1862, calling upon the Sec. of War for information relative to the homicide. In response to the letter of Secretary Stanton, Gen. Geary made the following report, which will be found in Ex. Doc., 37th U. S. Cong., 2d Sess., No. 113, Vol. 9, 1861–2.

"Headquarters Detached Brigade, near Rectortown, Va.,
May 13, 1862.

"*Sir:* Various versions of the recent shooting of Robert E. Scott and John Matthews, citizens of Fauquier Co., Va., having obtained currency, I herewith respectfully beg to submit to you a correct statement of the occurrence, a detailed account of which was furnished by me to Major General Banks. It was reported to me that two deserters from another branch of our army were committing depredations between Salem and Warrenton, when I immediately detailed Lt. Wells, with a detachment of 1st Mich. Cav., to trace them up. Guerrilla cavalry infesting the neighborhood, a squad was sent forward in advance, who returned and reported to the Lt. that Messrs. Scott and Matthews had been killed by the two men in question, when the whole party hurried to the scene of action, which was on the farm of Franklin Smith, about 5 miles from Warrenton. They there found the bodies of the two citizens and that of one of the supposed deserters, and ascertained that the two soldiers had been occupying a house for some time, when upon this day (May 3) Robert E. Scott, dec'd, led a party to capture them, among which were John Matthews, dec'd, Robert Hames, George Riley, Winter Payne, Alfred Perkins, Edward Briggs, J. W. Heflin, and Tibley Page, all residents of Warrenton and vicinity. Mr. Scott was shot while entering the house at the head of the party, gun in hand, and Mr. Matthews in the melee consequent upon the attempted escape of the two soldiers. One of the soldiers was shot by a citizen in attempting to escape; the other escaped to the mountains, where Lt. Wells did not deem it safe to pursue him owing to the presence of bodies of guerrilla cavalry.

"I have since learned that the remaining soldier voluntarily gave himself up to the commanding officer at White Plains. His name is J. H. Bayard, and that of his comrade who was shot was William C. Franklin. He represented that they were both privates in Capt. A. Gordon's Co. of 7th Reg. Wisconsin Vols., Gen. King's Brigade. The initials of the names and their identity with the regiment named, are shown upon the blankets found upon the site of the melee. Bayard stated that they had been taken prisoner by scouts of the enemy, from whom they had escaped, and that they were in search of the command to which they belonged when the attempt was made by the citizens to capture them.

"It appears, however, that they had been guilty of marauding in the section through which they passed.   Very respectfully, yr. ob't serv't,

"JOHN W. GEARY, Brig. Gen. Com'g."

Another account has been sent to me by a member of the Fauquier bar :

"In the spring of 1862 two deserters from the U. S. Army were plundering the people in lower Carter's valley, Fauq'r Co., and frightening women and children. The citizens appealed in vain to the Federal Commander for protection or for men to arrest and remove the marauders. The officers replied that they could not risk a small squad of soldiers for such a purpose, and advised the citizens to arrest and take before them the lawless parties for punishment. Accordingly Mr. Scott and some ten other elderly gentlemen of that region went in search of the deserters, and traced them to the Winchester road, opposite G. W. F. Smith's house, where they had been the previous night. In going from Mr. Smith's gate to his house they had to pass that of one of his servants. The tramp of horses brought from the cabin one of the deserters without arms. Mr. Scott, who was at the head of the column, said to him, 'You are my prisoner,' whereupon he promptly replied, 'I surrender, but won't you let me speak with my comrade in the house?' Mr. Scott rejoined, 'Yes, but we'll see him first.' Whereupon Mr. S. turned to Thomas Digges, familiarly known as Bishop, and said, 'Bishop, won't you take charge of this prisoner?' and retaining his position in front, Mr. Matthews and he riding side by side, moved to the cabin, where they immediately dismounted. Without waiting for the others to come up they walked upon the porch, and had scarcely opened the front door sufficiently to show Mr. Scott's form when a shot from within pierced his heart, and he fell back on the porch a dead man, exclaiming as he fell, 'I'm shot, fire into the house!' Matthews, who was immediately behind him, stepped forward, but ere his foot touched the sill of the door a second shot entered his brain and he fell dead on the porch. The murderer had his own gun and that of his comrade, both of which he used in his deadly purpose. As soon as the firing began the prisoner bolted and ran into the garden back of the house, when those who had not dismounted pursued him on horseback. At the lower end of the garden a stone fence prevented further pursuit with horses. The prisoner leaped the fence and started up the hill, when one of the party shot and killed him. In the meantime the murderer, reloading his two guns, opened the back door wide enough to admit his gun and fired at the party by the stone wall. Whereupon they put the hill between themselves and the house, and despatched a messenger to the Federal officers in Salem, six miles off, for soldiers to capture the murderer, and one to Warrenton, seven miles away. A troop of 20 cavalry from Salem reached there first, only to find that the murderer had escaped. As soon as he found himself screened from view by the hill, he broke the guns of Mess. Scott and Matthews, and with his own guns made good his retreat to his command near Thoroughfare. In the death of Mr. Scott was lost to us the wisest, best and most valuable man in the county."

In corroboration of all that has been said of Hon. R. E. Scott's eminent abilities and exalted character, also of the correctness of the accounts of his brutal murder and its effect upon the people at large, much will be found in the McDowell Court of Inquiry, Nov., 1862, "Official Records of the Union and Confederate Armies, Series, I., Vol. XII., pt. I., Reports," (Serial No. Vol. 15), pp. 47-49, 78, 294, 326.)

Children, first marriage (F. B.):

+ 143.   i.   ROBERT TAYLOR,[6] b. Mar. 10, 1834; m. May 25, 1858, Fanny Scott Carter.

Second marriage:

144.   ii.   ELIZA GAWIN, b. Aug. 20, 1839; m. Nov., 1860, John Henry Rives. P. O., Lynchburg.

145.   iii.   JOHN, b. Apr. 17, 1845; d. —, 1883.

146.   iv.   ROBERT EDEN, b. June 23, 1846; d. May 19, 1847.

147.   v.   ANN MORSON, b. June 29, 1841, m. July 1, 1868, Capt. Alexander Dixon Payne, C. S. A.; lawyer; P. O., Warrenton, Va.; b. 1837; son of Richard and Alice (Dixon) Payne, gr. son of Daniel and Elizabeth Hooe (Winter) Payne. (WALLACE 36; HOOE ——.) He grad. M. A., W. and M. Coll., 1856; studied law, Univ. Va., 1857; practiced Warrenton. In 1861 entered C. S. Army as 3d Lt. Black Horse Cav. Co., Wm. H. Payne, Capt.; made Capt. of his Co. 1863; was in command, as sen'r officer of his Reg't, 4th Va. Cav., April 9, 1865, at the surrender of Gen'l Lee, and succeeded in saving the colours of his reg't; returned to his practice at W. 1865; was mem. Va. Leg. 1885-7. (Payne note, p. 654.)

        Children:

      i. Robert Eden Scott, b. Mar. 31, 1869.

      ii. Alice Dixon, b. Dec. 23, 1870.

      iii. Margaret Lee, b. Dec. 21, 1872; d. June 29, 1873.

      iv. Eliza Rives, b. Apr. 29, 1874.

      v. Ann Morson, b. Jan. 21, 1876.

      vi. Richard Winter, b. Aug. 2, 1877; d. Aug. 13, 1877.

      vii. Agnes Lee, d. June 3, 1878.

      viii. Mason, b. July 10, 1881; d. July 10, 1871.

148.   vi.   SUSAN, b. July 6, 1843; m. —, 1868, William Herbert. P. O., Alexandria.

Third marriage:

149.   vii.   HENINGHAM, b. —; m. —— Spillman.

150.   viii.   CAMILLA, b. —; unm.

151.   ix.   ROBERT EDEN, b. —; m. —, Mary Hall of Loudoun.

152.   x.   JOSEPHINE, b. —; m. —, Tazewell Ellett.

153.   xi.   IMOGEN, b. —; unm.

93. MARIA MARTIN[5] SCOTT (*John,[4] John,[3] James,[2] John[1]*), of Warrenton, Va., b. July —, 1814; m. May 8, 1833, by Rev. George Lemon, "Oakwood," Fauquier county, ARTHUR ALEXANDER MORSON, b. —, 1801; d. Jan. 13, 1864; son of Hon. Alexander and Ann Casson (Alexander) Morson, of "Hollywood," Stafford county, Va. (BROWN 90, p. 192; R. S., 7, 24, '80.)

Children (MORSON), F. B.:

155.   i.   ELIZABETH SCOTT,[6] b. Fredericksburg, Va., May 8, 1834; d. July 9, 1835.

156.   ii.   MARIA SCOTT, b. F., Feb. 24, 1836; d. July 4, 1875; m. —, William Ballard Bruce, Charlotte, Va.

        Children:

      i. Rosalie. ii. Sallie. iii. Maria.

157.   iii.   ARTHUR ALEXANDER, b. F., Feb. 27, 1838; d. May 5, 1847.

158. iv. ANNE, b. F., Mar. 24, 1840; d. Citronella, Ala., Feb. 29, 1884; m. —, Prof. Scott Shipp, C. S. A. He grad. V. M. I., July 4, 1859; entered C. S. Army Apr. 20, 1861, with the Corps of Cadets at the Camp of Instruction, Richmond: Capt. P. A. C. S. and Ass't Adj't Gen'l, Camp of Instruction, June, 1861; promoted Major 21st Va. Reg't Inf., serving in the campaigns of West Va. and the Valley of Va.; appointed Commander of the Cadets and Professor of Tactics, V. M. I., 1862, and was ordered by the Sec. of War C. S. to report to the V. M. I. for special duty there. (Rep. Adj't Gen'l Va., 1862.) Major Shipp has been Professor at the V. M. I. continuously since 1862.

159. v. JOHN SCOTT, b. F., Jan. 17, 1842; d. Ky., May 26, 1886.
160. vi. WILLIAM, b. F., Dec. 12, 1843.
161. vii. MARGARET LEE, b. Richmond, Mar. 11, 1846.
162. viii. LILIAS GORDON, b. R., Nov. 11, 1848; d. July 22, 1877; m. —, Hon. James Keith. (See 165.)
163. ix. ROSALIE, b. R., Dec. 18, 1851; d. July 5, 1856.
164. x. ROBERTA WELFORD, b. R., Nov. 18, 1853.
165. xi. FRANCES BARKSDALE, b. R., Sep. 18, 1855; m. Feb. 6, 1887, Hon. James Keith (see 162), his 2d wife. (CONWAY, p. 267-8.)
166. xii. ROBERT EDEN LEE, b. R., Aug. 10, 1857; d. Mar. 20, 1864.

EXCURSUS—MORSON,—PAYNE.

1. ARTHUR MORSON, b. Greenock, Scotland, Jan. 3, 1734; d. "Hartwood," Stafford Co., Va., May 23, 1798. He sailed for Va. on board the "Greenock Snow" Feb. 14, 1751; arrived in Rapp'k R., Va., June 29, 1751; m. Aug. 31, 1758, Marion Andrew of Staff'd, b. 1734; d. "Hartwood," Dec. 30, 1808. Child.—2. *Alexander.* 3. Margaret, b. Falmouth. Dec. 12, 1763. 4. *Marian Andrews.*

2. ALEXANDER MORSON, b. Sep. 24, 1761; d. July 28, 18—; m. July 3, 1800, Anne Casson Alexander, b. Dec. 28, 1781, eldest dau. of William Alexander of Snowden. Child.— 5. Martin Andrew, b. "Hartwood," June 24, 1801. 6. Arthur Alexander, b. Falmouth, Jan. 23, 1803-4. 7. Alexander, b. Hollywood, Aug. 28, 1805. 8. William, b. Dec. 14, 1806. 9. James, b. do. Feb. 21, 1808; d. Oct. 3, 1816. 11. John Andrew, b. Oct. 25, 1809. 11. Hugh, b. Oct. 2, 1811. 12. Ann, b. Aug. 3, 1813; m. Oct. 18, 1838, *Hon. Robert E. Scott,* No. 91. 13. Susanna, b. July 8, 1815. 14. James Marion, b. —, 1817.

4. MARIAN ANDREW MORSON, b. Falmouth, Feb. 11, 1765; m. (I.) Apr. 14, 1781, William Love, Falmouth; d. Nov. 3, 1781; had 1 child, b. Dec. 1781. (II.) Apr. 19, 1801, Captain William Payne, of Clifton, Fauq'r Co., b. 1755, Child—15 *Arthur Alexander Morson.*

15. ARTHUR ALEXANDER MORSON PAYNE,* b. 1804; m. —, Mason Fitzhugh, dau. of Hon. Nicholas Fitzhugh of Alex'a, and his wife Sarah Washington, dau. of Col. Burdett and Anne (Washington) Ashton (Ashton, p. 632.)

Child 16. General William H. Payne, C. S. A., b. "Clifton," Fauq. Co., Jan. 27, 1830; m. Sep. 29, 1852, Mary Elizabeth, dau. of Wm. W. and Minerva West (Winston) Payne. He was ed. Univ. Md. and V. M. I. (of which he was made an alumnus, 1867), and Univ. Va., 1848-9. In 1851 he was admitted to the bar; elected, 1856, State's Att'y for his Co., Fauq., his opponent being Hon. Robert E. Scott, whose family had held the office, and con.

---

* The Paynes are of English descent. Sir Robert Payne purchased lands in Va. and located thereon his two brothers, William and John Payne, who, with Sir Robert, were among the "Adventurers of Va., 1620." Brown in his "Genesis," p. 962, gives "John Payne, gent., Pd. £12.10. He sold his shares to Dr. Theodore Guleton, Dec. 15, 1619. William Payne, Esq., of the 2d Charter, sub. £37.10; pd. £100 of the E. I. and N. W. P. companies. Pro. the Wm. P., Esq., Highgate, 1618." "Sir Robert Payne of the 2d Chart., sub. —; pd. £25; M. P., Huntingdonshire, 1614, 1621-22, 1626 and 1628-29; knighted at Greenwich, May 22, 1605. Either Robert of St. Neots m. Elizabeth, dau. of Dr. Jno. Bleiby, or his cos. Robert of Medloe m. Elizabeth, dau. of Geo. Rotherham of Somery, Bedford, both living 1613."

Arms—"Gu. on a fesse betw two lions pass. ar." Crest—"A lion's gamb couped ar. grasping a broken tilting lance, the spear end pendent gu." Motto—"Malo mori quam foedari."

General William H. Payne wrote me that, William Payne settled near Lynchburg, Va., John, near Leedstown, Northern Neck. 1. John Payne had—2. Richard, North'd Co., b. 1633, who had—3. John, Lane'r Co., b. 1670, who had—4. George, West'd Co., b. 1716, who had—5. John, ancestor of Bp. Payne, of Va. 6. Richard, Culp. Co. 7. Captain William of Clifton, b. 1775; Commander "Falmouth Blues," Yorktown, 1783; rec'd 4,000 a. from Va., for 3 years services Va. line, and d. 1837. He had by his 1st wife—i. Daniel, m. July 9, 1805, Elizabeth Hooe Winter (p. 165 f), and had Richard, b. 1808; m. Alice Dixon, C. S. A. (SCOTT, 147.) Dr. Wm. W., C. S. A., and others (v. M. II., 164-6. S. M. 193); by his 2d wife—ii. Arthur Alexander Morson, supra. (v. M. II., 164-6. S. M., 193.)

ferred honours upon it, for over 80 years. He was a disunionist before the War between the States, and as such was a candidate for the Va. Conv. of 1861, but was defeated by Hon. Robert E. Scott. Early in 1861 he entered as private in the Black Horse Cavalry Co. of Fauq.; was elected Captain, and commanded the Co. until Sep., 1861. He was promoted to successive ranks until made Brigadier General of Cav., Nov. 1, 1864, commanding 1st Div., Cav., C. S. A.; wounded at Williamsburg, Va., Hanover, Pa., and Five Forks, Va. he fell into the enemy's hands each time, and was prisoner at Old Point, Johnson's Is., and the Old Capitol. He is now Att'y for the Va. Mid., and the Washington and Ohio R. R.'s. Has had 10 children.

John Paine and wife Marg't, Rapp'k Co., made deed 1659. Robert Payne and Katherine, his wife, named in Rapp'k 1689; Justice, Essex, 1699; will dat. May, 1695; pro. Nov., 1701; names child. Lawson, Robert, Elizabeth, and wife Cath'e. Robert Payne, Jr., will dat. Dec. 29. 1724; pro. Sep. 21. 1725; names son Lawson, dau. Elizabeth, wife Moneca. John Paine, vestryman Sittingbourne par., 1665. Robert P., Rapp'k Co., will dat. 1671. Robert P. and wife Elizabeth, dau. of Epaphroditus Lawson, elder bro. of Rich'd L., who pat. the land conveyed, made deed 1667. George P., Sr., Rich'd Co., will dat. 1710–11; pro. 1711; names son Thomas, and children unnamed, also "my father, Thos. Pacey, and bro. Geo. White, ex'rs." (See also BALL, p. 124.)

97. COLONEL JOHN⁵ SCOTT, C. S. A. (*John,⁴ John,³ James,² John¹*), of Warrenton, Va., b. Fauquier county, Va., April 23, 1820; m. Nov. 14, 1850, HARRIET AUGUSTA CASKEY, b. Feb. 6, 1833, daughter of James and Eliza Randolph (Pincham) Caskey, of Stewarton, Scotland. Her father coming to Va., became President of the Exchange Bank, also of the Bank of Virginia, Richmond.

Colonel John Scott was ed. Warrenton; studied law for two years under his father, Judge Jno. Scott; grad. B. L., Univ. Va., and was admitted to the bar 1841. Among his associates in the Law School of the Univ. Va. were Judge Wm. J. Robertson, Va. Court of Appeals; Edmund Randolph, of the California bar; Gen. Geo. W. Randolph, Sec. of War, C. S. A.; Hon. Jno. S. Barbour, U. S. Senator from Va.; Gov. Thomas Watts, Ala., &c., &c. Col. Scott became editor Richmond *Whig* 1850, but in 1851 retired to his plantation, near Warrenton, inherited from his father, and entered upon a course of political reading. This resulted in his publishing, in 1860, his first literary work, entitled "The Lost Principles of the Federal Government, or the Sectional Equilibrium: How it was created, how destroyed, and how it may be restored, by Barbarossa." &c. 8°, p. 350. Richmond, 1860.

"The object of the work was to show that the true nature of the U. S. Constitution was a compact between the free soil and the slave sections based on a balance between them of political power and influence."

Col. Scott recruited and organized, about 1857–8, the famous "Black Horse Cavalry" of Fauquier Co., and commanded the company at Charlestown, Va., when John Brown, Cook and Coppick were hung for murder and attempting to excite a slave insurrection at Harper's Ferry. This was the only volunteer company which Gov. Wise had ordered to assemble at Charlestown to prevent an apprehended rescue of John Brown and his associates in crime. In 1861, before Va. seceded, Col. Scott resigned command of the Black Horse Cavalry, went to Montgomery, Ala., and tendered his service to the Confederate States. President Davis appointed him Captain of Cavalry, P. A. C. S. He recruited a battalion of cavalry and was appointed Major. Later still he was promoted to a Colonelcy and ordered to the Trans-Miss. Dept. After the battle of Gettysburg he applied to be ordered to Richmond, but Gen. E. Kirby Smith, who commanded the Dept., refused his request, stating that "Col. Scott was a valuable officer and could not be spared without detriment to the public service."

After the war Col. Scott published "Partisan Life with Mosby," 8°, Harper Bros., N. Y., 1867. In 1870 elected Commonwealth's Att'y for Fauq'r Co., he was re-elected each successive term until July 1, 1891, holding the office for twenty-one years. In 1887, as State's Att'y, he was a defendant in a most important suit, and imprisoned in the Richmond jail by the famous Judge Hugh L. Bond, whose action was reversed by the United States Supreme Court. The case, as stated by the present Attorney General of Va., was as follows:

"Virginia was compelled to protect her treasury against the use of coupons cut from bonds issued in settlement of her "Public Debt" in order to provide for her asylums, schools, colleges, courts, &c., and various statutes passed to this end; among them a statute known in vulgar phrase as "the coupon crusher." This law required the Attorney General and Commonwealth's Attorneys to proceed by motion against all tax payers who tendered coupons in payment of taxes and obtain judgments.

"James P. Cooper, an Englishman, claiming to represent the bondholders of Great Britain, brought suit in the Federal Court, presided over by Judge Hugh L. Bond, against the Auditor of the Commonwealth, her Attorney General, and various Commonwealth's Attorneys, to enjoin and restrain them from executing this law. The injunction was granted and the restraining order served upon the defendants. Major John Scott, Attorney General Rufus A. Ayres, and J. B. McCabe, Commonwealth's Attorney for Loudoun County, disregarded the injunction. They were summoned before Judge Bond in Richmond to answer for contempt, fined and imprisoned in the public jail. Writs of 'Habeas Corpus' were applied for and obtained from the Supreme Court of the U. S., the cases argued by able counsel, Roscoe Conkling and John Randolph Tucker appearing for the petitioners. Judge Bond was reversed and his prisoners discharged. Report of these cases will be found in 123 U. S. S. Reports, 443, and known as 'Ex parte Ayres, Scott, and McCabe.'

"The General Assembly of Virginia recognized the patriotic, brave and firm stand of these gentlemen, and complimented them by a series of 'Joint Resolutions,' which the Governor was directed to communicate and cause copies to be transmitted to them. These resolutions will be found in the Acts of 1887-8, p. 579."

Col. Scott's reply to the resolutions of the Gen. Ass'y, published in the Richmond *State*, was as follows:

WARRENTON, FAUQ'R CO., VA., March 3, 1888.

His Excellency, Fitzhugh Lee, Governor of Virginia:—Your Excellency: In due course of mail I received the resolutions of the General Assembly of Virginia approving my determination, as Commonwealth's Attorney for the county of Fauquier, to yield obedience to the Statute of the State, approved May 12, 1887, which directs suits to be brought by the Commonwealth's Attorney for each county on the tax bills of such persons as had tendered coupons in payment, rather than to the restraining order of the Judge of the Circuit Court of the United States for the Eastern District of Virginia, which forbade us to institute those suits. The Legislature in adopting, and your Excellency in sending to me those resolutions, accompanied by your Excellency's letter, commending the course which, on that occasion, I thought it my duty to pursue, have produced in me feelings of profound satisfaction. The testimonial and the letter by which I have been so greatly honored, will be preserved by me whilst I live, and when I die will be transmitted to my descendants as an heirloom and admonition of public duty, to be kept and guarded with religious respect and attention: But my action in reference to the occurrence which has attracted the attention and received the approbation of the Governor and Legislature of Virginia resulted from the deep conviction of my understanding that in all collisions under our double form of government it is the first duty of a citizen of Virginia to obey the mandate of the State. The State is the citizen's natural sovereign. It pre-existed the Federal Government, which, history informs us, originated in a bargain among politicians, which adverse circumstances may destroy, or the consent of the contracting parties may dissolve.

But the State is a natural body, the joint product of time and events, and is indestructible, save by conquest or absorption. It will not be forgotten by any man born on Virginian soil that it was only by the assent and command of the State of Virginia that any of her citizens owed duties to the external authorities situated at Washington.

If the local or State authority be not preferred by the citizen in cases where the right of jurisdiction is disputed, a dangerous, indeed a fatal blow is struck at the State's autonomy, and it may be, at the existence of the United States themselves, the aggregation and organization of which constitute the Government of the Union. If the citizen deserts his natural flag the resisting force to Federal usurpation is destroyed and consolidation is the result. If, under any pretext, he fail in obedience to his State, it logically follows that he forfeits the protection of person and property afforded by State law, for, under every mode of political life known to civilized or savage men, obedience is the price of protection. If the refractory citizen will not give the one, he loses his right to the other. The option is obey or emigrate. If this be the correct doctrine, the preferred obedience to State authority in the contingency mentioned is the foundation stone of our American system of government.

I have the honor to be your Excellency's ob't serv't,   JOHN SCOTT, of Fauquier.

A full account of the trial, with Col. Scott's answer to Judge Bond's rule, was published in the Richmond *Despatch*, Sep. 23, 1887. See also the other Virginia papers of the day. It was thought at the time, by many prominent men of Va., as Gov. Lee said, that Judge Bond's action was "not only an insult to the county of Fauquier, but to the whole State of Va., and that Col. Scott's years, eminent abilities as a soldier and citizen, and above all his position before the court, should have protected him." (Alexandria *Gazette*, Oct. 13, 1887.)

In 1890 Col. Scott published his last work, "The Republic as a Form of Government, or the Evolution of Democracy in America," 8°, London, 1890. In the "Appendix" to this work Col. S. has published his "Answer" to Judge Bond's rule. The decision of the U. S. Supreme Court, in favour of Mr. Scott, was delivered by Mr. Justice Matthews.

Children, b. Warrenton (J. S):

167.   i. ELIZA CASKEY,[6] b. June 14, 1852; m. Nov. 14, 1872, Richard Clark Scott, son of Col. George Lee Scott, C. S. A., of No. Ca. Is a commissionn mcht., Petersburg, Va.
Children :
i. Richard Clarke. ii. George Lee.
iii. Nannie Caskey. iv. John Gordon.
v. William Clarke. vi. James Caskey. vii. Arthur.
168.   ii. CHARLES FRANCIS, b. July —, 1854; m. —, Caroline Parker; ed. Rock Hill Coll., Howard Co., Md.; is planter, Franklin, Texas; has five child.
169.   iii. JAMES CASKEY, b. Feb. —, 1856; m. —, Jenny Pickett Dade; lawyer, Franklin, Texas; ed. Rock Hill Coll.
Children :
i. Dade. ii. Alice.
170.   iv. JOHN GORDON, b. July —, 1859; ed. Bethel Acad., Fauq'r Co.; lawyer, Madisonville, Texas.
171-174.   v. MARY ELLEN, b. July 24, 1869.

101. MARY ANN[5] SCOTT (*John C.,[4] Gustavus,[3] James,[2] John[1]*), b. "Strawberry Vale," Fairfax county, Va., January 10, 1804; d. Chillicothe, O., Oct. 23, 1842; m. "Western View," Culpeper county, Va., Sep. 25, 1827, WILLIAM BUSSARD FRANKLIN,* b. Georgetown, D. C., Oct. 29, 1804; B. Nov. 21, 1804; d. Jan. 4, 1879. He m. (II.) Aug. 5, 1845, ELIZABETH LEE BELL, daughter of Charles Bell, Fauquier county, Va.

Mr. Franklin grad. A. B., Coll. of N. J., 1822; A. M. 1825; was mem. Am. Whig Soc. 1820; studied law with Hon. Francis Scott Key. In 1831 he removed

---

* FRANKLIN, son of Daniel and Catherine (Knode) Bussard of Fred'k Co., Md., and gr. son of Daniel and Sophia (Reuner) Bussard, of Huguenot stock, who settled on the Monocacy R. in Md. early in the 18th century. In 1840 the name was changed by Act of the Leg. of Ohio from Bussard to Franklin.

to Chillicothe, O., and practiced law, but disliking the profession, he taught school in the Old Academy at C. with great success. In 1840 he was elected Auditor of Ross Co., O., serving until 1858, when he was made Register of the Land Office, Ohio, holding the office until it was abolished, 1876; was for 40 years a School Examiner, and also an Elder in the 1st Presbyterian Church.

" He was a gentleman of the old school, a man of pure, elevated and noble character. He was a charming companion, his varied attainments, wealth of information, and polished manners affording him great conversational abilities."

Children, first marriage (FRANKLIN):

175.   i.   CATHERINE,[6] b. D. C., July 21, 1828. P. O., Chillicothe.
176. ii.   JOHN SCOTT, b. D. C., Nov. 20, 1829; d. Chillicothe, Oct. 28, 1836.
177. iii. ANN LOVE, b. D. C., Aug. 27, 1831; m. Oct. 2, 1851, Robert George Dun, a large landholder of Madison Co., O., brother of Mrs. Senator Thurman.

        Children :
      i. Mary Scott, b. Dec. 1, 1852; m. Nov. 18, 1880, Edward Denmead, Columbus, O.; had Edward Graham, b. 1881.
      ii. Lucy Angus, b. Dec. 12, 1854; m. June 12, 1879, Stephen J. Patterson, Dayton, O.; had Robert Dun, b. 1882; Julia, b. 1884; Annie Love, b. 1886.
      iii. Walter Angus, b. Mar. 1, 1857; physician. P. O., Cin., O.
      iv. Hattie Franklin, b. June 10, 1859.
      v. Nancy Angus, b. Nov. 2, 1861.
      vi. Katherine Thompson, b. Dec. 29, 1863.

178. iv. WILLIAM WALLACE, b. C., Jan. 16, 1834. P. O., Columbus.
179. v.   HARRIET LOVE, b. Sep. 11, 1835.
180. vi. GUSTAVUS SCOTT, M. D., U. S. N., b. Nov. 22, 1837; m. Oct. 20, 1870, Mary Steele Foulke of Chillicothe, dau. of Dr. Lewis W. Foulke, gr. d. of Dr. G. D. Foulke,* of Carlisle, Pa.; grad. M. D., Columbia Coll., N.Y., 1862; appointed Asst. Surgeon; U. S. N., May 22, 1862; Passed A. Surg., Oct. 30, 1865; resigned Nov. 2, 1868.

        Children :
      i. Elizabeth McCoy, b. June 12, 1872.
      ii. Charles Love, b. May 1, 1875.
      iii. Marianne Scott, b. Sep. 15, 1877.

181. vii. CHARLES LOVE, U. S. N., b. Aug. 19, 1839; B. Feb. 19, 1840; d. Sep. 18, 1874; m. July 18, 1864, Sarah B. Thatcher, dau. of Dr. N. W. Thatcher, Chillicothe, and his wife, Sarah Bedinger Swearingen; grad. U. S. Naval Acad., Oct. 23, 1854; Acting Midshipman, same date; Midshipman, June 11, 1858; Lieut., Apr. 19, 1861; Lieut. Commander, Mar. 3, 1865; Commander, May 24, 1872. He d. of yellow fever, U. S. Navy Yard, Pensacola, Fla.

        Children :
      i. Marion, b. May 13, 1866.
      ii. Charles Love, b. Sep. 30, 1868; d. Aug., 1859.
      iii. William Wallace, b. Jan. 16, 1870.
      iv. Robert Scott, b. Feb. 1, 1872.

182. viii. ASAHEL RENICK, b. Aug. 2, 1841; d. unm. by R. R. accident, Buffalo, N.Y., Oct. 14, 1866.

---

* 1. STEPHEN FOULKE, b. 1702; d. 1760 (?); m. 1723, Esther Willis. If he was son of Edward Foulke of Gwynedd, Wales, it does not so appear in Edward Foulkes' record of his children. (Jenkins' Gwynedd Pa.) He had—2. Priscilla, b. 1724. 3. Esther, b. 1726. 4. Susannah, b. 1730. 5. *Stephen*, b. 1732. 6. John, b 1735. 7. Aeneas, b. 1740.

5. STEPHEN FOULKE, b. 1732; d. 1800; m. (I.) 1754, Margaret Carson, b. 1733; d. 1735; (II.) Catherine Themburgh, d. s. p.; (III.) Sarah Delap. Had by 1st mar.—8. Stephen, b. 1756; d. 1827; m. Jane Godfrey, b. 1757; d. 1803. 9. Moses, b. 1758. 10. Lewis, b. 1763 11. Esther, b. 1765. 12. Margaret, b. 1767. 13. John, b. 1770. 14. Susannah, b. 1772. 15. Priscilla, b. 1774; d. 1790. 3d mar.—16. William, b. 1779; d. 1811. 17. *George Delap*. 18. Sarah, b. 1783. 19. Aeneas, b. 1786; d. 1806. 20. Willis, b. 1788; m. Elizabeth Logan. 21. Priscilla, b. 1790. 22. Margaret, b. 1793. m. Henry Burkholder.

17. GEORGE DELAP FOULKE, M. D., b. 1780; d. 1849; m. 1804, Mary Steele. Had—23. Harriet May, b. 1805. 24. Stephen Aeneas, b. 1807; d. 1818. 25 Lewis William, b. 1809; d. 1887; m. 1836, Elizabeth McCoy, and had John McCoy, b. 1837, d. 1842, and *Mary Steele, supra*, m. DR. G. S. FRANKLIN. 26 Sarah Margaret, b. 1812; d. 1888; m. John Reber, Lanc'r, O. 27. Esther Rebecca, b. 1815; m. Dan'l Kutz, Lanc'r, O. 28. George Willis, b. 1818; d. 1818. 29. Stephen Aeneas, b. 1820. 30. George Willis, b. 1822; d. 1850. 31. Caroline Jane, b. 1826; m. Dr. James McCulloch. (Foulke-Fowke Ex., No. 2, p. 200 A.)

COMMANDER CHARLES L. FRANKLIN, U. S. N.

ASAHEL RENICK FRANKLIN.

DR. GUSTAVUS SCOTT FRANKLIN, U. S. N.

Second marriage (FRANKLIN):
183. ix. RICHARD HENRY LEE, b. 1846; d. 1846.
184. x. JAMES TAYLOR, b. May 28, 1847; d. Erie, Apr. 14, 1882; m. —, Norah Hutchins; grad. Theo. Sem., Kenyon Coll., O., 1869; ordered Deacon, 1869; Priest, 1870; Asst. Min. All Saints, Portsmouth, O., under Rev. E. Burr, D. D., 1869; Rector Christ's Ch., Portsmouth, 1870; St. Stephen's, Middlebury, Vt., 1877-1879; St. Paul's, Erie, Pa., 1879-1882.

Children:
i. Karl. ii. Paul.
185. xi. MARY, b. May 11, 1849; m. Chester W. Merrill.

Children:
i. Bessie. ii. Julia.
186. xii. HENRY COLIGNY, b. Feb. 21, 1851.
187. xiii. SENECA ELY, b. Mar. 7, 1853.
188-9. xiv. AGATHA EUSTACE, b. June 21, 1855.

108. JANE SELDEN[6] SCOTT (*John C.,[4] Gustavus,[3] James,[2] John[1]*), b. "Strawberry Vale," Fairfax county, Va., Oct. 16, 1806; d. Columbus, O., Sep. 21, 1881; m. "Western View," Culpeper county, Va., Oct. 20, 1825, WILLIAM BALLARD BROWN, b. Norfolk, Va., —, 1803; d. Columbus, O., 1863; son of John Brown, Norfolk, Va., and his wife, Elizabeth Hutchins, grand-daughter of Col. John Hutchins, a founder of Norfolk.

In 1827-8 Mr. Brown moved with his family to Chillicothe, O., whence he moved, 1849, to Columbus, O. They were life long members of the Prot. Epis. Church.

Children (BROWN):
190. i. ANN ELIZA,[6] b. Culp'r Co., Va., May 5, 1827; d. Jan. 17, 1878; m. (I). Circleville. O., Feb. 10, 1845, Nathaniel Willis Doddridge, b. Jan. 23, 1822; d. Columbus, O., Oct. 22, 1856; son of Philip Bukey and Matilda (Willis) Doddridge (SCOTT 110, Excursus—Doddridge, No. 11); m. (II.) Columbus, O., May 24, 1870, George Fairchild, Danbury, Conn., d. Chambersburg, Pa., Oct. 15, 1875.

Children, 1st mar.:
i. Matilda Willis, b. Circleville, O., May 7, 1846; m. Oct. 16, 1877, William B. Haycock, M. D., Chambersburg, Pa.
ii. William Brown, b. C., Oct. 9, 1848; m. —, 1869, Frances Barnum, Columbus, Neb.; was for years Agt. Salt Lake, Union and Cent. Pac. R. R., Ogden, Utah.
191. ii. ALBERT ALLMAND, b. Pickaway Co., O., Oct. 1, 1838.
192. iii. WILLIAM PRESTON, b. Circleville, Mar. 25, 1842; m. Apr. 30, 1873, Maria Louisa Hess, b. Mar. 7, 1847, dau. of John Moses and Elizabeth (Graylis) Hess.*

Children:
i. Edward. Cole, b. June 11, 1874.
ii. Mary Hess, b. Dec. 4, 1876.
iii. William Ballard, b. Nov. 12, 1878.
iv. Jessie Louisa, b. Oct. 12, 1880.
193. iv. JAMES FINLEY, b. C., Feb. 4, 1848; ed. V. M. I., 1867-1869. Is editor of *The Columbus Record.*

* JOHN M. HESS was son of Balser Hess, who em. from Bedford Co., Pa., to Franklin Co., O., 1801, and bought, 1802-3, of Gen. Jonathan Dayton, N. J., a large tract of land adjoining Columbus, O., where he d. 1806. Maj Frank W. Hess, U. S. A.. is of the same family.

104. GUSTAVUS⁵ SCOTT (*John C.,⁴ Gustavus,³ James,² John¹*),
b. "Strawberry Vale," Nov. 11, 1807; d. Gallatin, Mo., Jan. 25. 1867;
m. Jan. 21, 1847, ELIZABETH DANOLDS, Chillicothe, O.

Children :
      195.   i.   WILLIAM DANOLDS,⁶ b. Nov. 17, 1847; d. Mar. 22, 1853.
      196.   ii.   ANNA M., b. Aug. 23, 1849.
      197.   iii. JOHN CAILE, b. Mar. 11, 1851; m. Mar. 11, 1878, Alice Hughes.
      198.   iv. CHARLES LOVE, b. Dec. 22, 1852; m. Sep. 24, 1879, Mary Wilter.
      199.   v.   HENRY S., b. Aug. 9, 1855.
      200.   vi. MARY E., b. Sep. 12, 1857; m. Nov. 5, 1874, John F. Henderson.
      201.   vii. WILLIAM DANOLDS, b. Aug. 3, 1861.
      202.   viii. GEORGE C., b. May 25, 1864; d. Oct. 30, 1884.

105. JOHN CAILE⁵ SCOTT (*John C.,⁴ Gustavus,³ James,² John¹*),
b. "Strawberry Vale," Fairfax county, Va., July 17, 1809; d. Philadelphia, Pa., Feb. 5, 1875; m. Oct. 18, 1832, LOUISIANNA ELEANOR
SLESMAN, b. Philadelphia, Nov. 26, 1807, daughter of George and Elizabeth (Scull) Slesman, Philadelphia, Pa.

Children :
      205.   i.   ANNIE ELIZABETH,⁶ b. Chillicothe, O., Nov. 26, 1834; d. Boston, Mass.,
                  July 5, 1873; m. Oct. 15, 1856, Capt. William Talbot Truxton, U. S.
                  N., b. Phila., Mar. 11, 1824; d. Feb. 25, 1887; grad. U. S. Naval Acad.,
                  Feb. 4, 1841; Midshipman, Feb. 9, 1841; passed M., Aug. 10, 1847;
                  Master, Sep. 14, 1855; Lieut., Sep. 15, 1855; Lieut. Commander, July
                  16, 1862; Commander, July 25, 1866; Captain, Sep. 25, 1873; Commo-
                  dore, May 11, 1882; Rear Admiral, Feb. 18, 1886, but action was delayed
                  and he was retired as Commodore, Mar. 11, 1886. (App. Cyc. Am. Biog.,
                  also Hamersly's Naval Encyclopedia, p. 878.)
      206.   ii.   GEORGE SLESMAN, b. C., Jan. 25, 1837; m. —, Augusta Isham.
                        Children :
                        i. Isabell Isham.   ii. Louise.
                        iii. George.   iv. Charles Henry.
      207.   iii. WILLIAM BIDDLE, b. C., Mar. 16, 1839; m. (I.) —, Sarah Carpenter.   (II.)
                  Mrs. Eliza Harkness.
                        Children, first marriage :
                        i. William Carpenter. ii. John Carte.
      208.   iv. THERESA, b. Mar. 25, 1842.
      209.   v.   JOHN CAILE, b. Phila., May 29, 1844; m. —, Elizabeth Hacker.
                        Children :
                        i. Lloyd Mifflin.   ii. Theresa.
                        iii. Louis.   iv. Anita.
      210.   vi. CHARLES MEIGS, b. P., June 18, 1847; d. July 2, 1849.
      210a. vii. CHARLES HENRY, b. P., June 29, 1849; m. —, Margaret Geary.
                        Children :
                        i. Charles Henry, Jr., b. July 30, 1877.

106. HARRIET LOVE⁵ SCOTT, (*John C.,⁴ Gustavus,³ James,²
John¹*), b. Alexandria, Virginia, Feb. 7, 1811; d. Columbus, Ohio,
Feb. 18, 1865; m. (I.) Jan. 21, 1835, ASAHEL RENICK, b. —; d. s. p.
—, 1840; of Pickaway county, Ohio. (II.) Mar. 5, 1844, REV.
THOMAS WOODROW, D. D., Chillicothe, O., son of Rev. James Wood-
row of Georgia.

Rev. Thomas Woodrow is a clergyman of the Presbyterian Church, North.
His father was a minister of the Presbyterian Church, South.

Children, second marriage (WOODROW):

211. i. EDWARD RENICK,⁶ b. Chillicothe, Oct. 13, 1845; m. June 16, 1886, Jennie Curlette, Larned, Kan.
212. ii. HENRY WILLS, b. Mar. 8, 1847; m. Dec. 30, 1869, Elizabeth C. Miner, Columbus, O.
   Children:
    i. Harriet Love, b. 1871.
    ii. William Miner, b. 1873.
213. iii. CAILE SCOTT, b. Apr. 21, 1849; d. July 2, 1849.
214. iv. CHARLES SCOTT, b. Mar. 27, 1850; m. Apr., 1870, Ella Hess, Columbus, O.
   Children:
    i. Gay. ii. Joseph Scott. iii. Scott.
215. v. MARY ANN LOVE, b. May 19, 1853; m. Dec. 23, 1875, Frank C. Hunt.
   Children:
    i. Claude Banning, b. 1876.
    ii. Edward Renick, b. 1878.
    iii. Charles Scott, b. 1880.
    iv. Helen Bennett, b. 1884.
    v. William Franklin, b. 1886.

107. CHARLES LOVE⁵ SCOTT (*John C.,⁴ Gustavus,³ James,²*
John¹), b. "Bush Hill," Va., Sept. 20, 1812; d. Germantown, Pa., Jan.
24, 1861; m. May 8, 1834, ELIZABETH ELLEN SLESMAN, b. Philadelphia, Jan. 7, 1815; d. Germantown, Dec. 31, 1873; dau. of George
and Elizabeth (Scull) Slesman.

Children:

216. i. CATHERINE S.,⁶ b. Mt. Hope, Tenn., Apr. 2, 1835; m. Sep. 11, 1856, John H. Tingley, b. Phila., June 16, 1833.
   Children:
    i. Clem Henry, b. June 25, 1857; m. June 4, 1886, Mattie Rathmal of Ohio.
    ii. Charles Love S——., b. Apr. 27, 1861; d. Mar. 19, 1865.
    iii. Samuel, b. June 24, 1865; d. June 26, 1865.
    iv. Arthur S., b. Sep. 4, 1867.
    v. Elizabeth S., b. Nov. 13, 1871.
    vi. Edward C., b. Oct. 6, 1873.
217. ii. LOUISA H——, b. "Rose Lawn," Ohio, Mar. 23, 1837; m. Sep. 11, 1856, Clement Tingley, b. Phila., Oct. 21, 1832; d. Merchantville, N. J., Oct. 27, 1876.
   Children:
    i. Benjamin W., b. Aug. 6, 1857; m. Apr. 24, 1884, Margaretta Ashmead; had—Clement Fingley, b. Jan. 13, 1886.
    ii. Charles Love S., b. June 8, 1865.
218. iii. JOHN CAILE, b. do. Feb. 25, 1839; m. Sep. 18, 1878, Lizzie S. Stevenson, b. Reading, Pa., Feb. 9, 1857.
   Children:
    i. Charles Love, b. Aug. 15, 1879. ii. Mary S., b. Aug. 8, 1886.
219. iv. ARTHUR WATTS, b. Chillicothe, O., July 30, 1841; m. Nov. 9, 1870, Mary G. Taws, b. Phila., Feb. 11, 1847; d. Oct. 1, 1876.
   Children:
    i. Lewis T., b. June 5, 1872.
220. v. CHARLES LOVE, b. do., Jan. 12, 1845; d. s. p., Phila., Apr. 16, 1880; m. Oct. 15, 1874, Helen D. Raiguel.
221. vi. ELIZABETH S., b. do., Mar. 30, 1847; m. Jan. 18, 1875, Joseph T. Bradshaw, b. —; d. Phila., Apr. 7, 1881.
   Children:
    i. Elizabeth Ellen, b. Jan. 10, 1876.
    ii. Joseph T., b. Feb. 7, 1877; d. July 16, 1880.
    iii. Shelburne, b. Aug. 8, 1880.

222. vii. EDWARD W., b. Phila., July 25, 1849; m. Sep. 9, 1875, Cynthia Renick, dau. of John and Amanda Renick, b. "Darby," near Circleville, O., May 30, 1851.*

Children :
     i. Minnie Renick, b. May 16, 1878.
223. viii. ANNA STONE, b. Germantown, July 29, 1853; m. (I.) Jan. 18, 1882, Wm. H. Moore, d. Phila., Apr. 17, 1883; (II.) June 12, 1884, Charles R. Rowley.
224. ix. GEORGE SLESMAN, b. G., Aug. 28, 1860.

110. **ELLEN SELDEN[5] SCOTT** (*John C.,[4] Gustavus,[3] James,[2] John[1]*), b. "Western View," Fauquier county, Virginia, April 2, 1817; d. Covington, Ky., Feb. 26, 1857; m. Chillicothe, O., March 2, 1848, PHILIP ALEXANDER DODDRIDGE, b. April 14, 1816; d. July 28, 1885; son of Hon. Philip and Julianna (Musser) Doddridge. (Excursus—Doddridge, 30.)

Children (DODDRIDGE) :
225.   i. JULIANNA PHILLIPA,[6] b. July 31, 1849; m. (I.) Jan. 19, 1870, James T. Lackey, Rockbridge Co., Va., b. —; d. —, 1878; (ii.) Jan. 8, 1885, Hon. Anderson A. Rock, St. Albans, Wt. Va.
     Children, 1st marriage :
    i. William Doddridge.
    ii. John Scott. iii. James Henry. iv. Kate Selden.
     2d marriage :
    v. Philip Doddridge.

EXCURSUS—DODDRIDGE.

1. JOHN DODDRIDGE, of Maryland, b. —; d. Feb., 1791; m. (I.) Mary Wells, dau. of Richard Wells, and niece of Alexander Wells, Washington Co., Pa.; (II.) Elizabeth Reeves. He moved to Bedford Co., Pa., and, 1773, to Independence Township, Washington Co., Pa. (*v.* Crumrine's His. Washington Co., Pa., 825, &c.) His brother, Philip Doddridge, of Western Va., 1770, lost part of his family by the Indians. He had 1 son, John, and 5 daughters to survive. (*v.* Doddridge's Notes of Western Pa.) Child., 1st mar.—2. *Joseph.* 3. *Philip.* 4. Ann, m. Nathan Reeves. 5. Ruth, m. —— Carson. 2d mar.—6. Josiah. 7. Benjamin. 8. Enoch. 9. John. 10. *Eleanor.*

2. REV. JOSEPH DODDRIDGE, D. D., b. Oct. 14, 1769; d. Nov. 9, 1826; m. —, Jemima Bukey, b. —, 1777; d. Sep., 1829; dau. of John Bukey, Western Va. Dr. Doddridge was a Presbyter of the Prot. Epis. Church in Va., and a man of marked ability. He began to preach the gospel before he was of age. In 1788 he was a traveling preacher in the Wesleyan Connexion labouring on the Holstein, and on the West River, and in the Pittsburgh circuit. When his father died, 1791, he found it necessary to lay aside his ministerial work in order to provide for his stepmother and his brothers and sisters. But he did not relinquish his intention to enter the ministry. In 1791 he and his brother Philip entered Jefferson Academy, Canonsburg, Pa., where they were "remarkable for original genius, intellectual strength, and close investigation of any subject that came before them." Joseph, after his academic studies were ended, offered himself as a candidate for orders in the Prot. Epis. Ch. He was ordained Deacon by Bishop White, March 4, 1791, and Priest by the same, March, 1800. He also devoted himself to the study of medicine in Philadelphia in order to fit himself more thoroughly for his work on the frontiers. In both professions, the ministry and medicine, he attained eminent success. In 1793 he ministered to three parishes in Virginia, West Liberty, Ohio Co., and St. John's and St. Paul's, Brooke Co. He also extended his labours to Ohio, and was the first Christian minister to officiate in Steubenville, where he ministered from 1796 to 1820. St. Jame's Ch., Cross Creek, Jefferson Co., O., St. Clairsville, Belmont Co., and Zanesville, O., were all children of his labours. In 1813 he organized the Zanesville Church, and became the Rector in 1818. Of the ten churches represented in the first annual Convention of the Diocese of Ohio, "four had been organized by Dr. D., and this while he had charge of several churches in Va., and was extensively engaged in the practice of medicine."

* For Renick *v.* Egle's Notes and Queries, II., 79, 1887, where a pedigree is given of Thomas Renick, who came from Ireland to Pa. 1733, and settled in Dauphin Co. His son William left six sons.

Dr. Doddridge was an Honourary Member of the Medico-Surgical Society of O. He was elected, Dec. 1, 1812, Cor. Mem. of the Academy of Natural Science, Philada. He was an active Freemason, and W. M. of the Wellsburg Lodge. In addition to his well known "Notes on the Settlement and Indian Wars of the Western Parts of Virginia and Pennsylvania, 1761–1783," he published, 1813, a "Treatise on the Culture of Bees," "Logan, the Last of the Race of Shikellimus," and left manuscripts of other works. (*v.* his Memoirs in 2d ed. Doddridge's "Notes on the settlement and Indian Wars of the Western Country in 1763–83.") Child.—11. Philip Bukey, b. —, 1797; d. Columbus, O., Sep. 9, 1860; m. —, Matilda Willis, and had Nathaniel Willis, b. Jan. 23, 1822; d. Oct. 22, 1856; m. Feb. 19, 1845, Ann Eliza Brown. (SCOTT 190.) 12. Joseph, living Chicago, Ill., 1886. 13. Susan A., m. Capt. Robert Larimore, Chillicothe, O. 14. Ann. 15. Ruth. 16. Narcissa. 17. Eliza M., b. —, 1800; d. Jan., 1819. 18. R. Reeves, b. 1813; d. Jan., 1829. 19. Charles Hammond, b. 1816; d. Oct., 1834. 20. Harriet T., m. Major Wm. Duval, d. Jan., 1841. 21. Mary, b. 1823; m. B. T. Brannan, Cin., O., d. April, 1857. 22. Matilda, m. John Winters, N. Y.

3. HON. PHILIP DODDRIDGE, b. Wellsburg, Va., —, 1771; d. Washington, D. C., Nov. 19, 1832; m. Lancaster, Pa., Apr. 30, 1800, Julianna Musser.* He was one of the most eminent lawyers of his day; mem. Va. Leg., 1815–20; mem. Va. Conv., 1829–30; mem. U. S. Congress, 1829–1832. Lanman says "he commanded great influence in Congress." (*v.* very interesting incident of his life in American Pioneer, I., 134; also App. Cyc. Am. Biog.) Child.—23. Jasper Yates, b. July 22, 1801. 24. Joseph John Musser, b. Pa., Dec. 3, 1802. 25. Benjamin Zaccheus Biggs, b. Va., June 17, 1804. 26. Sarah Mary Musser, b. Va., Feb. 8, 1806. 27. Eleanor Sophia, b. Aug. 3, 1808; m. Mr. Plattenburg. 28. Cadwallader Evans, b. Va., Dec. 11, 1811. 29. Juliana Adeline, b. O., May 30, 1814. 30. Philip Alexander, b. O., Apr. 14, 1816; m. ELLEN SELDEN SCOTT, *supra.* 31. Harriet Varina, b. O., July 29, 1818. 32. Ann Ruth, b. July 30, 1820; m. —— Meek.

10. ELEANOR DODDRIDGE, b. Washington Co., Pa., Oct. 26, 1780; m. (I.) John Gantt Frederick, Md.; (II.) 1800, John Brown, son of Captain Oliver and Abigail (Richardson) Brown of the Revolutionary War. Had by 1st mar.—33. Juliana Doddridge. By 2d mar.—34. Catherine, b. June 7, 1807; d. Jan. 11, 1809. 35. Eliza Vilette, b. June 16, 1809; d. Dec. 5, 1879; m. Hon. Daniel Polsley, Pt. Pleasant, Wt. Va.; Judge and Mem. U. S. Cong.; had issue. 36. Caroline R., b. Oct. 22, 1811; d. Sep., 1881. 37. John, b. Feb. 12, 1814; d. July 19, 1814. 38. Louisa, b. Feb. 3, 1816. 39. Harriet, b. Nov. 20, 1818; d. Jan. 26, 1841. 40. John Doddridge, b. Oct. 8, 1821; d. Apr. 10, 1860. 41. Danforth, b. June 25, 1824. Captain Brown, the father of Mr. John Brown, is buried at Wellsburg, W. Va. His monument bears this inscription, written by himself: "Captain Oliver Brown of the Artillery of the Massachusetts Line, Revolutionary War. Born in Lexington, Mass., 1752. He stood in front of the first cannon fired by the British on the Americans in the affray at Lexington. Witnessed the Tea Party, Boston Harbor. Was at the battle of Bunker's Hill. Commissioned by Congress 16th of January, 1776. Commanded the volunteer party that bore off the leaden statue of King George from the Battery of New York, and made it into bullets for the American Army. Bore a conspicuous part in command of Artillery at the Battles of White Plains, Harlem Heights, Trenton, Princeton, Brandywine, Germantown and Monmouth. After serving his country, he enlisted in the Armies of the Son of God, and surrendered to the last enemy on the 17th of February, 1846, in the full assurance of a never ending Peace." Capt. Brown's brother, Deacon Solomon Brown, was a participator in the battle of Lexington, and "had the unrivalled honour of having shed the first British blood in defence of American liberty, at the battle of Lexington, on the morning of the 19th of April, 1775." (*v.* A Biographical Sketch of Captain Oliver Brown, an Officer of the Revolutionary Army, &c., &c., by the Rev. Horace Edwin Hayden, &c., 1882.)

226. ii. JOHN SCOTT, b. Sep. 9, 1850.
227. iii. ELLEN SCOTT, b. Mar. 22, 1852; m. Dec. 14, 1876, Samuel L. Smith, Brownstown, W. Va.
      Children:
        i. Eva Dawson, b. Oct. 29, 1877. ii. Mary Taylor, b. Jan. 4, 1881. iii. Ellen Selden, b. Nov. 7, 1884. iv. dau., b. Nov., 1886.
228. iv. PHILIP, b. Feb. 18, 1857; m. Nov. 18, 1886, Sallie Hansford, eldest dau. of Frazier Hansford, St. Albans.
      Children:
        i. Bettie Middleton.

---

* The Musser family was quite prominent in Lancaster Co., Penn'a. having given twelve members to the medical profession alone. (*v.* Evans' His. of Lancaster Co., Pa.)

115. REAR ADMIRAL GUSTAVUS HALL[5] SCOTT, U. S. N. (*Gustavus H.,[4] Gustavus,[3] James,[2] John[1]*), b. "Mulberry Hill," Fairfax county, Virginia, July 13, 1812; d. Washington, D. C., March 23, 1882; m. Port Mahon, Island of Minorca, May 3, 1843, JULIA TODD, b. —, of Philadelphia.

Admiral Scott was appointed Midshipman, U. S. N., Aug. 1, 1828; frigate "Guerriere," Pacific Squadron, 1829–31; schooner "Experiment," Chesapeake Bay, 1833; Passed Midshipman, June 14, 1834; sloop "Vandalia," W. I. Squadron, 1835–6; waiting orders, 1837; W. I. Squadron, 1839–40; Lieut. Feb. 25, 1841; frigate "Columbus," Mediterranean Squadron, 1843–44; special duty, 1845; frigate "United States," Med. Squad., 1846–47; ordnance duty, 1848–9; waiting orders, 1850; ordnance duty, 1851; frigate "St. Lawrence," Pacific Squadron, 1852–53; steamer "Michigan," in the Lakes, 1855–7; Commander, Dec. 27, 1856; Lt. House Inspector, 1858–60; commanding steamer "Keystone State," special service, 1861; commanding steam gunboat "Maratanza," North Atlantic Blockading Squad., 1862–3; Captain, Nov. 4, 1863, steamer "DeSoto," Blockading Squad, 1864; do. steam sloop "Canandaigua," Blockading Squad., 1865; do. "Saranac," Pacific Squad., 1866–7; mem. Examining Board, Phila., 1868; Lt. House Inspector, 1869–71; Commodore, Feb. 10, 1869; Rear Admiral, Feb. 14, 1873; commanding North Atlantic Station, 1873; retired, June 13, 1874. (Hamersly's Naval Encyc.)

Children:

230.   i. GUSTAVUS HENRY[6], b. Sep. 27, 1845; d. Sep. 7, 1861.
231.   ii. DOUGLAS MARSHALL, U. S. A., b. Dec. 31, 1846; m. —, 1871, ——; appt'd 2d Lt., 4th U. S. Cav., June 19, 1867; transf'd to 1st Inf., Sept. 16, 1869; 1st Lieut., June 28, 1878; Captain, 1st U. S. Inf.

                Children:

            i. William L., b. Dec. 7, 1872.
            ii. Julia Todd, b. Oct. 27, 1877.

123. HON. WILLIAM LAWRENCE[5] SCOTT (*Robert J.,[4] Gustavus,[3] James,[2] John[1]*), of Erie, Penna., b. Washington, D. C., July 2, 1828; d. Sep. 19, 1891; m. Sep. 19, 1853, MARY MATILDA TRACY, b. —; daughter of John A. Tracy.

As a public man the life of Mr. Scott has been more than once published in the press of Penna., but with so many erroneous statements that it is the purpose of his friends to prepare and publish a full sketch of his successful career

Mr. Scott lost his father while he was a boy in his seventh year, but his mother a devoted and an intelligent lady, was spared to him until her death in 1879 He was not, therefore, "turned out into the world as a boy to shift for himself." To the early and careful training of his mother he owed much of his success in life. He attended the Academy at Hampton, Va., near his home, Fort Monroe, where his mother lived for 30 years, until the Civil War began, 1861, when, losing her home, she went to Erie and lived there until her death. Mr. Scott also passed a great deal of time at Mount Vernon by reason of his family connexions through the Blackburns. At the age of 12, in 1840, he received an appointment as a page in the U. S. Congress serving there four years, until 1846. It was during this service that he attracted the attention of Gen. C. M. Reed, M. C., 1843–45. The following

HON. WILLIAM LAWRENCE SCOTT.

SCOTT FAMILY.

sketch of Mr. Scott's life from this period to its close is condensed from the columns of the Erie *Herald* of Sep. 26, 1891, the editor of which was a personal friend of Mr. Scott :

"Through the influence of Gen. Reed, Mr. Scott came to Erie in 1847, attended school in this city for about three months, and then was employed as a clerk in the shipping business at Reed's docks. In 1850 he made his first business venture, entering into the coal trade with the late M. B. Lowry, under the firm name of Lowry & Scott. This firm dissolving in 1851, Mr. Scott entered into a partnership with Mr. John Hearn in the coal business, under the firm name of John Hearn & Co. At the death of Mr. H. was formed the firm of W. L. Scott & Co. Through the great executive and financial ability of Mr. Scott this firm has become the largest producing and shipping coal firm in the world, owning thousands of acres of hard and soft coal lands in Pa., Ill., Iowa and Mo. Mr. Scott was interested in the ownership of upwards of 70,000 acres of coal land, and gave employment to some 12,000 people. At the time of his death he was the principal owner of the Youghiogheny Coal Co. and the Union Coal Co. of Pa. and the Spring Valley Coal Co. of Ill.

"In 1861 he contracted to build that portion of the Erie and Pitts. R. R. which extends from Jamestown to New Castle, and in 1863 and '64 he secured the contract and constructed the E. & P. road to New Castle, on completion of which he built the link from the latter place to the Fort Wayne road, becoming a large owner of same. Soon afterward he was elected president of the E. & P. R. R. and held this position up the time of his death.

"In 1862 Mr. Scott was engaged with his brother-in-law, Mr. John F. Tracy, in extending the Chicago, Rock Island & Pacific R. R. from Grinnell, Iowa, to the Mo. River, that being the first railroad that had ever been built to the Missouri.

"Mr. Scott and Mr. J. F. Tracy were largely interested in establishing the first elevated road in N. Y. city. The legislature of the state was not at first kindly disposed toward granting the innovation, and Mr. Scott did much hard personal and persuasive work before the privileges desired were granted. Mr. Scott was one of the most active builders and a director of the N. Y., Pa. & Norfolk R. R. in 1884, which was the first railroad constructed on the peninsula of Virginia. The development of both the Canadian South. and the Canadian Pac. R. R. was largely due to Mr. Scott. It was owing to his enthusiasm and strong arguments, backed by his own willingness to furnish money, that these roads were placed in a prosperous condition. When he died he was the oldest, and only living original, director in the Lake Shore & Mich. South. R. R. He was a director and mem. of the executive committee Chicago & N. W. R. R.; a director of the Pitt., Cin., Chi. & St. Louis R. R.; the New Castle & Beaver Valley R. R.; the Mich. Cent. R. R., and a director in the Albemarle & Chesapeake Canal Co. Until lately Mr. Scott was connected officially with other railroads, but his poor health compelled him to withdraw from active participation therein.

"He was largely engaged in the manufacture of iron in the Shenango Valley, and in Missouri, and some years ago took an active interest in the rolling mill in Erie. He was a large owner in the N. W. Fuel Asso. of Chicago, St. Paul and Duluth, and had controlling interests in the Mo. Iron and Coal Co., the Sligo Furnace Co., Mo., and the What Cheer Coal Co., Iowa.

"Mr. S. took great pride in developing his farm at Cape Charles, Va. This land lies opposite to his old boyhood home, between the Chesapeake Bay and the Atlantic Ocean. He used to refer to this land as the 'Garden spot of America.' He owned 2,000 acres there, from which during the past year there has been shipped over 80,000 barrels of the best garden truck. Mr. S. had large and varied interests in Erie city and county, all of which received his special care. He was one of the heaviest stockholders in the Second National Bank of Erie, and its original president, serving continuously until he could no longer do so.

"Mr. Scott was president and stockholder of the Eureka Tempered Copper Co. of North East, one of the most prosperous manufacturing concerns in the state of Pa. He owned 2,000 acres of farming land in Erie county, which he was having brought to the highest possible development. The Algeria Stud Farm is one of the largest and best equipped establishments in the country for the breeding of thoroughbred running horses. It was from these stables that the famous horse Chaos, who won the Futurity stakes in 1889, came; also the celebrated horses Tenny, Tea Tray, Banquet and Bolero; and the Frontier Farm was noted for having the largest and best herd of thoroughbred short-horn cattle in western Pennsylvania. He was also sole owner of Massassauga Point, one of the most beautiful summer resorts on Lake Erie.

"The record which Mr. Scott leaves is its own best commentary on his life as a public citizen. Although always heavily engrossed with business cares, he never shrank from bearing his full share of burdens of public life, and to all positions which he was called upon to fill he devoted the same care and energy that characterized his personal affairs. He was elected mayor of Erie 1866 and 1871. His share in giving to the city the very best water works system possible was very great, and he served as one of the water commissioners upon the first board. For many years one of the accepted leaders of the national and state Democracy, his interest in and loyalty to his party in this city and county never flagged, but he took no very active part in general political affairs until 1876. He was nominated by the Democracy of this district for Congress in 1866 and 1876, but made no contest for the office, devoting his entire time during the campaign of the latter year to the interests of Samuel J. Tilden, Democratic candidate for President, of whom Mr. Scott was an ardent admirer. He was a del. to the Nat. Dem. Conv. 1876, 1880 and 1888; serving on some of the most important committees, and his counsels generally prevailed. In 1884 Mr. Scott was elected to Congress from the 27th district, and re-elected in 1886. In 1888 and 1890 he was renominated, but declined to be a candidate, as his health was beginning to fail.

"Mr. Scott took a very active part in Congress. His ability and good judgment were quickly recognized by his fellow members and by President Cleveland, between whom and Mr. S. a strong personal friendship existed. As a member of the most important committee of the House (Ways and Means), he took a prominent part in the preparation of the Mills bill and was one of its most earnest advocates. To him was largely due the credit of uniting the Democratic party, in securing a majority for it in the House. His speech in favor of the bill, in which he devoted special attention to the iron industry, was widely circulated as a campaign document. His denunciation of the Randall tariff bill in 1888 was a bit of invective as strong as was ever uttered in Congress. Mr. S. was a steadfast advocate of a sound monetary system, and delivered a speech on the silver question which showed exhaustive study of the problem, and attracted the attention of the country. He was the originator of the oleomargarine bill, for protection of American farmers and dairymen; he addressed the House in its favor, and mainly through his efforts the bill became a law. He originated the bill for the transfer of the Peninsula to the U. S. government, thus securing its permanent preservation, necessary work on it not now being dependent on the passage of a river and harbor appropriation bill.

"When the news came that China had rejected the treaty regulating immigration from the latter country, Mr. S. illustrated his capacity for prompt action in an emergency by the immediate introduction of the Chinese exclusion bill, which passed both houses the day it was introduced, under suspension of the rules. Mr. S. supported all the bills for the forfeiture and restoration to the people of lands granted to railroads by the government on conditions with which the R. R. Cos. had failed to comply. In every instance during his service in Congress when the question at issue involved the interests of the people on the one hand, and the corporations on the other, Mr. Scott's vote and influence were on the side of the people.

"As a member of the Nat. Dem. Com. Mr. Scott's services were always regarded as equally valuable. It has been said that he was one of the most untiring and unselfish workers upon the committee, and that the influence he exerted was almost universal.

"He was a great admirer of Samuel J. Tilden, and was one of Mr. T.'s most confidential advisers. He labored zealously for the election of the Democratic nominee, and after he had won the fight and Mr. Tilden was counted out, Mr. S. insisted that Mr. Tilden should again lead the ticket in 1880. His counsel did not prevail, but the wisdom of his views was never questioned after the campaign of 1880.

"In 1884 Grover Cleveland had no stauncher friend than W. L. Scott for the nomination and election to the presidency. And, although Mr. S. had the hottest congressional fight in the country upon his hands, he was one of the most important factors in Mr. Cleveland's election, and after the inauguration of the Democratic administration he was one of Mr. Cleveland's most trusted advisers. The friendship between Mr. Cleveland and Mr. S. ended only when the light of life left the latter. He regarded the ex-President as one of the greatest statesmen the country ever produced. He admired his rugged honesty and his unflinching adherence under all circumstances to duty, as it was given him to see his duty.

"For many years Mr. S. was an active member of the Board of Trade of Erie, had served as President. He was also a member and contributor to the Erie Liedertafel and Mænnerchor societies. During the early days of the Civil War he was instrumental in raising and equipping an artillery company, and when the U. S. was sorely in need of money he came forward and invested more than half of all he was worth in government bonds. This was at a time when the credit of the government was at the lowest ebb.

"Mr. Scott was one of the most self-reliant men in the country. He never undertook to accomplish a thing which he did not thoroughly understand, and this had the tendency to make him a vigorous advocate for or against whatever he undertook. He was undoubtedly one of the best informed men in the successful management of railroads. Not many years ago during a directors' meeting of one of the largest railroad corporations in the world, when the policy of the road was to be decided upon for the next year, all of the directors excepting Mr. Scott at first had settled convictions in one direction. Mr. Scott differed with them radically, and for half an hour argued with the directors, stating his reasons for differing with them. At the close of his address he produced such convincing proof of the correctness of his position that one of the leading directors exclaimed, "Scott knows more about running a railroad than all of us put together." Mr. Scott's ideas prevailed, his predictions were verified, and the policy of that road was the most popular and financially the most prosperous of any in the country."

Col. Thompson, in his address before the Erie City Council, said of Mr. Scott:

"In his private life was a man of generous disposition and large charities. He was one of the very few rich men of whom it can be said that riches did not dry up the bowels of compassion. Always ready to give, and give generously to worthy charitable causes, he was not sectarian in his deeds of charity. Nor were his deeds of charity confined to public institutions. He gave much in charities the public knew nothing of. He was pleased to do it in a quiet way and unknown. I remember one severe winter, while having my office in Scott's Block, noticing poorly clad women and children moving up and down the stairs with baskets on their arms. On inquiring I found that Mr. Scott had a private bureau for the relief of the poor. Tons upon tons and carload after carload of coal was by his orders distributed among the poor of our city. Few, very few, knew of his liberal charities. He preferred to do his acts of charity in silence, and for him there must be laid up in the world beyond a great reward. He has kept the wolf from the door of many an humble family. He has given them warmth as well as food; and many a family in our city will feel the loss this coming winter."

At the time of Mr. Scott's death Ex-President Cleveland, in conversation with a reporter of the Erie *Herald*, spoke of his late friend in the following words, which Mr. Cleveland has assured me are correctly reported:

"My acquaintance with Mr. Scott dates no farther back than his prominence in public life. That acquaintance, however, rapidly grew to a close intimacy, which was only interrupted by his death. I learned to love him for his sincerity and for his steadfastness in his relations to his friends. He was not one of those who opened the way to the inner circles of his friendship to anyone who would flatter him and truckle to him.

"His preference for people was based upon something he saw in them of sturdy usefulness and upon qualites of independent strength that commanded his respect, and so it happened that having once selected a friend, and based his selection upon solid ground, he remained a friend in all circumstances and without the shadow of turning. It is most pleasant to think of him in the light of these qualities.

"But there was another phase of his character which should endear his memory not only to his personal friends, but to every true American. As a public servant he was patriotic, disinterested, honest and sincere. As a member of Congress he spent his efforts and his thought in advancing those measures and objects which he deemed for the good of the entire country, and he never belittled his position nor diminished his usefulness by seeking to accomplish legislation which had relation to his own benefit or to interests merely local and circumscribed.

"It was certainly true of him that having determined that a certain course of conduct led to the promotion of the public good, his private interests and all personal considerations were set aside as he followed in the way of public duty.

"If his life had only been valuable for the example he set for the faithful performance of the trust the people repose in their public servants, he should be remembered with gratitude and affection; and when we recall his other traits of mind and heart, those who loved him cannot fail to be comforted by the precious memories he has left to them."

Children:

235.   i. MINNIE TRACY,[6] b. —; m. —, Richard D. Townsend, Philadelphia, Pa.
                Children:
                  i. Mary Matilda, b. 1884.
236.   ii. ANNIE WAINWRIGHT, b. —; m. —, Charles H. Strong, Erie, Pa.
                Children:
                  i. Thora Wainwright, b. —.

143. MAJOR ROBERT TAYLOR[6] SCOTT, C. S. A. (*Robert E.,[5] John,[4] John,[3] James,[2] John[1]*), of Warrenton, Virginia, b. March 10, 1834; m. "Glen Welby," Fauquier county, Va., May 25, 1858, FANNY-SCOTT CARTER, b. July 4, 1838; daughter of Richard Henry and Mary Welby (De Butts) Carter of "Glen Welby" (SCOTT, 131, p. 649), gr. dau. of Edward[5] and Janet (Hamilton) Carter of John[4], Landon,[3] Robert,[2] John,[1] of Corotoman, 1649.

Major Scott was ed. Univ. Va., 1851-54; studied law and was admitted to the Fauquier bar. In 1861 he entered the C. S. Army as Captain, Co. K., 8th Reg., Va. Inf. In 1862 he was app'd Major and Quarter Master on Staff of General Pickett, serving through the War. He was elected a mem. Va. Constit'l Conv., 1867-8, and of the Va. Leg., 1882. In 1889 he was elected Attorney General of Virginia for four years, entering upon his duties as such, Jan. 1, 1890. He is a member of the law firm of Scott & Scott, Richmond, Va., his son Richard being associated with him.

Children, b. Warrenton (F. B.):

238. i. RICHARD HENRY CARTER,[7] b. July 23, 1859.
239. ii. ELIZABETH TAYLOR, b. Apr. 23, 1861; d. Feb. 27, 1862.
240. iii. ROBERT EDEN, b. Mch. 22, 1866; d. Jan. 20, 1867.
241. iv. MARY WELBY, b. Jan. 3, 1870.
242. v. ROSALIE TAYLOR, b. Oct. 21, 1871.
243. vi. JULIAN TAYLOR, b. Apr. 16, 1873; d. Apr. 20, 1873.
244. vii. FANNY CARTER, b. Apr. 14, 1877; d. Apr. 16, 1879. (S. C.)
245. viii. ROBERT TAYLOR, b. May 25, 1880; d. Apr. 22, 1884.
246. ix. EDWARD CARTER, b. Jan. 14, 1885; d. Sep. 23, 1885.

It is an odd coincidence that James Scott of Mattox, Westmoreland Co., Va., merchant, left will dat. May 28, 1700, in which he names his two sisters, Jane and Rebecca Scott, in Ireland, his brother *Gustavus Scott* of Bristol, his brother James, son Gustavus, son John, wife Sarah, daughter Jane. Two letters from his brother, Gustavus Scott, dated 1702, are published in the N. E. His. Gen. Reg., XIII., 305-7.

www.ingramcontent.com/pod-product-compliance
Lightning Source LLC
Chambersburg PA
CBHW081159270326
41930CB00014B/3224